ADVANCE PRAISE FOR

Autoethnography in Undergraduate Writing Courses

"Hopkins provides a helpful and comprehensive resource for doing and teaching autoethnography. He engages several key topics related to autoethnography including how to conceptualize, research, compose, report, and evaluate autoethnographic texts. By providing diverse examples of autoethnographies written by students, as well as students' feedback about the practice of autoethnography, Hopkins also demonstrates how autoethnography can improve writing and literacy skills."

—Tony Adams, Professor, Bradley University

"With a creative and engaging narrative of his own, Justin Hopkins tempts composition instructors to adopt autoethnography to enhance the writing and learning of their students. Interspersing actual drafts from students, he lucidly demonstrates how student research, composing, voice, and ideologies can be addressed transformatively by teachers. He makes a compelling case for the rhetorical and intellectual value of this genre, wiping out any lingering doubts on the academic relevance of the personal and narrative."

—Suresh Canagarajah, Professor, Pennsylvania State University

"Autoethnographic writing gives composition students voice and power, helping them critically engage and communicate the narrative of the self. Hopkins powerfully models the genre by diving into his own life while rightfully devoting the majority of his book to the work of his students. This reflective personal inquiry is the inspiring and important work many of us have devoted our scholarly lives to nurturing. I applaud Hopkins' accessible and thoughtful contribution to its evolution."

—Melissa Tombro, Professor, SUNY, The Fashion Institute of Technology

Autoethnography in Undergraduate Writing Courses

This book is part of the Peter Lang Education list.
Every volume is peer reviewed and meets
the highest quality standards for content and production.

PETER LANG
New York • Bern • Berlin
Brussels • Vienna • Oxford • Warsaw

Justin B. Hopkins

Autoethnography in Undergraduate Writing Courses

PETER LANG
New York • Bern • Berlin
Brussels • Vienna • Oxford • Warsaw

Library of Congress Cataloging-in-Publication Data

Names: Hopkins, Justin B., author.
Title: Autoethnography in undergraduate writing courses/Justin B. Hopkins.
Description: New York: Peter Lang, 2020.
Includes bibliographical references and index.
Identifiers: LCCN 2020018810 (print) | LCCN 2020018811 (ebook)
ISBN 978-1-4331-8143-6 (paperback) | ISBN 978-1-4331-8144-3 (ebook pdf)
ISBN 978-1-4331-8145-0 (epub) | ISBN 978-1-4331-8146-7 (mobi)
Subjects: LCSH: English language—Rhetoric—Study and teaching (Higher) |
Academic writing—Study and teaching. | Ethnology—Biographical methods.
| Autobiography—Authorship. | Social sciences—Research—Methodology.
Classification: LCC PE1404 .H664 2020 (print) | LCC PE1404 (ebook) |
DDC 808.06/6378—dc23
LC record available at https://lccn.loc.gov/2020018810
LC ebook record available at https://lccn.loc.gov/2020018811
DOI 10.3726/b17184

Bibliographic information published by **Die Deutsche Nationalbibliothek**.
Die Deutsche Nationalbibliothek lists this publication in the "Deutsche
Nationalbibliografie"; detailed bibliographic data are available
on the Internet at http://dnb.d-nb.de/.

The paper in this book meets the guidelines for permanence and durability
of the Committee on Production Guidelines for Book Longevity
of the Council of Library Resources.

© 2020 Peter Lang Publishing, Inc., New York
80 Broad Street, 5th floor, New York, NY 10004
www.peterlang.com

All rights reserved.
Reprint or reproduction, even partially, in all forms such as microfilm,
xerography, microfiche, microcard, and offset strictly prohibited.

Printed in the United States of America

To Hayley and Hal
"Never was such a sudden scholar made" (William Shakespeare, *Henry V*)

Table of Contents

Foreword ix
Preface xiii
Acknowledgments xix

Chapter One: Introduction 1
Chapter Two: "What Is That?" Defining Autoethnography 9
Chapter Three: "How Do You Do That?" Practicing Autoethnography 21
Chapter Four: "How Do You Teach That" Autoethnographic Pedagogy 31
Interchapter: "What's Next?" Outcomes of Practicing Autoethnography 45
Chapter Five: Self and Context: Increasing Reflexivity 49
Chapter Six: Audience Awareness: Improving Writing Skills 59
Chapter Seven: Relevant References: Improving Research Skills 69
Chapter Eight: Writing Rightly: Ethical Consideration 81
Chapter Nine: Writing Wrongs: Critical Empowerment 91
Chapter Ten: Creative Catharsis: Therapeutic Potential 99
Chapter Eleven: Enjoyment and A Sense of Community 109
Chapter Twelve: "What Could Go Wrong?" Critique and Concern 121
Chapter Thirteen: Conclusion 131

Appendix A: *Invitation to Interview and Interview Questions*   139
Appendix B: *Sample Course Syllabus*   143
Appendix C: *Sample Course Assignments*   149
Appendix D: *Additional Student Autoethnographies*   153
    Reflexivity   153
    Writing   157
    Research   159
    Ethics   161
    Empowerment   164
    Catharsis   167
Appendix E: *Author's Autoethnography*   173
Index   187

Foreword

A Reflection by David I. Hanauer on Autoethnography and the Meaning of Life

There is an interesting paradox at the heart of all lived experience. The paradox, simply put, is that while there is a constant onslaught of events to which each of us is a participant, these experiences do not come with a preassigned meaning. This is true even (or perhaps especially) of those events to which we have the strongest emotional reactions. The world and our lives are, to a large extent, a mystery even to ourselves.

Against this backdrop, society, our parents, schools, religious institutions, the news, social media, the government, our cultural heritage, and every other powerful discursive system aim to fill this void of meaning with their own ideological interpretations. Essentially, our lives are interpreted for us, and we often blindly and seemingly naturally believe the stories we are told about our own lives. Except there is nearly always a problem with this. The problem is that each of our lives is not easily reducible to the narrative meanings imposed upon it. There is often a sense of discomfort, alienation, and distance from the ways in which personal experience is experienced and the way it is discursively presented. This problem is further exacerbated by the fact that there are multiple meanings and interpretations present within any given experience. Rather than a single meaning, experience comes both without meaning and simultaneously with multiple potential meanings. As I have argued elsewhere (Hanauer, 2003), there is a uniqueness in every individual's life that is just not reducible to the stereotypical norm of society. We are just not fully the stories imposed upon us. There is always a space and a feeling of unease with ourselves.

This puts the consciousness of all of us, every human alive, in the difficult situation of being the locus of a long personal history of experienced events to which meanings have been assigned, which in many cases are only partial and sometimes problematic. There is a space between the experience of the event, the bodily imagistic memory of what happened and the way a person explains this to themselves, drawing upon the discursive resources to which they have been exposed. This space and unease make themselves known at points of crisis and significance in an individual's life. The need to explain one's own experiences and what they mean happens to everyone eventually. Life is full of drama, trauma, parting, danger, death, love, caring, and emotion.

Unfortunately, most education systems do not prepare individuals for these types of experience. Currently, higher education increasingly sees itself, in accordance with neo-liberal ideas, as a job agency and not as a site for the development of critical, self-reflective abilities. Even writing instruction, which historically has been the site of self-exploration, has been shifted to the role of "support" course designed to provide students with the types of academic writing that their disciplines and future employers require. While I have nothing against this beneficial function of a writing class, there is at this moment in history a far more important role that writing instruction can play. A brief purview of the current political and societal trends reveals the rise of populist, nationalist ideologies promising individual agency through group ideology. We have not seen such an increase in this sort of ideological positioning for a hundred years, and with it comes the specter and realities of xenophobia, division, hate, racism, and warmongering.

The power of these discourses to supersede the insecurity of a partial interpretation of self with a totality of self cannot be underestimated. The desire for an overriding interpretation of the meaning of one's life is a powerful force, which attracts many who feel it as a simple solution to the problem of self. Of course, these types of populist, nationalist, and fascist interpretations come at the price of a stereotypical sense of self and other. To align oneself with such positions requires violence and distortion in relation to one's own history. Specifically, one is required to mold and force the self to meet a predefined stereotype of self and to see others using the same ideological lens.

It is against this context that writing instruction is crucial and a potential bulwark against the slippage of identity into stereotypical group membership. Writing can, when conducted seriously, be an influential source of self-exploration that counters the symbolic attacks of a variety of societal discourses. I am not talking about the multitude of self-presentation performances enacted on a range of social media platforms. That type of writing is primarily a rehearsal of a stereotypical sense of self. Rather, I am talking about the writing research methodologies under the heading of meaningful literacy instruction (Hanauer, 2012) which allow individual students to explore and explicate the meanings of their lives and to understand the ways in which they are uniquely positioned between a range of existing discourses and their own experiences. Primary among these approaches is the writing of interpretive autoethnographies (Denzin, 2014).

As such, I am very pleased to write the foreword for Justin Hopkins' important book on the usage of autoethnography in the college composition classroom. The book carefully explicates and exemplifies autoethnography as a writing methodology and pedagogy that allows for the exploration of self in order to understand the different strands of meaning and feeling that are inherent in each experience and in our lives more broadly. Autoethnography allows the individual writer the option of really delving into the paradoxes and complexities of lived experience, not a simplistic imposition of a grand discursive meaning, but rather the careful explication of the complications of being oneself.

Hopkins' book, in the tradition of all quality composition scholarship, is grounded within his own experiences as a writing instructor who has taught extensively using autoethnography and is an autoethnographer himself. The book provides a concrete sense of how this type of pedagogy can be used in the classroom and what outcomes can be expected. For any writing instructor, Hopkins provides the resources necessary to use autoethnography in the classroom setting. Simply put, this book lays the groundwork for the broad educational implementation of a program of autoethnographic writing for a wide range of student populations. This is the importance of the current publication.

At this time, as we face the rise of nationalism and its correlated racism and loss of self, writing instruction has a central role to play in helping students find a more honest and grounded meaning for their lives. Hopkins, through this book, shows a way in which this can be enacted. I cannot think of a more important contribution to literacy education at this present time.

David Ian Hanauer
Professor of Applied Linguistics/English
Indiana University of Pennsylvania

References

Denzin, N. (2014). *Interpretive autoethnography*. London: SAGE.

Hanauer, D. (2003). Multicultural moments in Poetry: The importance of the unique. *Canadian Modern Language Review, 60*(1), 27–54.

Hanauer, D. (2012). Meaningful literacy: Writing poetry in the language classroom. *Language Teaching: Surveys and Studies, 45*(1), 105–115.

Preface

If the course had been titled "Autoethnography," I might not have taken it.

I'd never heard of autoethnography before. It sounded kind of silly, frankly—oxymoronic, even: "auto-" meaning "self" and ethnography, as far as I knew, being the study of others. A professor I admired—a prominent compositionist—scoffed at the idea, waving a dismissive hand, and calling it a contradiction in terms.

Yet as I glanced over the offerings for the second summer of my Ph.D. coursework, the subtitle of the last class on the list intrigued me: "Life Writing."

I'd liked writing about my life ever since I'd started keeping a (more or less) daily journal in a dark blue, wide-lined Mead notebook in sixth grade. I remember writing about building Lego castles, playing capture the flag, and getting a letter that had heart-dotted Js and Is and smelled of perfume. I wonder whatever happened to the girl who wrote that letter …

But that kind of writing, that free-form, reflexive, recursive, cursive scribbling was completely different from the kind of formal, sturdily-structured composition I'd been practicing for more than half my life since—academic prose, trying to join the academic pros.

I had no idea that these two kinds of writing could coexist.

Dr. David Hanauer's "Life Writing" seminar introduced me to the genre of autoethnography: studying the self in relation to social/cultural context through a combination of personal reflection, artistic representation, and academic research (Ellis & Bochner, 2000, 2016).

We read Hanauer's own autoethnography, about his experience as the son of a Holocaust survivor, in which he asserts: "Writing and the act of witnessing one's own life offers the option of exploring the complexities of personal experience and presenting it for observation by another" (2012, pp. 845–846). Hanauer blends his own poetry, interviews with his father, and historical research to show the complex relationship he has with his heritage.

We read many examples of autoethnography, including Nora Murad's (2005) on being a mother in an American-Jewish-Palestinian-Muslim family; Yuri Han's (2012) on losing an ex-lover and colleague to cancer; Maria Daskalaki's (2012) on being a scholar crossing geographic borders; Miriam Sobre-Denton's (2012) on workplace bullying; Sunguen Yang's (2012) on the significance of her decision to remain childless in South Korea; Benny LeMaster's (2014) on coming out of the closet. I was simply astonished by the breadth of possible topics, and the intellectual and emotional depth of the writing.

As required, I wrote an autoethnography for the course. I decided to examine my experience of leaving Senegal, West Africa, to live in the United States. Born in New Jersey, I had grown up in Senegal as the child of missionary linguists, but when I graduated from high school, I returned to my passport country.

Concentrating specifically on what David Pollock and Ruth Van Reken (2009) call Third Culture Kid (TCK) "reentry," and following Hanauer's (2010, 2012) methodological lead, I wrote poetry representing my time of transition from living in Africa to living in America. I framed those poems with analysis of scholarship on the TCK phenomenon. (I will describe my process in greater detail in Chapter Three.)

I learned a lot about myself and my social/cultural context, discovering that I was both similar to and different from other TCKs. Researching and writing my autoethnography was, without doubt and by far, the most meaningful academic assignment I had ever completed.

After the course, I submitted my autoethnography to the journal *Qualitative Inquiry*, expecting a rejection but hoping for some useful feedback to rewrite and resubmit elsewhere. I was astonished and elated when the essay was accepted, conditionally, on minor revision. It needed an ending, according to reviewer and prominent autoethnographer Tony Adams, who wrote: "The topic is important, the writing and poetry are engaging, and I like the analysis."

I wrote the ending, and I celebrated the publication.

I presented the final version at an autoethnography conference in San Angelo, Texas, where Tony Adams co-key-noted during a snowstorm so severe, the local airport was shut down. To get home, I had to rent a van with several fellow autoethnographers and drive to Dallas overnight, hoping to catch an early morning flight. Under normal conditions, that trip would take around four hours, but the roads were so slick, it took nine.

Inching down the icy highway at 1:30 a.m.—trying to ignore the tractor trailers that had skidded, jackknifed, and overturned off the side of the highway—and thinking about everything I had encountered in the past days and months, I knew I wanted to continue my work with autoethnography.

But how, exactly?

At first, I wanted to follow the example of autoethnographic pioneer Carolyn Ellis. A decade into her work establishing autoethnography as an academic genre, Ellis (2004) wrote a book, *The Ethnographic I*, about teaching a graduate-level class on autoethnography. I wanted to teach such a course, but to undergraduate students.

As far as I could tell at that time, autoethnography had mostly been the practice of professional scholars. I believed the genre could and maybe should be practiced by less advanced writers as well.

My reason: Autoethnography might provide an ideal bridge between the kind of personal writing often done in high school and the academic writing required in college. Also, it could serve as an introduction to research methods through a subject that students find genuinely interesting: themselves. Researching and writing about their own experiences might motivate students more than any assigned topic.

There were obstacles along the way. More about those later, but eventually I was able to teach autoethnography to my first-year undergraduate students. I wrote my doctoral dissertation about the outcomes of their practice of the genre, based on analysis of the students' essays, as well as their answers to interview and survey questions. The outcomes I identified were predominantly and powerfully positive:

- Increased reflexivity
- Improved writing skills
- Improved research skills
- Ethical consideration
- Critical empowerment
- Therapeutic catharsis
- Enjoyment
- Development of a sense of community

I decided to teach autoethnography again. And again, and again.

At the time of this writing, I have taught the course seven times, and I plan to continue. While each iteration varies slightly, the outcomes remain consistent. Here are just a few of the comments from student interviews and from anonymous surveys, supporting my conclusions:

- Christa: "I learned what I'm capable of....I accomplished this piece, and I'm proud of it."
- Betty: "I discover[ed] my passion about writing again."
- Cooper: "I think it was definitely a really good course to have as part of the curriculum....It really touches on a lot of different aspects like research, writing, and almost psychological aspects....So, I think especially for freshman, those are good to have under your belt, just to get through the rest of the college experience."
- Lynne: "It helped me discover myself, and I'm sure it helped others."
- Anonymous Student Survey: "Although I do not like writing classes, this class helped me enhance my intellectual development [because] of the interesting material."
- Anonymous Student Survey: "I can't articulate how much I loved this course."

There are many more such comments—not to mention the autoethnographies themselves—which I will share in the following chapters.

My experience indicates that not only is practicing autoethnography valuable, for many reasons, it is unusually or even uniquely well suited to first-year undergraduate courses. Certainly, teaching autoethnography has been uniquely rewarding for me. I hope this book will help others have similar experiences.

References

Daskalaki, M. (2012). Personal narratives and cosmopolitan identities: An autobiographical approach. *Journal of Management Inquiry, 21*(4), 430–441.

Ellis, C. (2004). *The ethnographic I: A methodological novel about autethnography*. Walnut Creek, CA: AltaMira Press.

Ellis, C., & Bochner, A. P. (2000). Autoethnography, personal narrative, reflexivity: Researcher as subject. In N. K. Denzin & Y. S. Lincoln (Eds.), *Handbook of qualitative research* (2nd ed., pp. 733–768). Thousand Oaks, CA: SAGE.

Ellis, C. S., & Bochner, A. P. (2016). *Evocative autoethnography: Writing lives and telling stories*. New York, NY: Routledge.

Han, Y. (2012). Grief and work: The experience of losing a close coworker by cancer. *Journal of Management Inquiry, 21*(3), 288–396.

Hanauer, D. I. (2010). *Poetry as research: Exploring second language poetry writing*. Philadelphia: John Benjamins.

Hanauer, D. I. (2012). Growing up in the unseen shadow of the Kindertransport: A poetic-narrative autoethnography. *Qualitative Inquiry, 18*(10), 845–851.

LeMaster, B. (2014). Telling multiracial tales: An autoethnography of coming out home. *Qualitative Inquiry, 20*(1), 51–60.

Murad, N. L. (2005). The politics of mothering in a "mixed" family: An autoethnographic exploration. *Identities: Global Studies in Culture and Power, 12*(4), 479–503.

Pollock, D. C., & Van Reken, R. E. (2009). *Third Culture Kids: The experience of growing up among worlds* (Revised ed.). Boston, MA: Nicholas Brealey.

Sobre-Denton, M. S. (2012). Stories from the cage: Autoethnographic sensemaking of workplace bullying, gender discrimination, and white privilege. *Journal of Contemporary Ethnography, 41*(2), 220–250.

Yang, S. (2012). An autoethnography of a childless woman in Korea. *Affilia: Journal of Women and Social Work, 27*(4), 371–380.

Acknowledgments

Shakespeare wrote: "Ingratitude is monstrous" (*Coriolanus* 2.3.9). My gratitude is great, and I express it humbly and happily to my friends and family, fellow artists and academics, without whom this book would not be.

To Dr. David Hanauer, who introduced me to autoethnography, something that seemed both strangely familiar and at the same time radically and wonderfully different from anything I had encountered before.

To my many former teachers, from those of École des Enfants de la Croix-Rouge, whose aggressive pedagogy introduced me to cross-cultural learning, all the way to Dr. Gloria Park, who was far gentler, but who still pushed me to push myself.

To my many former students, from whom I have probably learned as much as, if not more than I taught, and especially to those students who contributed to this book: Edward, Betty, Kaitlyn, Kim, Spencer, Taylor, Christa, Elizabeth, Cooper, Tania, Lydia, Sam, Caroline, Jocelyne, Selena, Marian, Mariama, Allison, Emily, Lynne, Hannah, Sophie, and Haley. You all have made this work possible.

To the Franklin & Marshall community, for years of investment in me, and especially to the Writing Center—Dan and the tutors: You have made me a better writer, and many times a better person, at every stage of my education and employment since I started at F&M, almost half my life ago.

To my many mates, from many places, with whom I have lived, learned, laughed, cried, and played: Alex, Ryan, Matt, Maria, Marko, Lu, Summer.

To the Wismers—there really are no words.

To Ibu.

To Tonton Soly and to Aida—*kasumaay* and *abaraka*.

To my grandparents, who loved me all ways and always.

To my brother, who is as good a man and has as fine a mind as any I know—Sean, you should write more, and I hope you will.

To my parents, who were the first to make me want to know more about the world, myself and others, who taught me to read and to write, and to love.

To anyone who was there along the way, and to the one I hope will be here soon, but mostly to Hayley. I'm happy we're here now.

CHAPTER ONE

Introduction

I had rarely laughed while reading students' essays before, and I had certainly never cried.

I had chuckled—sometimes with pleasure at a clever turn of phrase or an amusing idea, more often ruefully and shaking my head, bemused more than amused. Not infrequently, I had ground my teeth and groaned, frustrated, wondering whether this was my students' fault—for procrastinating and not paying attention—or mine, for just not knowing how to prompt better work.

Often, the essays seemed to show what the students hadn't learned, rather than what they had. Both bemusement and frustration were especially frequent when reading research essays. Most often—though it felt unfair to say so—these consisted of chunks of information imported from the minimum number of sources, often apparently unconnected and largely uninterpreted. Sentence-level coherence and absence of plagiarism could be considered a success, but these were discouragingly low bars to clear.

My experience is not unusual. Students at the undergraduate level, especially in their first year, often struggle to write meaningful research essays. In both editions of his pedagogical guidebook *Engaging Ideas*, published 15 years apart, John Bean (1996, 2011) notes: "The question we face, then, is how to transform students from writers of uninspired, pseudo-academic research papers into engaged undergraduate researchers" (p. 198, 225). A decade and a half hadn't changed a word of the problem Bean articulated, and since then, it would be hard to assert the situation has greatly improved.

And again, it feels unfair to blame the students, who are, understandably, not motivated by assigned topics that are often irrelevant or uninteresting to them. You know the kind: "Write an eight- to ten-page paper on therapeutic touch. Follow APA conventions for documentation" (Bean, 2011, p. 232). Apart from the desire to get a good grade, odds are that students just don't have a reason to invest much in these kinds of assignments.

So the work is underwhelming.

Like many writing teachers, I had tried hard to craft assignments that allowed for some choice in topic. For example, in my course with an African literature theme, students picked an African country and some aspect of culture or society to explore, depending on their interests: economics, politics, environmental conservation, sports. In my course with the theme of heroes in literature, students picked a personal hero to examine: a parent, a politician, a comic book character. During those years, I read plenty about Somalian pirates, Nelson Mandela (in both courses), and Spiderman, and I felt *okay* about the students' level of investment and accomplishment.

Still, the results—while adequate and even occasionally engaging or informative—were rarely profound, or passionate. I remember spending many Thanksgiving and Spring Breaks responding to too many drafts clearly cobbled together at the last possible moment from only marginally related sources with listless prose, little thought, and less feeling.

But the autoethnographies that my students submitted—even the first drafts—amazed me.

Sure, there were plenty of grammatical hiccups, and many organizational and expressive elements that students needed to push further in revision. Yet these were, almost without exception, riveting accounts of important personal experiences framed by substantial research and analysis. The topics ranged widely: family conflicts and family celebrations; grieving a grandmother, a dear friend, a father; coping with illness, injury, and injustice; witnessing a religious riot; participating in political protest; surviving a car accident; recognizing educational privilege; overcoming educational obstacles; battling social stigma, peer pressure, and nightmares.

I laughed—not bemused or befuddled, but with genuine enjoyment of the sharp prose and (albeit sometimes morbid) humor. I cried, truly moved by the powerful representations of the experiences and the insights into their significance. And I learned—more than I ever had about Tanzanian jazz or Elizabeth Bennet.

These autoethnographies were different.

****

Autoethnography, according to the genre's foremost pioneers, Carolyn Ellis and Art Bochner, is a study of the self in relation to social/cultural context through a combination of personal reflection, aesthetic representation, and academic research (Ellis & Bochner, 2000, 2016). I will expand on that definition in Chapters Two and Three, providing an overview of the genre's evolution—especially relating to composition—as well as a description of my own approach to practicing autoethnography.

For now, however, I want to emphasize that autoethnography is a blending of concepts that are often perceived as binaries, or polar opposites: artistic *and* scientific, subjective *and* objective, emotional *and* intellectual, personal *and* academic.

The potential of blending academic and personal writing is not new to compositionists. For years, prominent expressivists like Donald Murray, Peter Elbow, and Wendy Bishop championed personal writing in an academic context. Though their influence has somewhat diminished over the years, enthusiasm for expressivist pedagogy remains. In a special issue of *College Composition and Communication* devoted to personal writing, Eli Goldblatt (2017) observes: "many demonstrate a preference for personal writing and narrative, for teaching keyed to individual development" (p. 440).

Narrative is foundational to autoethnography. While not every autoethnography is wholly story, there must be some narrative component, or at least some artistic aspect to engage the reader. Autoethnographers strive for accessibility, rejecting the idea that academic writing must be dense, difficult, and dull. While it appears on scholarly platforms, the genre is intended to engage a wider audience. As Goldblatt (2017) notes, many teachers of writing are familiar with narrative writing. Though not an autoethnographer himself, Gian Pagnucci (2004) argues for narrative's acceptance by the academy: "We are telling stories to figure out who we are and where our place is in the world" (p. 68). For autoethnographers, the artistic can also be analytical.

Furthermore, artistic, personal writing need not be "only" personal. It can also be compatible with the focus on political ideology preferred by proponents of the social turn in composition studies. Many autoethnographers point out that the genre can give a voice to those who might otherwise struggle to be heard. For example, Gloria Park (2013) asserts: "by encouraging genres of writing such as … autoethnography … there is a collective push toward revealing how gendered, racial, linguistic, and classed arguments have further (dis)enfranchised individuals" (p. 9). Autoethnography can serve to enfranchise or empower individuals otherwise absent from scholarly conversations. Goldblatt (2017) also observes the potential of blending personal and political lest we "forget the importance of two impulses that compel writers: the desire to speak out of your most intimate experiences and to connect with communities in need" (p. 442).

Teaching autoethnography offers the opportunity to address those impulses and satisfy those desires, connecting the individual with the communal need. Indeed, the great difference between autoethnography and other forms of expressivism is the fundamental *necessity* to frame personal writing with social/cultural research and analysis.

I'll give an example. My student Emily wrote an autoethnography titled "Sweet Dreams (Are Made of This): Media's Effect on Nightmares." Emily could have crafted an effective, purely personal account of her experience of night terrors, communicating her thoughts and feelings about how her affinity for horror films might have influenced the terrifying dreams that have afflicted her since childhood. However, it is Emily's investigation into how and why night terrors are experienced by *others* that makes her account autoethnographic.

Emily examined the phenomenon not only from her own but also from myriad other perspectives, ranging from psychological studies to literary criticism to online support fora. Emily recognizes the value of this approach in the introduction to her autoethnography:

> As a blend between the artistic and the scientific, I can weave my dreaming experiences into my current and past reflections as well as providing research which supports my position that dreams are relevant to the waking world. The strict, clinical structure of purely scientific writing does not allow for the emotional writing and responses this story evokes in me, while purely personal writing does not often allow for the numerous sources (scientific and otherwise) that I wish to use in this piece.

Emily's essay perfectly demonstrates the potential of practicing autoethnography when connecting the self to the social/cultural context with rigorous research and analysis.

One might look to some interesting numbers for further evidence of Emily's investment, and results. The minimum requirement of the assignment (available in Appendix C) was 2,700 words, with references to at least six sources. Emily's first draft included over 6,000 words, with references to a dozen different texts. Her graded draft was 7,324 words, and—like many of my students—Emily continued to revise the autoethnography even after receiving a grade.

While I recognize that quantity is no guarantee of quality, it is interesting to calculate the average length of the essays written by the students who contributed to this book: over 4,500 words—again, well beyond the requirement. Plainly, these students felt motivated to go above and beyond—a welcome change from the usual approach of barely scraping out the minimum. I suspect many writing teachers would be delighted to read such enthusiastically composed prose.

Some writing teachers are already aware of the genre. As Chapter Two describes in more detail, autoethnography has appeared in composition scholarship for many years. David Bartholomae mentioned it as early as 1993, and in a survey of 11 composition journals, I found almost 100 other articles that include references to autoethnography. Most of these references (e.g., Dixon, 1995; Spigelman, 2001) present autoethnography as a genre used by compositionists in their own research, not as a pedagogical tool. A few (e.g., Brodkey, 1997; Camangian, 2010; Danielewicz, 2008) have taught the genre, and with success. Jane Danielewicz (2008), for example, documents her efforts to bring out her students' personal and academic voices, asserting: "students gain a sense of themselves only when they stand in relation to others" (p. 440).

However, in a survey conducted by Carra Hood (2010), autoethnography appeared to constitute just over 1% of alternative research assignments—nearly the same (in)frequency of occurrence as, for example, brochures and action plans. Since Hood's study, several more compositionists have advocated adopting autoethnography into writing pedagogy, including Steven Alvarez (2012), Suresh Canagarajah (2013, 2020), and maybe most substantially, Melissa Tombro in her 2016 textbook *Teaching Autoethnography: Personal Writing in the Classroom*. Still, I suspect if Hood's study were updated, there wouldn't be much of a change, at least regarding autoethnography.

I want to add my voice to those of Tombro, Danielewicz, Canagarajah, and the others who believe that more compositionists should consider teaching autoethnography, either in addition to or instead of more traditional research writing assignments.

I should emphasize now that this is not a how-to book. Much of the text, especially in Chapters Five through Eleven is student writing, which I hope will inspire readers to recognize the potential of practicing autoethnography and explore the possibilities of teaching the genre. In these first few chapters, however, I do offer some pedagogical possibilities, as well as some necessary context.

Chapter Two provides further background on the genre of autoethnography. I sketch autoethnography's history. I provide a definition. I acknowledge and address some critiques of autoethnographic practice. I note the ways in which the genre has already appeared in composition scholarship.

In Chapter Three, I describe my own autoethnographic process. There is no one right way to practice autoethnography, but I share some guidelines offered by Heewon Chang (2008) and David Hanauer, and I show how I followed them.

Chapter Four describes the circumstances under which I came to my conclusions about teaching autoethnography. I provide an overview of the course I designed: a first-year undergraduate seminar in the general education curriculum of a small, liberal arts college.

Chapters Five through Eleven demonstrate specific outcomes of practicing autoethnography:

- Increased reflexivity
- Improved writing skills
- Improved research skills
- Ethical consideration
- Critical empowerment
- Therapeutic catharsis
- Enjoyment
- Development of a sense of community

Each chapter includes evidence of the relevant outcome from multiple sources, mainly selections from the students' autoethnographic essays, supplemented by student interviews and anonymous end-of-semester teacher evaluation surveys.

As an example, let me return to Emily, who demonstrated the outcome of increased reflexivity. In her interview, Emily commented explicitly on the "'aha' moment of realizing your small role is part of a bigger piece in your culture." In her autoethnography, not only does Emily describe her own personal experience with nightmares, and the experiences of others, she also turns her reflexive eye to the connections between the two. Specifically, she contextualizes her nightmares with film theory about the horror genre:

> Without our nightmares, there would be no fear to incite, nothing unnerving waiting to be triggered. Thus, "the nightmare is a culturally established framework for ... understanding the horror genre" and is necessary to grasp the concept of these monsters (Carroll, 1981, p. 17). Dreams are the source of artistic invention; their notes of whimsy provide the dreamer with a fanciful reality where anything is possible.
>
> Conversely, nightmares give the dreamer a glimpse of a world where anything they fear comes to life, a striking quality. Indeed, it is "the unforgettable nature of nightmares that makes them potent cultural phenomena" explaining their widespread application. (McNamara, 2008, p. 111)

Emily's reflexivity—her critical consideration of her own experience in its social/cultural context—is evident in this passage. There is much more evidence of reflexivity—and the other outcomes of practicing autoethnography—in Emily's and other students' work.

However, there are risks and costs as well. Chapter Twelve acknowledges the concerns and challenges involved in teaching autoethnography. Some challenges are unsurprising: Autoethnography, like any serious scholarly endeavor, is hard work, and students do not always relish hard work. (Though many do embrace the hard work involved in this particular genre, as I will show.)

A more substantial concern is that some students indicated the possibility of feeling vulnerable, even anxious, about sharing aspects of their personal experiences. For example, Spencer, whose autoethnography explored his decision not to drink or do drugs, said in his interview that the genre might not suit everyone. While he was enthusiastic about his own work and generally supported autoethnography's inclusion in an undergraduate curriculum, he offered a caveat: "*if* students are made aware of the implications of autoethnographic writing beforehand." Chapter Twelve addresses these implications, offering options for reducing stress and pressure, while recognizing that eliminating them entirely may not be possible.

Chapter Thirteen concludes my account with some further reflection on autoethnography's place in composition history and current best practice, as well as some final thoughts from my students about their experiences. I believe the combination of evidence from students and scholars in this chapter—as throughout this book—shows how useful autoethnography can be in teaching writing at the undergraduate level, and I hope readers will consider adopting this remarkable genre into their pedagogy.

References

Alvarez, S. (2012). Arguing academic merit: Meritocracy and the rhetoric of the personal statement. *Journal of Basic Writing, 31*(2), 32–56.

Bartholomae, D. (1993). The tidy house: Basic writing in the American curriculum. *Journal of Basic Writing, 12*(1), 4–21.

Bean, J. C. (1996). *Engaging ideas: The professor's guide to integrating writing, critical thinking, and active learning in the classroom* (1st ed.). San Francisco, CA: Wiley.

Bean, J. C. (2011). *Engaging ideas: The professor's guide to integrating writing, critical thinking, and active learning in the classroom* (2nd ed.). San Francisco, CA: Wiley.

Brodkey, L. (1997). Remembering writing pedagogy. *Journal of Advanced Composition, 17*(3), 489–493.

Camangian, P. (2010). Starting with self: Teaching autoethnography to foster critically caring literacies. *Research in the Teaching of English, 45*(2), 179–204.

Canagarajah, A. S. (2013). Negotiating translingual literacy: An enactment. *Research in the Teaching of English, 48*(1), 40–67.

Canagarajah, S. (2020). *Transnational literacy autobiographies as translingual writing*. New York, NY: Routledge.

Carroll, N. (1981). Nightmare and the horror film: The symbolic biology of fantastic beings. *Film Quarterly, 34*(3), 16–25.

Chang, H. (2008). *Autoethnography as method*. Walnut Creek, CA: Left Coast Press.

Danielewicz, J. (2008). Personal genres, public voices. *College Composition and Communication, 59*(3), 420–450.

Dixon, K. (1995). Gendering the "personal." *College Composition and Communication, 46*(2), 255–275.

Ellis, C., & Bochner, A. P. (2000). Autoethnography, personal narrative, reflexivity: Researcher as subject. In N. K. Denzin & Y. S. Lincoln (Eds.), *Handbook of qualitative research* (2nd ed., pp. 733–768). Thousand Oaks, CA: SAGE.

Ellis, C. S., & Bochner, A. P. (2016). *Evocative autoethnography: Writing lives and telling stories*. New York, NY: Routledge.

Goldblatt, E. (2017). Don't call it expressivism: Legacies of a "tacit tradition." *College Composition and Communication, 68*(3), 438–465.

Hood, C. L. (2010). Ways of research: The status of the traditional research paper assignment in first-year writing/composition courses. *Composition Forum, 22*.

McNamara, P. (2008). *Nightmares: The science and solution of those frightening visions during sleep*. Westport, CT: Praeger.

Pagnucci, G. S. (2004). *Living the narrative life: Stories as a tool for meaning making*. Portsmouth, NH: Boynton/Cook Publishers.

Park, G. (2013). My autobiographical-poetic rendition: An inquiry into humanizing our teacher scholarship. *L2 Journal, 5*(1), 6–18.

Spigelman, C. (2001). Argument and evidence in the case of the personal. *College English, 64*(1), 63–87.

Tombro, M. (2016). *Teaching autoethnography: Personal writing in the classroom*. Geneseo, NY: Open SUNY Textbooks.

CHAPTER TWO

"What Is That?" Defining Autoethnography

While I was writing my dissertation, people would ask, politely, what it was about. When I told them "autoethnography," they almost always followed up with a more genuinely curious, if not confused, "What is that?"

I had a pat reply: "It's the combination of personal reflection, artistic representation, and academic research to study the self in relation to social/cultural context."

Not surprisingly, that only tended to prompt more questions.

Really, there is no perfect answer. Even (and especially) autoethnographic experts don't necessarily see eye to eye. In her introduction to an anthology of seminal works on autoethnography, Pat Sikes (2013) emphasizes the difficulty in defining the genre: "As leading commentators and exponents of autoethnography generally note, there is no consensus on what the term means or what the approach involves" (p. xxii). Now, I do see some common ground, but it is certainly true that there is plenty of disagreement as well.

In this chapter, I will try to sift through that disagreement, providing some general background information on autoethnography to orient any who might be unfamiliar with the genre, and to clarify my position on its more controversial issues. To do so, I will present a brief history of the genre's evolution, including its most prominent critics, and, more importantly, an overview of autoethnography's previous appearances in composition studies.

****

First, and fundamentally, autoethnography is a form of qualitative research. The genre prioritizes subjectivity over objectivity. Rather than numerical data, autoethnography depends on experiential accounts—stories instead of statistics. (I recognize that for many, including myself, the binary opposition between qualitative and quantitative is not always comfortable, but here it helps to distinguish the two.)

Second, autoethnography is interdisciplinary, with roots in the social sciences, humanities, and arts. Anthropologists Karl Heider (1975) and David Hayano (1979) were among the first to use the term in the 1970s, applying it to their ethnographic work. Later, literary scholar Françoise Lionnet (1989) referred to Zora Neale Hurston's work as autoethnography: "the defining of one's subjective ethnicity as mediated through language, history, and ethnographical analysis" (p. 99). Lionnet's definition approaches the one I will use, emphasizing the connection between self and social/cultural context.

In 1997, sociologist Carolyn Ellis and communications scholar Art Bochner published autoethnographies that helped establish the genre as it is most commonly, currently understood. Art Bochner wrote about his father's death and how that loss acted as a catalyst to change his professional life. Bochner (1997) critiqued academia as institutionally "impersonal, not intimate" and asserted: "the academic self frequently is cut off from the ordinary, experiential self" (p. 421). He pointed out, not incorrectly, that academics often hide their personal reasons for studying something and then spend their careers publishing work that almost no one reads. Bochner (1997) resolved to tell more stories for a wider audience and to "bring [his] academic and personal worlds closer together" (p. 434).

Bochner's work resonated with many, including Carolyn Ellis. Ellis (1997) illustrated the impersonal insularity of scholarship using her previous autoethnographies about her brother's and her former partner's deaths. Ellis emphasized how she wanted to break through the intellectual and emotional boundaries the academy erects, instead embracing the intersection of the personal and the scholarly. She argued that autoethnography "connects the autobiographical impulse with the ethnographic impulse … fluently mov[ing] back and forth, first looking inward, then outward, then backward, and forward … until the distinctions between the individual and social are blurred beyond recognition" (Ellis, 1997, pp. 132–133).

Ellis and Bochner, partners in life as in work, have continued championing the practice of autoethnography (2000, 2016), and it is their (ever-evolving) definition I use throughout this book.

Criticism of Autoethnography

Autoethnography is not without its critics. Early attacks on the genre came from some social scientists who considered autoethnography neither sufficiently social nor scientific, but instead overly sentimental. Their critiques were sharp. For example, sociologist Herbert Gans (1999) called the genre "the latest of the fads and fashions to which intellectual life, like show business, has always been subject" (p. 543). Such claims have been proven wrong by, if nothing else, the passage of time and the surviving and thriving of autoethnography in the academy.

Other critiques may carry more weight. Social anthropologist Sara Delamont, passionately opposed to the practice of autoethnography, called the genre "essentially lazy—literally lazy and also intellectually lazy" (2007, p. 2) and "an intellectual *cul de sac*" (2009, p. 51). Delamont (2009) correctly identified but also wrongly characterized the foundation of the genre: "Autoethnography focusses on social scientists who are not usually interesting or worth researching" (pp. 59–60). It is undeniable that autoethnography focuses on social scientists, and Delamont may, fairly, find nothing interesting or worth researching in their experiences. However, I, and many others, do.

Even as I reject Delamont's overall position, I do acknowledge that there are aspects of autoethnography that are potentially problematic. In the next sections, I will discuss several such issues: ethical implications, the question of analytic rigor, and the struggle to apply appropriate evaluative criteria to the genre.

Ethical Implications

Maybe the most important challenge to autoethnography comes from ethical concerns expressed by both its advocates and its antagonists.

In two separate 2007 publications, Ellis discussed the ethical implications of practicing autoethnography. After admitting to her own, earlier, ethically problematic research, she gave extensive advice on how to handle ethical issues in autoethnography. Some of her suggestions are abstract: "Seek the good….Be wise, but not cynical" (2007a, p. 213; 2007b, p. 23). But she also provides concrete, actionable steps, like letting subjects read anything written about them. She hedges, however, insisting there are exceptions to every rule. Ellis concludes with an impressive assertion: "autoethnography itself is an ethical practice" (2007a, p. 223; 2007b, p. 26).

However, not all scholars are favorably impressed with autoethnographers' ethical considerations. Martin Tolich (2010) indicted autoethnographers—including Ellis—for practices he considered indefensible, including assuming consent or obtaining only retrospective consent from research subjects. Tolich proposes 10 guidelines for ethical autoethnographic research, addressing issues of consent, consultation, and vulnerability of subjects. He concludes: "Autoethnographers can easily demonstrate their respect for persons by anticipating the needs of both the other and the self before the research writing begins" (Tolich, 2010, p. 1608).

"Easily" may be an exaggeration, but I do not disagree with certain points Tolich makes. On the other hand, I also agree with Jill Tullis' (2013) assertion that autoethnography is more ethically complicated than many more traditional types of research, and taking that complication seriously requires more complex consideration. For example, Tullis (2013) responds explicitly to one of Tolich's (2010) critiques: "While retrospective consent is less than ideal, I think calling this practice coercive lacks nuance" (Tullis, 2013, p. 248). Sometimes, specific circumstances make informed consent impossible to obtain before beginning research, and the value of the research outweighs the potential for harm. When I composed my own autoethnography, for example, I wrote about more and more subjects (i.e., friends and family members) along the way. While I did eventually request and receive their permission to publish representations of them, it would not have been possible to do so before beginning writing, as Tolich insists.

Overall, I respect the boundaries Tolich proposes, and I concur with Tullis' (2013) statement: "Doing autoethnography well means taking ethics seriously" (p. 257). After all, whether or not to engage ethically in research, of any kind, is a choice that must be made and practiced by every researcher.

Analytic Rigor

Another concern about autoethnography is the extent to which the genre must balance both of its core components—personal reflection and social/cultural research. The question behind this concern is blunt: How can autoethnographers go beyond the artistic genres of autobiography and memoir to achieve serious scholarly status?

Around halfway through autoethnography's evolution thus far, Leon Anderson (2006) incited controversy when he proposed a split between what he called "evocative" and "analytic" autoethnography. Basically, Anderson proposed, analytic autoethnography should be more intellectually rigorous than the more emotionally-driven (and artistic) evocative autoethnography; and autoethnographers should consider adopting one or the other.

The reason I mention the tension between evocative and analytic autoethnography is that this tension informs one of the most frequent and difficult challenges to the genre: Is autoethnography really academic work? In particular, I want to address the question of the necessity of conducting substantial scholarly research on the social/cultural context framing the personal experience. Most autoethnographers include that academic framework, but some do not feel the need for many (or any) such intrusions into their stories. Boiled down, as Robin Boylorn and Mark Orbe (2014) observe: "Some incorporate citations while others rely on the verisimilitude of the experience for confirmation" (p. 20).

But is verisimilitude sufficient to merit academic status?

My own position in this much-contested issue is that without some substantial elements of formal research and reference to an existing body of knowledge, autoethnographies are instead actually autobiographies or memoirs. I am not alone in that opinion. According to Heewon Chang (2008), for example: "Mere self-exposure without profound cultural analysis and interpretation leaves this writing at the level of descriptive autobiography or memoir" (p. 51). I do not, and I don't think Chang means to denigrate either autobiography or memoir, but if autoethnography is to distinguish itself from these non-academic genres, I believe it must remain grounded in the rigorous, analytical scholarship to which it aspires to contribute.

Evaluation

Though there are other criticisms of autoethnography, the last I will address is the difficulty of applying evaluative criteria to the genre. This challenge is especially relevant—and potentially discouraging—to any who would wish to teach autoethnography.

Part of the challenge is that autoethnography is fundamentally personal work, and evaluating a person's personal work can seem like evaluating that person's personal life. It can seem nearly a kind of violation, an almost violent passing of judgment on experience, rather than a detached assessment of aesthetics and analysis.

But surely the solution cannot be an "anything goes" attitude, of which autoethnographers have been accused—unfortunately, not always inaccurately. Sikes (2013) expresses concern for maintaining quality in autoethnographic discourse: "My view is that sometimes work does get through and get published on a 'pity' call, rather than on its stylistic or scholarly merit" (p. xxvi). Such a confession, frankly, may not inspire confidence in the genre.

Autoethnography can come across as relentlessly relativistic. Bochner (2000) argues against the value of *any* evaluative criteria and only reluctantly recommends several specific qualities he looks for when reviewing: "abundant, concrete detail … structurally complex narratives … emotional credibility, vulnerability, and honesty … a tale of two selves … ethical self-consciousness …[and] a story that moves me" (pp. 270–271). These are hardly objective criteria, though some scholars (including Bochner) would protest that assessment is never truly objective anyway.

Then there is Ellis' (2000) description of her process of reviewing a manuscript. She begins with an optimistic attitude: "looking forward to being engaged" (p. 273). While she asks critical questions throughout, she also concludes with positive reinforcement, regardless of her recommendations: "I go back through the review and try to rewrite it in a more encouraging manner" (p. 276). Many writers would be thrilled with such a sympathetic reader, but many scholars would shudder at such an apparently relaxed approach to peer review.

I must recognize that this final critique of autoethnography might make compositionists particularly hesitant to adopt the genre into their pedagogy. Writing teachers know that assessing writing is already awfully hard (Danielewicz & Elbow, 2015; Elbow, 2000; Inman & Powell, 2018; Rowntree, 2015). One might reasonably ask, why complicate things further?

Autoethnography in Composition

Yet, I contend, compositionists should indeed consider teaching autoethnography. Some already have, and do, and in this section, I briefly review the history of autoethnography in composition studies, particularly relating to its pedagogical application.

Personal writing assignments have long been a part of compositionists' repertoire, and some of these assignments bear striking resemblances to autoethnography. Allen Carey-Webb (2001) notes: "Rather like the 'I-Search' paper that Ken Macrorie [1988] has written about, multigenre autoethnographies allow my students to reflect on the process of research as well as on the product" (p. 143). And as early as 1993, before even Carolyn Ellis and Art Bochner had begun using the term *autoethnography* much in print, David Bartholomae named the genre while imagining an approach to basic writing that would affirm students' differing cultural backgrounds. He dismissed his own proposal as improbable if not impossible "caricature" because students would not be prepared for such a high level of discourse; but he admitted autoethnography was an appealing idea (Bartholomae, 1993, p. 14).

By five years later, autoethnography had become popular enough in composition studies for Krista Ratcliffe (1999) to comment on "the number of 1998 CCCC [Conference on College Composition and Communication] preconvention workshops on the topic" (p. 213). However, while Ratcliffe (1999) acknowledges autoethnography is "valuable," she also claims it is "limited in perspective" because it "risks lapsing into a narcissistic confessional solipsism ... unless we tie the personal to the cultural" (pp. 212–214). Advocates of autoethnography would reply that when practiced properly, the genre already does what follows Ratcliffe's "unless."

Regardless of Ratcliffe's hesitation, autoethnography has undeniably accrued a substantial following in composition studies. I had no idea how substantial when I began my dissertation literature review. During the summer of 2015, I searched the online archives of 11 composition journals and found 93 references to autoethnography. Of those 93 results, many mention autoethnography only in passing, and most refer only to the genre as used by compositionists in their own research, not in their teaching.

However, in several articles, compositionists do specifically describe teaching autoethnography. For example, Mary Soliday (1994) advocates the use of literacy narratives in composition courses and shares examples of her students' work: "Through writing her own response to [Richard Rodriguez's (1983)] *Hunger of Memory* Alisha practices a sort of autoethnography" (p. 519). Soliday's perspective is worth highlighting especially because of its emphasis on reflexivity, one of the outcomes I identified in my own study of practicing autoethnography: "When they are able to evaluate their experiences from an interpretive perspective, authors achieve narrative agency by discovering that their experience is, in fact, interpretable" (pp. 511–512). Soliday's students, like mine, found that autoethnography helped them understand themselves better.

Similarly, Daniel Mahala and Jody Swilky (1996) argue for the place of personal storytelling, including autoethnography, in academia, and specifically in the writing classroom. They trace the history of personal writing in composition studies, describing the conflict between its proponents and opponents, and laying the theoretical groundwork for their overall assertion: "When we advocate attention to the personal in writing, we are talking about discursive strategies through which writers can present themselves as historically situated subjects exploring how their knowledge has been shaped by lived experience" (Mahala & Swilky, 1996, p. 364). About autoethnography specifically, Mahala and Swilky (1996) observe: "Contemporary autoethnography integrates knowledge from different contexts that are never distinct, contesting the notion that the personal is ever outside of writing" (p. 375). They also share examples of autoethnography in the classroom, their students writing reflexively about their experiences with issues of gender and race in relation to popular culture.

Linda Brodkey (1997) also advocates the use of autoethnography in the classroom, albeit at a more advanced level. Building on her earlier theoretical and practical work with autoethnography (1987, 1994, 1996), Brodkey (1997) recounts her experience assigning graduate students autoethnographic literacy narratives: "The intellectual labor of writing autoethnographic accounts of literacy entails locating and exploring the sites where people learn to think of themselves as readers and writers" (p. 493). Earlier, Brodkey (1994) had presented such a project herself, comparing her experience of writing to "finding and following the bias" (p. 546). By bias, she means the line of fabric one must use as an orientation point in stitching—though certainly she puns, too. She uses the bias as a metaphor for image-rich narrative inquiry, asserting: "I wish everyone were taught to write on the bias … it is as critical to writing as to sewing" (Brodkey, 1994, p. 546).

Over a decade later, Jane Danielewicz (2008) discussed the use of personal genres, including autoethnography, in the undergraduate composition classroom. She echoes and advances the theoretical positions articulated by Brodkey (1997) and Mahala and Swilky (1996), emphasizing the reflexivity of autoethnography, as well as the creative and critical capacity of personal writing in general, which "not only develops voice and cultivates identity but also enhances authority" (Danielewicz, 2008, p. 421). Like Mahala and Swilky (1996), Danielewicz shares stories written by students about family, friendship, fashion, and religion. In an endnote, she reemphasizes autoethnography's pedagogical potential for promoting independent thought: "Writing an autoethnography … can be a form of radical critique as well as a way for the writer to escape the totality of cultural determinism" (Danielewicz, 2008, p. 447). Here we see hints of critical empowerment, another outcome I identified in my own study.

Patrick Camangian (2010) concurs. Citing the work of Paulo Freire (1970), he advocates a critical pedagogy of caring: "As cultural narratives that build toward critical social analysis, autoethnographies promote self and social reflection as well as establish compassionate classroom communities among youth with fractured collective identities" (Camangian, 2010, p. 179). Here Camangian combines the ideas of critical empowerment and therapeutic confrontation of difficult situations, yet another of the outcomes I identified in my study. He concludes by noting the impact of the genre: "For most students in the focal class, writing and performing autoethnographies was one of the first times they were deeply invested in meaningful social inquiry and intellectual interrogation of their own lives while producing academic work" (Camangian, 2010, p. 200).

Steven Alvarez (2012) cites Freire too, but his main focus is on how Pierre Bourdieu's (1973) theory of cultural capital informs autoethnographic work. Alvarez (2012) presents the positive results of his teaching autoethnography in basic writing and first-year composition courses as "a practical alternative to standardized writing assignments" (p. 36). Specifically, he assigned his students autoethnographic personal statements to be used in applications for school scholarships.

Thus, their writing was invested with immediate material significance, as well as a Bourdieusian critique of academic merit as cultural capital. Alvarez (2012) shares examples of his students' writing, examining issues of age and language barriers to advanced education, and he notes their success: "Their writing about changes in life choices have produced qualitative inquiry for each, in addition to writing with purposes and for audiences" (p. 52).

Finally, Suresh Canagarajah (2013) expands on his earlier (1997) pedagogical exploration of autoethnography. Promoting a translingual orientation to language differences in writing courses, Canagarajah (2013) assigned his students a literacy autobiography, one option of which was autoethnography: "the genre can accommodate introspective research on one's memory, archival research on one's writing development, discourse analysis of one's literate artifacts, and library research to interpret the ramifications of one's literacy development" (p. 48). In this description—beyond reflexivity—one can recognize the results of improved writing and research skills, both outcomes I identified in my study. Canagarajah has continued his work with literacy autobiography, asserting: "Autoethnographies can enable marginalized people to represent their own literacy practices and experiences in their own voices, resisting the knowledge constructed about them" (2020, p. 22). Once again, we see the potential for critical empowerment as an outcome of practicing autoethnography.

****

One might wonder why autoethnography is not taught more often, if practicing the genre produces such positive outcomes. Of the nearly 100 appearances of autoethnography I found in composition journals, almost all are entirely complimentary.

Yet despite the overwhelmingly positive references to autoethnography in composition scholarship, the genre remains a relatively rare presence on undergraduate writing teachers' syllabi. In Stephen Brown and Sidney Dobrin's (2004) anthology on ethnography in composition studies, Susan Hanson (2004), who has defended the pedagogical value of autoethnography, nevertheless expresses frustration that still "the term is largely pejorative" (p. 185), the genre underappreciated.

More recently, Carra Hood (2010) presented results of a survey indicating, on the one hand, a dramatic drop in the number of traditional research assignments in the composition classroom. Her results might mean there is more room for alternatives, and indeed, autoethnography is included as one such alternative. But at less than 1% usage. Given the nearly universal and enthusiastic approval of autoethnography in composition scholarship, it seems a shame that more compositionists do not teach the genre.

A recently published textbook by Melissa Tombro may help to change that. Released in August 2016, *Teaching Autoethnography: Personal Writing in the Classroom* advocates the teaching of autoethnography:

> the melding of our traditional composition practices and new ideas from qualitative inquiry can help our field strike an ethical balance and critical awareness in teaching and utilization of personal writing in our classrooms and scholarship. We can combine writing intensive assignments with community engagement and analysis of positionality to create a holistic education model. (Tombro, 2016, p. 15)

Tombro does not discount the difficulties of prioritizing personal writing; she recognizes the risks, and she acknowledges teaching autoethnography requires significant preparation and flexibility. Yet it is worth it, she writes:

> Asking students to draw on visceral experiences as well as textual evidence complicates their analysis and keeps them constantly involved in what is being communicated. … In this way the writing carries an impact that extends beyond the scope of the assignment. (Tombro, 2016, pp. 44–45)

Tombro (2016) concludes: "We have an obligation to prepare our students by devising courses that allow them to engage in personally relevant research and then share it with larger audiences" (p. 51). I wholeheartedly agree.

References

Alvarez, S. (2012). Arguing academic merit: Meritocracy and the rhetoric of the personal statement. *Journal of Basic Writing, 31*(2), 32–56.

Anderson, L. (2006). Analytic autoethnography. *Journal of Contemporary Ethnography, 35*(4), 373–395.

Bartholomae, D. (1993). The tidy house: Basic writing in the American curriculum. *Journal of Basic Writing, 12*(1), 4–21.

Bochner, A. P. (1997). It's about time: Narrative and the divided self. *Qualitative Inquiry, 3*(4), 418–438.

Bochner, A. P. (2000). Criteria against ourselves. *Qualitative Inquiry, 6*(2), 266–272.

Bourdieu, P. (1973). Cultural reproduction and social reproduction. In R. K. Brown (Ed.), *Knowledge, education and cultural change*. London: Tavistock Publications.

Boylorn, R. M., & Orbe, M. P. (2014). Introduction: Critical autoethnography as a method of choice. In R. M. Boylorn & M. P. Orbe (Eds.), *Critical autoethnography: Intersecting cultural identities in everyday life* (pp. 13–32). Walnut Creek, CA: Left Coast Press.

Brodkey, L. (1987). Writing critical ethnographic narratives. *Anthropology & Education Quarterly, 18*(2), 67–76.

Brodkey, L. (1994). Writing on the bias. *College English, 56*(5), 527–547.

Brodkey, L. (1996). *Writing permitted in designated areas only.* Minneapolis: University of Minnesota Press.

Brodkey, L. (1997). Remembering writing pedagogy. *Journal of Advanced Composition, 17*(3), 489–493.

Camangian, P. (2010). Starting with self: Teaching autoethnography to foster critically caring literacies. *Research in the Teaching of English, 45*(2), 179–204.

Canagarajah, A. S. (1997). Safe house in the contact zone: Coping strategies of African-American students in the academy. *College Composition and Communication, 48*(2), 173–196.

Canagarajah, A. S. (2013). Negotiating translingual literacy: An enactment. *Research in the Teaching of English, 48*(1), 40–67.

Canagarajah, S. (2020). *Transnational literacy autobiographies as translingual writing.* New York, NY: Routledge.

Carey-Webb, A. (2001). *Literature & lives: A response-based cultural studies approach to teaching English.* Urbana, IL: NCTE.

Chang, H. (2008). *Autoethnography as method.* Walnut Creek, CA: Left Coast Press.

Danielewicz, J. (2008). Personal genres, public voices. *College Composition and Communication, 59*(3), 420–450.

Danielewicz, J., & Elbow, P. (2015). A unilateral grading contract to improve learning and teaching. *College Composition and Communication, 61*(2), 244–268.

Delamont, S. (2007). Arguments against auto-ethnography. *Qualitative Researcher, 4,* 2–4.

Delamont, S. (2009). The only honest thing: Autoethnography, reflexivity, and small crises in fieldwork. *Ethnography and Education, 4*(1), 51–63.

Elbow, P. (2000). *Everyone can write.* New York, NY: Oxford University Press.

Ellis, C. (1997). Evocative autoethnography: Writing emotionally about our lives. In W. G. Tierney & Y. S. Lincoln (Eds.), *Representation and the text: Re-framing the narrative voice account* (pp. 115–140). Albany: State University of New York Press.

Ellis, C. (2000). Creating criteria: An ethnographic short story. *Qualitative Inquiry, 6*(2), 273–277.

Ellis, C. (2007a). "I just want to tell my story": Mentoring students about relational ethics in writing about intimate others. In N. K. Denzin & M. D. Giardina (Eds.), *Ethical futures in qualitative research* (pp. 209–227). Walnut Creek, CA: Left Coast Press.

Ellis, C. (2007b). Telling secrets, revealing lives: Relational ethics in research with intimate others. *Qualitative Inquiry, 13*(1), 3–29.

Ellis, C., & Bochner, A. P. (2000). Autoethnography, personal narrative, reflexivity: Researcher as subject. In N. K. Denzin & Y. S. Lincoln (Eds.), *Handbook of qualitative research* (2nd ed., pp. 733–768). Thousand Oaks, CA: SAGE.

Ellis, C. S., & Bochner, A. P. (2016). *Evocative autoethnography: Writing lives and telling stories.* New York, NY: Routledge.

Freire, P. (1970). *Pedagogy of the oppressed.* New York, NY: Herder and Herder.

Gans, H. J. (1999). Participant observation in the era of "ethnography." *Journal of Contemporary Ethnography, 28*(5), 540–548.

Hanson, S. S. (2004). Critical auto/ethnography: A constructive approach to research in the composition classroom. In S. G. Brown & S. I. Dobrin (Eds.), *Ethnography unbound: From theory shock to critical praxis* (pp. 183–200). Albany: State University of New York Press.

Hayano, D. M. (1979). Auto-ethnography: Paradigms, problems, and prospects. *Human Organizations, 38*(1), 99–104.

Heider, K. G. (1975). What do people do? Dani auto-ethnography. *Journal of Anthropological Research, 31*(1), 3–17.

Hood, C. L. (2010). Ways of research: The status of the traditional research paper assignment in first-year writing/composition courses. *Composition Forum, 22*.

Inman, J. O., & Powell, R. A. (2018). In the absence of grades: Dissonance and desire in course-contract classrooms. *College Composition and Communication, 70*(1), 30–56.

Lionnet, F. (1989). *Autobiographical voices: Race, gender, self-portraiture*. Ithaca, NY: Cornell University Press.

Macrorie, K. (1988). *The I-search paper*. Portsmouth, NH: Boynton/Cook Publishers.

Mahala, D., & Swilky, J. (1996). Telling stories, speaking personally: Reconsidering the place of lived experience in composition. *Journal of Advanced Composition, 16*(3), 363–388.

Ratcliffe, K. (1999). Rhetorical listening: A trope for interpretive invention and a "code of cross-cultural conduct." *College Composition and Communication, 51*(2), 195–224.

Rodriguez, R. (1983). *Hunger of memory: The education of Richard Rodriguez*. New York, NY: Bantam.

Rowntree, D. (2015). *Assessing students: How shall we know them?* New York, NY: Routledge.

Sikes, P. (2013). Editor's introduction: An autoethnographic preamble. In P. Sikes (Ed.), *Autoethnography* (pp. xxi–lii). London: SAGE.

Soliday, M. (1994). Translating self and difference through literacy narratives. *College English, 56*(5), 511–526.

Tolich, M. (2010). A critique of current practice: Ten foundational guidelines for autoethnographers. *Qualitative Health Research, 20*(12), 1599–1610.

Tombro, M. (2016). *Teaching autoethnography: Personal writing in the classroom*. Geneseo, NY: Open SUNY Textbooks.

Tullis, J. A. (2013). Self and others: Ethics in autoethnographic research. In S. Holman Jones, T. E. Adams, & C. Ellis (Eds.), *Handbook of autoethnography* (pp. 244–261). Walnut Creek, CA: Left Coast Press.

CHAPTER THREE

"How Do You Do That?" Practicing Autoethnography

The most common question about autoethnography I've answered—after "What's that?"—is "How do you do that?"

It's another good question, and also without a simple answer. Just as there are many definitions of autoethnography, there are a wide variety of methods for practicing it. In this chapter I'll share my own process. That process, naturally, influences how I teach the genre, which I will describe in more detail in the next chapter.

I will illustrate my process by referring to my own autoethnography, published in *Qualitative Inquiry* in 2015 and available in Appendix E. I'll refer also to Heewon Chang's (2008) handbook, *Autoethnography as Method*. Chang provides a solid structure for autoethnographic methodology, with many specific suggestions for strategies and exercises.

I wrote my autoethnography during a summer term graduate course taught by David Hanauer. The course was a short one. Hanauer had only four weeks to introduce us to autoethnography and guide us through the process of producing our own. I might have preferred more time, though there is also something to be said for the intensity and urgency of imminent deadlines, as many researchers and writers can attest.

Picking a Topic

Picking a topic may be the most important part of any research project. A topic in which a researcher has little interest will hardly motivate them to do good work, beyond the minimum requirements. Autoethnography benefits from its fundamental focus on topics that should interest any person: their own experiences. However, it can still be hard to choose the right experience to research.

When picking a topic, Heewon Chang (2008) recommends first casting a big net: "virtually any aspect of one's life can become a research focus" (p. 49). Chang suggests a shortlist of five possible areas of interest, which one can rate based on the criteria of personal interest, professional significance, manageability, and ethical standards. That is, how important is the topic to you, both personally and professionally; how likely is it that you can complete the project, given the resources available; and what ethical issues does the topic raise?

David Hanauer asked our class for a proposal of at least three possible topics. I was confident I wanted to write about my experience of growing up in Senegal as a Third Culture Kid (TCK), but I wasn't sure precisely what aspect of that experience I would explore. Hanauer encouraged me to stick with the TCK study. He offered an initial research question: "What was the experience of growing up in Senegal as the child of a missionary family?"

It was the right choice, and a good starting point. Being a TCK is an important part of my identity, of high personal interest, in Chang's (2008) terms. It felt manageable, even given the limited time available. I wasn't sure what ethical issues the study might raise, but I couldn't think of anything prohibitively problematic, and I felt very motivated to learn more about how my experience might connect with the social/cultural context of being a TCK.

Data Collection

Autoethnography differs from more traditional research in that the data come mostly from the self, from memories of one's own experience. However, personal memory alone is not sufficient—at least not for the way I practice autoethnography. It is also crucial to be able to frame that data with substantial external information about the social/cultural context of one's personal experience.

Chang (2008) distinguishes between two approaches to research: "the specific-to-general and the general-to-specific" (p. 62). In the former, an autoethnographer begins with their own experience. They start gathering memories from their lives before trying to connect them with the social/cultural context. In the latter, an autoethnographer looks first to the context. They might read scholarly literature or conduct interviews, establishing a broad overview of a topic before narrowing in. Probably because our course time was so short, Hanauer prompted us to conduct both kinds of research simultaneously. I found that approach worked well for me, and I have subsequently adopted it into my own pedagogy.

I started searching for literature on the TCK experience. I found a variety of sources, scholarly and non-scholarly. For example, I found a psychological study on how "reentry"—the return of a TCK to their home (or "passport") country—could cause anxiety, stress, and depression (Davis, Suarez, Crawford, & Rehfuss, 2013). I could relate to that, having felt all those on my own return to the United States, years earlier. I found a monograph published by the U.S. Department of State Family Liaison Office with observations and advice for TCK reentry (Eakin, 1998). I wished I had found that monograph before my own reentry—it could have helped.

Most importantly, I found, or rather re-discovered the work of David Pollock and Ruth Van Reken (2009). Their book *Third Culture Kids: The Experience of Growing Up Among Worlds* is widely acknowledged as authoritative in the TCK community. I had met David Pollock, even attended one of his seminars, but I had never read the book before. I was excited, finally, to do so, and it proved invaluable, providing a good foundation for my further research. For example, Pollock and Van Reken (2009) identify five stages of TCK reentry: involvement (in the "old" culture), leaving, transition, entering, reinvolvement (in the "new" culture). These stages would prove especially useful in my later writing stage.

Meanwhile, I also began to identify memories of meaningful experiences in my own life that might serve as data sources. These memories I recorded in relatively rough form. For example, during one in-class exercise, I free-wrote about one of the more traumatic days of my life in Senegal, when soldiers and tanks entered the village where my family lived, looking for rebel fighters.

Other memories were happier. I jotted notes about building giant mudbrick forts for my Micro Machines, and about playing pretend Swiss Family Robinson shipwreck. I did a lot of listing, with gerund-driven bullet points like "Almost stepping on the snake" and "Dropping the pot of hot water." Many of these memories did not make their way into my final autoethnography, but they informed my process, nonetheless.

Some of Chang's (2008) specific suggestions for data collection were not practical for the quick work we had to do in Hanauer's class. For example, there was no time to obtain Institutional Review Board approval for formal interviews, which can be excellent sources of data. But there were other strategies I did use. For example, Chang (2008) suggests looking at artifacts, like photographs, which can prompt memories: "Visual data make long-term impressions" (p. 109). I looked through many photographs of my childhood in Senegal.

Eventually, one of these photos became the first image in my autoethnography: a picture of my teenage self, just days before leaving Senegal, reclining in the frangipani tree in which I had played as a much younger child—the trunk served as the mast in my Swiss Family Robinson shipwrecking. I remembered vividly when the picture was taken, how I had been reflecting on my life in Senegal and my imminent departure.

Data Analysis

As I continued gathering data, from both my own memories and external sources, I realized that my focus was gradually shifting from the many years I had spent growing up in Senegal towards the briefer time of transition, or reentry: leaving Senegal and returning to live in the United States. In particular, I realized, I was concentrating on the sense of pain and loss I felt from difficulty of adjusting from life in Africa to life in America. This realization came from following Chang's (2008) guidelines for data analysis. She proposes ten strategies, several of which I present here.

"Compare with Social Science Constructs" (Chang, 2008, p. 136)

The term "TCK" is itself a social science construct, coined by anthropologists John and Ruth Hill Useem and used in both academic and non-academic contexts. Defining what it means to be a TCK, for myself as for my readers, was crucial. Here, the work of Pollock and Van Reken (2009) was useful. Though not scholars themselves, Pollock and Van Reken (2009) extensively theorized the TCK experience and crafted the generally accepted definition: "a person who has spent a significant part of his or her developmental years outside the parents' culture … build[ing] relationships to all of the cultures, while not having full ownership in any" (p. 13). Born in New Jersey, raised in West Africa, but with the expectation to eventually return to live in the United States, I was a pretty standard issue TCK.

"Identify Exceptional Occurrences" (Chang, 2008, p. 133)

Exceptional occurrences—or, as some autoethnographers call them, "epiphanies" (Adams, Holman Jones, & Ellis, 2015)—are the most common subjects of autoethnographies. One can also write about more everyday life experiences, but it is natural to focus on the extraordinary. For me, leaving Senegal was one of the most significant events of my life, thus far.

It was also surprisingly hard. I had anticipated returning to the United States as a time of excitement, new opportunities—not to mention conveniences and comforts like fast food and consistent electricity. But reentry hurt. A lot. I found out that's common, according to Kathleen Gilbert's (2008) psychological study of TCK grief:

> Moving from the country they lived in as TCKs was a commonly cited loss. The smells, tastes, cultural rituals, site-specific opportunities, in addition to the physical aspect of the country—geography and climate—were noted as elements of what was then missing in their lives. (p. 100)

Between the literature and my own memories, to write about that time made perfect sense.

My own departure, though, was preceded and followed by other important moments. For example, I wrote about my childhood friend Ibu, another American TCK who had adopted a Senegalese name, and who left Senegal shortly before I did. I also wrote about my eighteenth birthday, which I celebrated just days after returning to the United States; and the terrorist attacks of September 11, which occurred less than three months later. These were all exceptionally important occurrences in my transition to life in America.

"Search for Recurring Topics" and "Look for Cultural Themes" (Chang, 2008, p. 132)

These closely related guidelines were not hard to follow. Not surprisingly, relationships emerged as a frequently recurring topic/cultural theme in my research, both personal and contextual. Several researchers comment on how hard it is for many TCKs to make long-lasting friendships. For example, Anastasia Lijadi and Gertina van Shalkwyk (2014) found that many TCKs "could not reach a deep level of friendship as they were constantly on the move" (p. 11). However, others noted that once they make friends, those relationships are especially strong and important to TCKs: "TCKs usually place a high value on their relationships" (Pollock & Van Reken, 2009, p. 136). Consequently, leaving relationships behind, or being left behind, may be particularly painful for TCKs: "every farewell was difficult, as it entailed grieving the loss of friends" (Lijadi & van Shalkwyk, 2014, p. 13).

These themes in the literature corresponded closely to my friendship with Ibu. As I wrote in my autoethnography: "His parents were my parents' work partners, and their moves often mirrored ours. In the village, his family lived only about a 40-minute drive away. In the city, they were even closer" (Hopkins, 2015, p. 3). Growing up nearby, "Playing Legos,/Practicing martial arts" (Hopkins, 2015, p. 3), we had become close friends, and we both left Senegal at nearly the same time. Saying goodbye to Ibu was hard, maybe more so because it was also saying goodbye to the place we had both lived, as I noted: "After Ibu left, I felt as though I wasn't really present anymore in Africa. It was like an out-of-body experience—an out-of-country, off-of continent experience" (Hopkins, 2015, p. 4).

"Connect the Present with the Past" (Chang, 2008, p. 134)

One of the weaknesses of the autoethnography I wrote for Hanauer's class was the lack of a satisfying conclusion. When I submitted the draft for publication, the reviewer's strongest suggestion for revision was to provide a better ending. I crafted that ending by deliberately and explicitly showing how my (then) current experience connected with my past experience.

I wrote a poem called "Anymore" in which I reflected on how I had changed, and on how aspects of my Senegalese upbringing still affect me. For example, I wrote about how I now (then and still) binge watch television shows—"Very American"—but how I also still (then and now) use Senegalese expletives and gestures: "When I like something, I snap my tongue against my soft palate in a glottal click" (Hopkins, 2015, p. 7).

And in my ending—at the very end, actually—I also wrote about how my Senegalese upbringing influences my pedagogy:

> One of the ways I have incorporated my past into my present identity is by teaching a course called "In and Out of Africa." In this seminar, in which we explore writing from and about Africa, we encounter the poetry of Léopold Sédar Senghor (1991), Senegal's first president, and one of its finest artists and academics. In "Que m'accompagnent koras et balafong" ["To the music of Koras and Balaphon"] Senghor evokes "Paradis mon enfance africaine" (p. 282) ["Paradise my African childhood" (p. 17)] and how his home "reçoit l'enfant toujours enfant, que douze ans d'errances n'ont pas vielli" (p. 291) [Receive the eternally childlike child who has not aged/In twelve years of wandering" (p. 24)]. I never considered my African childhood Paradise, and when I returned after not quite a dozen years away, I felt comfortable, but not at home. I've moved on, or moved forward, or moved away, or something. (Hopkins, 2015, p. 7)

This ending directly connected my present and past, and it felt satisfying despite—or maybe because of—its ambiguity. The uncertainty, the lack of closure, aptly captured my enduringly complicated sense of home.

Writing

Chang (2008) notes that writing should not begin only once data collection and analysis are complete. Rather, it must be part of the process throughout. At some point, however, one must step away from collection and begin to concentrate primarily on making sense of the many pieces one has gathered. Chang (2008) writes about this step: "Your focus needs to shift from sifting through masses of fragmented details to stringing discovered gems together in an intriguing pattern so that the finished product will sound cohesive and interesting" (p. 139). She offers several broad approaches, while acknowledging that styles may blend. Chang's (2008) suggested styles include Descriptive-Realistic, Confessional-Emotive, Analytical-Interpretive, and Imaginative-Creative. As Chang indicated was likely, my autoethnography blended elements of each.

For example, the work was Imaginative-Creative in that I used poetry to present my memories. This style is what Chang (2008) might consider "the boldest departure from traditional academic writing" (p. 148). It was certainly well outside my comfort zone. I do not consider myself a poet, but Hanauer asked us to at least try to use the form in our drafting. I discovered, happily, the concentrated language allowed me to communicate efficiently and evocatively.

For example, I drafted the following short poem:

> I played soccer
> With my friends
> With my soccer ball
> Because no-one else had one

I distilled that into "Playing soccer with friends in the dusty twilight" and, still feeling self-conscious about overly-gilding the lily, adjusted that to "Playing soccer in the sand at twilight." The constant attempt to condense the text allowed me to express more with less. Or, as I put it in the autoethnography itself: "poetry goes where prose cannot, straight to the heart of the matter" (Hopkins, 2015, p. 3).

Despite the creative form, the poems also include some degree of the Descriptive Realistic, as defined by Chang (2008): "depict places, people, experiences, and events as 'accurately' as possible with minimal character judgment and evaluation" (p. 143). For example, in my poem about the night I left Senegal, most of the content is as objectively described as possible, concentrating on factual details: "I carry my beat-up backpack,/And other luggage …. I drink a Coke./I ride the bus to the plane." Only two lines could be considered subjective: "And I feel ready" and "18 years weighs a lot" (Hopkins, 2015, p. 5). In other poems, also, I emphasized detailed description of happenings over emotions.

Still, some of the content must be considered Confessional-Emotive, which, according to Chang (2008), can "expose confusions, problems, and dilemmas in life" (p. 145). In particular, the line "18 years weighs a lot" expresses the sense of burden I felt. The earlier poem about Ibu leaving Senegal is also full of pain, as clearly and as simply as I could present it: "I climb the wooden stairs to the roof,/Sit in a corner, alone,/And cry" (Hopkins, 2015, p. 4). Chang (2008) notes that this kind of "vulnerable self-exposure opens a door to readers' participation in the stories" (p. 145). Even if the reader is not a TCK, surely they have at some time had to say goodbye to a close friend, and they know how much that hurts.

However much my work may contain elements of the above categories, I think the dominant style of my autoethnography, and certainly the style for which I consciously strived, is Analytical-Interpretive. I wanted my autoethnography to do more than creatively and realistically convey my emotions. As Chang (2008) puts it: "In analytical writing, essential features transcending particular details are highlighted" (p. 146). I wanted my story to be truly scholarly, to show how I fit into a broader phenomenon.

For me, this style was most applicable to the structure of my autoethnography. Autoethnographers may employ a wide variety of structures, but the basic question is to what extent does one prioritize story (whether poetic or prose narrative) or analysis? Are the two presented separately, and if so, which comes first?

It was important to me to punctuate the poetic narrative description with passages of explicit social/cultural analysis, so a reader could never go too far without both features complementing each other. Though I respect and admire some autoethnographers' preference for separating story and research, for me it risks reinforcing the perception of art and science as opposites. I wanted the two side by side.

Another, more specific element of structure emerged during data collection, when I found Pollock and Van Reken's (2009) five stages of TCK reentry: involvement, leaving, transition, entering, reinvolvement. Serendipitously, I realized that these stages corresponded closely to the moments I had chosen to represent in poems. This realization was an immense help in structuring my autoethnography. I incorporated the stages into the poems themselves, and referred to Pollock and Van Reken in analyzing how each poem positioned me in my overall experience. For example, about the fifth stage, I wrote:

> The poem "Reinvolvement" positions me as a TCK in the final stage of transition, a time when "[I] once again become part of the permanent community" (Pollock & Van Reken, 2009, p. 73), settling, and experiencing a moment of identification with the culture around me. (Hopkins, 2015, p. 7)

The poem was an account of my experience watching the tragedy of September 11, 2001. The way I remembered and wrote about that day, and the days after, affected me in a surprising way:

> I believe it took 9–11 to truly bring me "home." Sharing the fear of a nation has a powerful acculturative effect. Now I find myself not entirely comfortable with this perception, as I have since confronted the problematic aspects of nationalism. Retrospectively, I balk at the particular brand of patriotism that flared during those days of shared fear. But it happened, and I was a part of it. (Hopkins, 2015, p. 7)

When I presented my autoethnography to my classmates at the end of the course, one of Hanauer's comments was that this was the first time he had perceived 9–11 as having had any positive personal effect. He did not mean in any way to trivialize the mass suffering, or to idealize my problematic reaction. But he noted that though the sense of belonging was inflected with less desirable elements, it did help me to feel more at home—as an individual, part of a community, sharing an identity, however uneasy.

This is exactly the sort of analysis and interpretation I hoped to experience and to prompt through practicing autoethnography.

****

Autoethnographic practice is extremely flexible, and while there are plenty of helpful guidelines, no two autoethnographers are likely to follow the same process. There are simply too many variables to expect conformity in methodology, and, indeed, the openness to variety is one of the attractions and the strengths of this genre.

On the other hand, the fundamental flexibility can also be unsettling, or even frightening to those who prefer more rigidly defined methodology. I know I was simultaneously scared and curious at many moments along the way, wondering how I could connect that odd assortment of poems with pieces of research and analysis, and fearing that there was no way it would make any sense. I have heard stories of the same sense of doubt from many other autoethnographers. Actually, I would probably be most concerned if someone began the process with complete confidence in how it would unfold. The uncertainty, and figuring out how to handle it, is part of the point.

References

Adams, T. E., Holman Jones, S., & Ellis, C. (2015). *Autoethnography: Understanding qualitative research*. New York, NY: Oxford University Press.

Chang, H. (2008). *Autoethnography as method*. Walnut Creek, CA: Left Coast Press.

Davis, P. S., Suarez, E. C., Crawford, N. A., & Rehfuss, M. C. (2013). Reentry program impact on missionary kid depression, anxiety, and stress: A three-year study. *Journal of Psychology and Theology, 41*(2), 128–140.

Eakin, K. B. (1998). *According to my passport, I'm coming home*. Washington, DC: Family Liaison Office, United States Department of State.

Gilbert, K. R. (2008). Loss and grief between and among cultures: The experience of Third Culture Kids. *Illness, Crisis, & Loss, 16*(2), 93–109.

Hopkins, J. B. (2015). Coming "home": An autoethnographic exploration of Third Culture Kid transition. *Qualitative Inquiry, 21*(19), 812–820.

Lijadi, A. A., & van Schalkwyk, G. J. (2014). Narratives of third culture kids: Commitment and reticence in social relationships. *The Qualitative Report, 19*(49), 1–18.

Pollock, D. C., & Van Reken, R. E. (2009). *Third Culture Kids: The experience of growing up among worlds*. Boston: Nicholas Brealey.

Senghor, L. S. (1991). Que m'accompagnent koras et balafong. In *Léopold Sédar Senghor: The collected poetry* (Dixon, M., Ed. and Trans.), Virginia: The University Press of Virginia.

CHAPTER FOUR

"How Do You Teach That?" Autoethnographic Pedagogy

For several chapters, I've been exhorting compositionists to consider teaching autoethnography. In Chapters Five through Eleven, I will show the outcomes of practicing autoethnography that I've observed from my own teaching. Though I indicated in Chapter One that this is not a how-to book, I do wish to share the ways I incorporated autoethnography into composition pedagogy.

Just as I would never claim there is only one way to practice autoethnography—or anything else, for that matter—I don't suggest I know the only way to teach it. However, in this chapter, I provide the context in which I have taught my course on autoethnography and an overview of the course itself. Hopefully this helps situate readers in the specific circumstances under which I observed the outcomes described in the following chapters. It should also provide pedagogical possibilities, including descriptions of readings, in-class exercises, and longer assignments.

****

I began teaching at Franklin & Marshall College, a small, residential, liberal arts, undergraduate-only school in Lancaster, Pennsylvania. Founded in 1787 and named for the fourth United States Supreme Court Chief Justice and the author of *Poor Richard's Almanac*, as of this writing, F&M admits around 625 students each year for a four-year course of study. That study begins with courses called "Connections."

Connections are a two-semester pair of seminars designed to transition students into the rigors of college academics. As the name hints, there is an emphasis on interdisciplinarity, on crossing intellectual borders and finding common academic ground all can share—an idea conveniently in line with autoethnographic principles.

Taught by faculty from every department, topics range from philosophy in film, to space exploration, to the World Cup. When registering, students indicate preference for topics they wish to study. Most get their first or second choice topic. All courses are mandated to develop certain crucial academic skills: reading, writing, speaking, critical thinking, and information literacy. Class size is limited to 16 students, to allow for more individual attention.

Though writing is technically just one of the skills Connections courses aim to develop, for many faculty, writing is the primary focus of the courses, especially since there is no other general education writing requirement at F&M. In this way, Connections are similar to the first-year composition courses required by many institutions.

Connections 1 courses, taken in the first fall semester, situate students to general expectations for college work, particularly writing analytical and argumentative essays. In the spring, Connections 2 courses focus on research skills. Students are expected to develop a research project throughout the course, culminating in an essay and presentation of their work. By completing both Connections courses, all first-year students are supposed to be ready for their further studies.

The Connections curriculum was introduced in the fall of 2014, coincidentally, just after the summer during which I first encountered autoethnography. I immediately recognized an opportunity to try something different. To my knowledge, autoethnography had not yet been taught at F&M. Since then, at least one other Connections course focusing on a version of autoethnography has been taught, and I have become aware of some sociologists and anthropologists incorporating autoethnographic assignments into their classes. At that time, however, as far as I knew, I was breaking some new ground.

That ground was not easy to break. As I mentioned in Chapter One, there were obstacles to teaching autoethnography at my institution. Chief amongst these obstacles was the misunderstanding of the genre by a curricular oversight committee. They thought this was a *solely* creative (i.e., artistic *rather than* analytical) writing course, which would not belong in the Connections curriculum.

The misunderstanding was quite understandable. The genre is unfamiliar to many, and its basic blending of academic and personal writing is paradoxical, if not apparently self-contradictory. I had to explain how my students would be doing *both* artistic representation of their personal experience *and* academic analysis of their social/cultural context.

Eventually my explanation worked, and I piloted two sections of "The Story of You: Autoethnography in Action." Both sections succeeded beyond even my expectations or hopes. After the courses were completed and grades posted—so there would be no possibility of coercion—I invited all students to contribute to my doctoral research. (The invitation and the interview questions are available in Appendix A.) I was pleased when 11 students—about a third of the total number in both sections—volunteered. I interviewed each, and all also agreed to have their autoethnographic essays analyzed and used as evidence and illustration of the outcomes of practicing the genre. A second pair of classes a year later was similarly successful, and a dozen more students volunteered.

Following chapters will present these students' opinions and their work in greater depth, showing how their practice of autoethnography produced the outcomes identified. For the remainder of this chapter, however, I will share an overview of the course during which the work was done. A sample syllabus is available in Appendix B, but here I will describe the progress through the semester, from beginning to end.

Weeks 1–3: Introduction and Basics

Since beginning teaching, I have always started my courses with a freewriting exercise. For example: "Take five minutes and write about Africa." (Or heroes, or Shakespeare, or whatever else the topic may be.) Students then use what they wrote in their self-introductions: "I'm James, from Philadelphia, planning to study Biology, and I wrote about how Ebola is in the news a lot lately …." I've found this is a good exercise to get students engaged with the topic, and writing right away.

For autoethnography, the exercise is especially important. I ask students to think of something that they did or that happened to them in the last 24 hours or so, and to describe it as vividly, as artistically as they can. To avoid embarrassment, I mention that they will be sharing this description, so they should pick something they are comfortable talking about with the class.

After the freewriting, but before the sharing, I briefly define autoethnography—exploring personal experience in a social/cultural context—and ask the students to share their writing and try to imagine how they might explore their experiences further in a social/cultural context.

Knowing that this is not an easy task, I model it first. In the past, for example, I have written about playing with my cat, or organizing the pieces in a collectible strategy game I play. These are relatively low-stakes, relaxed examples, which I picked deliberately for their relatability, before demonstrating more profound possibilities. I try to show how even these seemingly mundane experiences can have social/cultural significance by asking these kinds of questions:

- What is the place of pets in our society/culture? Why do we care so much for them? Are they a kind of replacement or substitute for more human contact and interaction?
- Why do we play games, especially complicated and expensive games that require a lot of time and money? Are they a way of channeling aggression through competition without the physical exertion of sports or actual war?

After this modeling, the students seem to understand—to some extent—what it means to connect their experiences with a social/cultural context. Many do so right away with surprising eloquence and insight, talking about their lacrosse practice, or their sorority bids, or saying goodbye to families before coming back to school, or eating supper with friends after arriving.

Some are harder: "I found black mold in my refrigerator." Even I struggled to make that one connect with any social/cultural context. But most manage.

I'm sure, both from my own observations and from what students reported in interviews, that after the first class, there is still plenty of confusion about what autoethnography actually *is*. I describe it in more detail after the sharing and introductions, but it is just not an easy thing to understand, and is quite easy to misunderstand. One student said: "You try to connect it with things you know, but it's only half of the things you know." Personal *and*—not *or*—academic.

Confusion can continue for several classes, along with skepticism about how practicing autoethnography will work. However, I also know, again from what students reported, that some of them are excited about this genre from the very beginning, and eager to learn more.

For the subsequent several classes, students read journal articles (e.g., Ellis, Adams, & Bochner, 2011) and book chapters (e.g., Adams, Holman Jones, & Ellis, 2015) describing autoethnography, as well as examples of autoethnographies. The first example I assign has always been the first autoethnography I ever read: David Hanauer's (2012) "Growing Up in the Unseen Shadow of the Kindertransport."

Using poetry and narrative alongside more traditional research and analysis, Hanauer describes how his father survived the Holocaust, and how David himself came to terms with his family history. For example, he describes a ghostly visitation from his long-dead grandparents, murdered by the Nazis, an experience he had as a young child, and as an adult. He writes:

> It does not matter whether this is a dream or real. For me the visitation was so visceral and physically present that it is a reality in my life and the mere fact that I know that

this cannot be true and that it must be a reality generated by my own mind is unimportant. (Hanauer, 2012, p. 847)

As it did with me, Hanauer's autoethnography seems to resonate powerfully with my students. Some students have said they can relate to Hanauer's experience, even though they have no personal connections to the Holocaust at all. One said that after reading Ellis et al.'s (2011) more theoretical description of autoethnography, she was nervous about the course, fearing it would be terribly abstract and boring. But then when she read Hanauer's account of being visited by the spirits of his grandparents, she was both reassured about how accessible and artistic the genre could be, and also shocked—a ghost story in a scholarly journal article?

Hanauer (2012) provides an excellent entry point into autoethnography, prompting productive conversations about format, methodology, ethics, and other aspects of the genre. I follow Hanauer with other examples, like Emma Dowling's (2012) account of waitressing at a high-end restaurant, and Damion Sturm's (2015) depiction of his multiple fandoms (e.g., Formula 1 racing, rugby, punk rock). These examples show students that any experience can be the subject of an autoethnography—even experiences that are not as dramatic as Hanauer's. Many students have worked in restaurants, or at least eaten in restaurants, and all of them are fans of something, if not of Formula 1. As they recognize themselves in these accounts, they also see models of different styles and structures for autoethnographies, realizing the remarkable flexibility of the genre.

During this time, students also write the first of the course's conventional essays, identifying what they think are the most important aspects of autoethnography. (The assignment is available in Appendix C.) One valid concern about teaching autoethnography is that it might *only* teach students autoethnography, rather than providing more breadth of practice in research and writing. But it is simple enough to integrate more traditional assignments alongside the autoethnographic work, requiring the students to develop the analytical and argumentative skills they will need in other coursework. It also can help keep the students from being overwhelmed by the unfamiliarity of the genre. Gradually, while they familiarize themselves through exposure and interpretation, students begin to recognize the range of possibilities for their own autoethnographic studies.

Weeks 4 & 5: Critiques, Ethics, and Picking a Topic

I suspect even from the first class, most students start thinking about what topic they will pick for their autoethnography. Some know right away, and others need more time. I assure them all that everyone *will* find something—at least, so far, everyone always has.

Some come to me to talk about potential topics, or for help generating an idea. If they are struggling to think of anything at all, I usually ask them what kinds of things they've done, either for a long time or just once. I ask them if they have played any sports, or participated in any artistic activities, or community service, or if they've travelled. I ask them about significant relationships and about how those relationships have changed over time. Just getting them talking about their experiences can help students realize that even if they can't think of any major, life-changing events, everyone has something they can write about.

Often students' most pressing concern is related to research, that they won't be able to find the kind of sources required to contextualize their experience. I assure them that they will. At least, again, so far everyone has.

Before the end of the first month, I lead an in-class adaptation of an exercise conceived by Della Pollock (cited in Adams et al., 2015, p. 53). I ask students to think about either an "epiphany"—a momentous experience that transformed the world for them—or a more mundane, everyday occurrence that still matters, even if it seems less important (Adams et al., 2015, p. 48). I instruct the students to spend ten minutes writing a description of their chosen epiphanic event or mundane moment.

This activity is similar to the exercise on the first day of class. Now, however, the students have more time, as well as the advantage of some knowledge about autoethnography. They also know that they may be working on the beginnings of their own essay.

Next, students pair up and read their descriptions aloud to each other. Having (hopefully) listened carefully, each partner retells the description they heard. After both have shared, we gather as a group and discuss how the telling and retelling differed.

Often students comment on how their partners emphasized different aspects of their description. Sometimes they say the retelling was much the same. Either way, this is an opportunity to realize what it feels like to have your story heard and interpreted, understood (or misunderstood), and retold.

It is also a chance to test a topic, to get a sense of how it feels to share it, and to decide whether or not it will become the research focus for the rest of the semester. Some topics may prove too emotionally challenging and need to be adjusted or even abandoned. I know of a few—but only a few—instances when this has been the case, and I will discuss this issue more in depth in Chapter Twelve. More often than not, though, the experience described during the exercise will become the first draft of the first part of the student's autoethnography.

During these weeks, we also discuss critiques of autoethnography, including some of those mentioned in Chapter Two (e.g., Delamont, 2009). I try to assure students at this point (and throughout), that it's ok to agree with these critiques, to dislike autoethnography, even. I note that the critics make some good points, including the ethical challenges of practicing autoethnography.

We spend a week reading about those ethical challenges and debating issues like consent and vulnerability. Students write the second of the course's conventional, argumentative essays, comparing two autoethnographies in how they handle the ethical implications of their research. (The assignment is available in Appendix C.)

In class, students also freewrite a reflection on any ethical implications of the story they shared with their classmate, answering these questions:

- Who else was in the story?
- What might they think of the way they are portrayed?
- Should they be consulted and/or asked for consent?

As I will show further in Chapter Eight, students often find the discussion of ethics one of the most eye-opening and important aspects of practicing autoethnography.

Weeks 6 & 7: Research and Representation

These weeks are the beginning of data collection—both the personal and contextual data. As I will illustrate further in Chapter Seven, though the research component is often not students' favorite part of practicing autoethnography, they do recognize its value, both as an academic exercise and, more meaningfully, as one of the unusual or even unique fundamentals of the genre: finding and showing how one's personal experience fits into the social/cultural context.

After a library workshop introducing students to research basics, students write several memos annotating the sources they are finding. Through the years, I have experimented with requiring fewer or more sources, but the least I have ever required has been six: two scholarly books, two scholarly articles, and two sources of some other kind. Usually, I have required more, mainly to try to ensure that the research portion of the project is as rigorous as possible.

Also during this time, we work in class to start developing the students' artistic representation of personal experience. So that we can all start on the same page, I assume the students will have had little or no training in creative writing. I lead a discussion of elements of narrative: plot, character, theme, dialogue, description, point-of-view. We talk about how the autoethnographies we've read thus far have employed these elements, always emphasizing the necessity of "showing" (artistically) alongside "telling" (analytically). So, for example, we recall how Hanauer's (2012) poetry and Dowling's (2012) prose narratives engaged us as readers, and how Sturm's (2015) experimental shifts in point-of-view and his passages of unattributed dialogue were disorienting, but could also be effective, depending on one's taste.

At this point, I tell students to begin writing a scene for their autoethnography. I ask them to keep the narrative elements in mind, but I don't provide many more instructions. I don't want to overburden students with too much direction, and I have found they do just fine without. After drafting, students share their scenes with partners for peer feedback, and with some revision, they send the scenes to me. I provide several sentences of praise and pushing, to encourage them and to demonstrate how they may take their work further.

To return to my exemplary student in Chapter One, Emily wrote a scene about the haunting of her childhood home, and how her family processed that phenomenon. Her elder sister, particularly, reinforced Emily's fears, telling her scary tales of ghostly apparitions:

> I believed this story for years. I don't feel like a "chowdah head," as my city of Boston might call me. My dad, brother, both sisters, and especially my mom suspect our house is haunted. ... What other evidence do you need? (I knew the truth ... My hamster escaped from its cage and is permanently missing. My one sister has gone to the hospital five times in her childhood! She's fallen down the stairs, my other sister dropped a radiator on her foot, she fell out of bed and bit through her lip, she drank too much cough syrup when my mother wasn't looking, and she swallowed a whole bunch of staples! My brother's wall knocks for an unknown reason at night, and he spends sleepless nights in fear as a result. And my parents are getting a divorce. What good is this ghost? It must be malevolent. I'm certain.)
>
> As if all this evidence wasn't enough to convince me, my babysitter Patricia sealed the deal. She was born with the caul over her head, a signal of connection to the supernatural in many cultures, although good or bad connotations differ globally. She was proud of her connection, and took it seriously, the most superstitious person I've met. She's seen the ghost, a pale woman in an old-fashioned dress, always silently hovering, as Patricia described her.

In my feedback, I praised Emily's engaging description of her family members as well as the atmosphere she creates through vivid details like the missing hamster and swallowed staples—both humorous and foreboding. I encouraged Emily, as I encourage most of my students, to consider breaking up long paragraphs into shorter, more dramatic units or "beats."

I also ask each student to pick a single sentence from their scene to share with the whole class for group feedback. I put these sentences into a PowerPoint presentation, without the students' names, and one by one, we talk through them as a class. I ask the students to lead with praise, identifying specific aspects of the sentence that they like. After several minutes, I ask the students to shift to pushing, identifying aspects of the sentence they think could be stronger, and how.

To continue to use Emily as an example, she picked the sentence that began her third paragraph, slightly modified: "My babysitter, Patricia, was born with the caul over her head, indicating her connection with the supernatural in Brazilian black magic." Students commented favorably on the elements of mystery, causing curiosity—most were unfamiliar with the word "caul" and intrigued by the idea of South American spiritualism. Some also complimented Emily on her alliteration. Suggestions for improvement included defining caul for readers, which Emily did, and replacing the somewhat awkward verb "indicates," which she also did.

Once everyone has had their chance to respond, I ask the writer of the sentence to identify themself, and I offer them the opportunity to respond to the feedback, answer any questions, and ask any of their own.

This exercise, which often takes two or more class sessions, has proven popular, and I find it an excellent way to train students in giving and receiving useful feedback. It also helps reinforce the ideas of artistic writing that are often unfamiliar to many, if not most students. The social/cultural significance of the sentences comes up occasionally, but it is not the focus of this exercise.

Weeks 8–10: Drafting

Students have now started the drafting process, but so far they have kept the research and the representation components separate. Combining those components is maybe the most intellectually difficult part of practicing autoethnography. Most students have been taught to keep academic and personal writing separate. Even by their first year of college, they are so ingrained in this mindset of objective science contrasting with, if not contradicting subjective art, they balk at blending the two. Even after reading many examples of autoethnography, when it comes time to do it themselves, they stall.

I don't fault them for it, one bit. I stalled too, when I wrote my first autoethnography. It's just that hard.

I dedicate an entire class to getting past this stalling. I tell students to bring all the sources they've found, and the scene they've drafted. I print out the instructions for an exercise called "Text Spinning and Collaging," which I copy here from Adams, Holman Jones, and Ellis (2015):

> Begin by gathering a few (3–5) books and/or essays that you have read recently or find yourself revisiting....
>
> 1. Read through these works, writing or typing passages that you have underlined or noted.
> 2. Work through each source, or work with multiple sources at one time, building and spinning out a collection of notable passages until you have several entries.
> 3. Look over this list of entries, connecting and grouping—collaging—the disparate material in ways that make sense to/interest you.
> 4. ... if you are already writing stories, look for moments to connect the citations into, alongside, before, or after your stories.
> 5. Do not worry if you do not use all of the material you have cited or all of the stories you have written. You can continue spinning and collaging in multiple writing sessions, beginning by reading over what you have done in a previous draft and then adding to the document you are creating.
> 6. Stay open and pay attention to the emerging logic of your choices, thinking about what connects the work and words you are writing. Over time, your collaging will develop into an internal through-line or logic. ... Use this logic as you continue to develop your writing project. (Adams et al., 2015, p. 72)

I talk them through these instructions, and I tell them to get going. I sit in the classroom, available to answer questions, but mostly I just listen to the typing clicks and the intermittent sighs, either of frustration or, occasionally, satisfaction.

An hour and change later, hopefully they've all made at least a bit of progress in connecting their collection of narrative and data dots, so seemingly far apart.

If they have made progress, from here, it's just a matter of time until they complete their first draft. (If they haven't made progress during the class—which is rare—I work with them individually, out of class, until they have.) In class, we continue to discuss examples of autoethnography on a variety of topics (e.g., family, gender/sexuality, race/ethnicity)—now increasingly focusing on which elements of these examples the students might want to employ or avoid in their own essays.

We do an in-class workshop on structure, responding to the following questions:

- Does one begin one's autoethnography with art or analysis, and why?
- Does one end one's autoethnography with art or analysis, and why?
- Does one keep the art and the analysis separate, and why?
- Does one follow a straightforward chronology, or jump from point to point?

Emily, for example, chose to begin with an artistic depiction of one of her recurring nightmares, in which she lies paralyzed while a stream of thousands of numbers pour from a dark cloud above her head: "They circle me: They grow and shrink, become bolder, more confident as I become more terrified, like sharks readying for a feeding frenzy." She then establishes a more-or-less chronological structure, progressing from childhood, when she watched her first horror movie (*Jaws*—the sharks are a theme) to the present, but with frequent temporal digressions. She incorporates her analysis alongside her narrative, alternating sections throughout.

We do a workshop on reflexivity, in which students brainstorm a list of aspects of identity (e.g., race/ethnicity, religion, politics, gender/sexuality, socioeconomic class), and then explicitly address select aspects in their drafts. For example, addressing her scene about the haunted home, Emily wrote:

> Reflecting on this, I see that my family structure made a huge impact upon my perception of this story. As the youngest, I was easy to convince and my siblings took advantage of that. I believed this story fully, and it ended up impacting my experience in that house as a child, my view of dreams/nightmares, haunted houses, and scary stories.

In this reflection, Emily considers the factors of family structure and age, specifically her position as the youngest of several siblings.

As the due date for the first draft approaches, students often express anxiety about meeting the minimum requirement of 2,700 words. I assure them that it's likely not going to be as hard as they think, that they may find it harder to stop, once they're started, than it was to start. Often the first drafts I receive substantially surpass the minimum. Remember, Emily's was over 6,000 words, and while that was unusual, it's not at all uncommon to receive drafts of several thousand words.

Many writing teachers might blanche at the idea of responding to that volume of text. It can be intimidating, and challenging, but I have found real pleasure in reading material motivated by genuine enthusiasm—even passion—as opposed to stumbling over the lowest possible bar an assignment allows.

Weeks 11 & 12: Revising

Now the students need to revise. But before I give them my own feedback, I require students to give feedback to each other. We have already practiced peer feedback throughout the semester, so the general format is familiar. Each student must respond, on each page, to one thing they like, and to one thing they think could be improved.

However, this time, the stakes of the feedback are higher. Once a student has received feedback from a partner, and from me, they *must* address *all* of that feedback in their revision. That is, they must either make the changes suggested, to the best of their ability, or they must indicate why they have chosen not to make changes in the email with which they submit their final draft.

With these parameters, I try to create, as close as possible, the process by which a scholar submits revisions to an editor. I emphasize, again, that writers need seriously to consider (and most often follow) the suggestions of a reviewer, but if they choose to disagree, they must take responsibility for explaining why. For example, Emily decided not to make one of the changes I suggested, and she explained:

> Page 3 of first draft: You said I should break up the long paragraph of my nightmare. I decided to leave it long as it gives the sense of being "stuck" in the nightmare; there's no break from it, as there is no break in the paragraph.

On re-reading Emily's long paragraph, I think she was right after all:

> The weight of dread sits on my chest like a herd of elephants. I'm not free to sit up in my bed, I'm not free to reach over and switch on the light, I'm not free to move. Air brushes my feet and I know they are not tucked under my blanket as they should be; I am exposed and vulnerable. Facing my ceiling, I struggle to look anywhere else. My eyes are not free to obey. I'm gripped by fear, knowing what happens next. My mind paints the ceiling a shade of deep black. An inky tone which exists only in my nightmare. A thunderstorm-gray cloud erupts from the black abyss' center. It encapsulates everything but the bed, blanket, pillow, and me. I wait in silent terror. It can take seconds, minutes, or hours until they surge out of the cloud that stores them in waking. Thousands of them, all different sizes, swirling around me. I sense some horrible intent and feel extraordinarily threatened by the numbers. One stream passes closely by my face:
>
> $$_2 \, _0 \, 9 \, 4 \, 7 \, _5 \, _1$$
>
> They circle me: they grow and shrink, become bolder, more confident as I become more terrified, like sharks readying for a feeding frenzy. Finally, when it seems they will strike, I wildly shut my eyes, breaking free of my paralysis and kick, awake in my bed. I immediately tuck my feet into my blanket, reinstating the sense of comfort and safety that it brings me. I breathe without the elephants, only to realize for what seems like a contemptible, re-run episode, that I must go back to sleep, and it's only a matter of time until I must face my nightmare again.

Weeks 13 & 14: Presentations

The final two weeks of the semester are devoted to student presentations. I have given the students a presentation of my own autoethnography (Hopkins, 2015), which they are assigned to read beforehand. I believe it is only fair that if I require students to share their personal experiences with the class, I also share my own.

I delay that sharing until late in the semester because I don't want students to think that my way is the only, or even the best way.

After the first time I taught the class, I have also invited students from past years to present their autoethnographies. Always, several have volunteered, and it seems the (then current) students appreciate and enjoy the (then former) students' examples. The former students seem to, too—several of them have volunteered to share their autoethnographies every semester until they have graduated.

I give the students rules and guidelines for the final presentation. Rules are simple. Don't go over the time limit, and refer to *both* your personal experience and your research. Without these rules, I know most students would focus exclusively on their experience, and many would go well over the limit. Guidelines include advice to consider the audience carefully, thinking about what you will be comfortable sharing.

I encourage students to provide a handout or to use a PowerPoint or whatever other visuals or audio appropriate, but I do not require these accompaniments. (Emily prepared a PowerPoint that incorporated visual and audio components illustrating her topic: the musical score from *Jaws*, for example.)

I tell students they are welcome to speak extemporaneously, or just to read their work, since I know how hard it can be to share some stories. I tell them that if they become emotional, it's fine: They should just pause and collect themselves and resume when ready.

I advise them—urge them, really—to rehearse, both for timing, and for some sense of the emotional element.

After each presentation, students are invited to respond verbally to the presentation. These responses are often as poignant as the presentations themselves, since students share the surprising ways in which they relate to the presenter's experience. I also ask all students to fill out a form with anonymous feedback for the presenter. By requiring these written responses, I guarantee that every presenter receives some comments on their presentation. As I will show further in Chapter Eleven, the two weeks of presentations are a highlight of the course for many students.

The fact that there is no final exam is also popular.

****

One of the questions I asked in my interviews of students is what suggestions they had for improving the course. Most had few, if any ideas for major changes. One suggested more in-class writing exercises, since she liked those. One suggested fewer theoretical readings, since those were not as engaging. One suggested inviting autoethnographers to class, which I did incorporate into subsequent teachings of the course. One urged me to consider providing more and earlier explanation of what the course entailed, which I have done, and which I will discuss further in Chapter Twelve.

I have made some other adjustments, and I remain open to further suggestions each year. But overall, students seemed pretty pleased with the course. As the following chapters will further show, so am I.

References

Adams, T. E., Holman Jones, S., & Ellis, C. (2015). *Autoethnography: Understanding qualitative research*. New York, NY: Oxford University Press.

Delamont, S. (2009). The only honest thing: Autoethnography, reflexivity, and small crises in fieldwork. *Ethnography and Education, 4*(1), 51–63.

Dowling, E. (2012). The waitress: On affect, method, and (re)presentation. *Cultural Studies⇔ Critical Methodologies, 12*(2), 109–117.

Ellis, C., Adams, T. E., & Bochner, A. P. (2011). Autoethnography: An overview. *Forum: Qualitative Social Research, 12*(1).

Hanauer, D. I. (2012). Growing up in the unseen shadow of the Kindertransport: A poetic-narrative autoethnography. *Qualitative Inquiry, 18*(10), 845–851.

Hopkins, J. B. (2015). Coming "home": An autoethnographic exploration of Third Culture Kid transition. *Qualitative Inquiry, 21*(19), 812–820.

Sturm, D. (2015). Playing with the autoethnographical: Performing and re-presenting the fan's voice. *Cultural Studies⇔ Critical Methodologies, 15*(3), 213–223.

INTERCHAPTER

"WHAT'S NEXT?" OUTCOMES OF PRACTICING AUTOETHNOGRAPHY

Thus far, I have provided some background on autoethnography and showed how I have practiced and taught autoethnography myself. Now I turn to the reasons other writing teachers should consider teaching autoethnography: the outcomes of its practice.

The first time I taught my course, I identified specific outcomes of practicing autoethnography, each supported by evidence in my students' essays, as well as by answers to interview and survey questions. I should note that these outcomes were mostly unsurprising. Most are commonly associated with autoethnography by leaders in the field, and, to some extent, I taught my courses with the outcomes already in mind. However, I was not prepared for just how powerfully the outcomes manifested.

Chapters Five through Eleven describe each outcome in detail:

- Increased reflexivity
- Improved writing skills
- Improved research skills
- Ethical consideration
- Critical empowerment
- Therapeutic catharsis
- Enjoyment
- Development of a sense of community

(I deliberately do not begin with improved writing skills. Though that would be the most obviously relevant outcome for compositionists, there are plenty of pedagogies that can improve writing skills. While the specific writing improvements from practicing autoethnography were, I think, unusual, the most remarkable outcome was undoubtedly the increased reflexivity nearly all my students experienced and expressed.)

Each chapter begins with a brief description of the outcome—how I understand it, and how it fits into my teaching of autoethnography. However, the bulk of the chapters consists of student writing, supplemented with answers to interview and anonymous end-of-semester teacher evaluation survey questions. Each chapter focuses primarily on an extended excerpt of one student's work.

I frame and interpret the student writing and answers to show how they support my understanding of the relevant outcome; but often, actually, I find it better just to get out of the way as much as possible. In many cases, my students' words don't need my explanation.

I can't possibly discuss in detail all 23 students who contributed to my research, but I also can't bear not to share at least part of their work. So Appendix D includes briefer excerpts from all the autoethnographies not covered in Chapters Five through Eleven. Perusing these excerpts may be of interest and use.

It's important to remember that the 23 students who contributed to these chapters were invited to participate *only after* their final grades were posted, to eliminate the possibility of coercion. (The invitation is available in Appendix A.) I also sent all the student participants multiple drafts of the manuscript, with requests for confirmation of continued participation, and offers to consider any changes the students thought necessary.

No students withdrew from the project or asked for any major changes. Only a few asked to make minor changes. One asked to include additional reflection.

In presenting excerpts of student essays, I have made only minor editorial modifications, correcting a few obvious typos, and adjusting formatting in places. I have tried accurately to represent students' authentic voices. In presenting excerpts from student interviews, I have edited for clarity and efficiency, excising distracting "likes" and "you knows."

As I've reread my students' essays, preparing to share them here, I've been impressed all over again by their intellect, insight, and passion. I wish I could share more of each essay.

I wish I could include examples from subsequent classes, as well. Topics through the years have ranged from playing video games, baseball, basketball, soccer, and golf; to struggling with a fading belief in Santa Claus and God; to visiting Disneyworld; to transferring colleges; to exploring gender identity and sexual orientation; to realizing an extraordinary emotional investment in film music; to surviving sepsis, chronic migraines, misophonia, depression and anxiety, and heartbreak; to competitive horse-riding; to recreational shopping; to taking Uber.

The topics are usually fascinating, and the students' work is consistently excellent, nearly always demonstrating the outcomes that the following chapters describe.

CHAPTER FIVE

Self and Context: Increasing Reflexivity

> In what ways do I respond to the social norms? In what situations did previously existing social structures impinge on my individuality? And in what ways were my ideas shaped today by the people around me in my past?
> —Tania, Student Autoethnographer

> The world is so much bigger than me, but my experiences have greater meaning in a cultural sense.
> —Anonymous Student Survey

Reflexivity rests at the center of autoethnographic practice. But just like autoethnography itself, one might well ask, what is reflexivity, exactly?

For autoethnographers, reflexivity refers to the deliberate examination of the self in its social/cultural context, and the insight individuals gain into their experiences by looking both inward and outward. Adams, Holman Jones, and Ellis (2015) posit: "[Autoethnography] uses deep and careful self-reflection—typically referred to as 'reflexivity'—to name and interrogate the intersections between self and society" (p. 2). More simply put: Reflexivity is learning about how you are like or unlike those around you.

Though it is a kind of self-examination, reflexivity should not mean—as some have suggested—self-centered, self-indulgent navel-gazing (Delamont, 2009). Autoethnographers should not be interested *only* in themselves. Rather, reflexivity contextualizes the self within the other, the person within the group. Reflexivity allows for recognition of similarities and differences between individuals, and resonance between writers and readers.

As with many of the outcomes of practicing autoethnography, I stress the crucial importance of reflexivity throughout my teaching. Most students seem not to have encountered the concept of reflexivity much before the course. Modern Western culture is not renowned for promoting reflexive habits, and it's not necessarily the easiest idea to understand, much less to practice. But students' understanding grows as they read theory and examples, and more so as they start to practice autoethnography themselves. Certain class activities, described in Chapter Four, are meant explicitly to prompt and push students' capacity for reflexivity. Given all this, it should be no surprise that students would report increased reflexivity. Indeed, without exception, students claimed and demonstrated substantial growth in this area.

In answering survey questions about the aspects of the course they liked best, several students indicated the increased insight into the self: "This course helped me … to discover more about myself through retrospective analysis" and "I liked that we were encouraged to explore our own lives and write things from our POV [point of view]." Even more indicated increased insight into their social/cultural context: "Helped me grasp a better understanding of my culture" and "I became very reflexive involving my own culture."

Indeed, there were many variations on this theme, with students emphasizing the value not only of embracing the subjectivity of one's own perspective, but also of recognizing other perspectives: "I have gained a better understanding of what it means to put yourself in someone else's shoes" and "helped me understand myself as well as change my view on others." And one of my favorites: "I analyzed my own life after every class and really thought about the broader connection."

With the rest of this chapter, I will share the work of one student who powerfully demonstrated increased reflexivity: Christa. Christa used her autoethnography to show her mental and emotional journey through cancer, depicting scenes from her diagnosis and from receiving news of remission, and referring to sources as varied as medical scholarship and an interview with Demi Lovato in *Cosmopolitan* magazine. Throughout, Christa demonstrates keen awareness of how her personal experience connects with her social/cultural context, from her family, to her greater Philadelphia community, to the (too) many others who have battled this disease.

Christa—"Coping with Cancer"

January 2016. I sat on tissue paper atop the table in the exam room, scrolling through my phone as I waited for the doctor to arrive. My mom did the same in a chair near the door. We were both exhausted, as we had spent a whole day at the Children's Hospital of Philadelphia (CHOP) together. This time, it was just an x-ray, although for the past few visits, occurring every three months, we had been alternating between x-rays and CT scans, which take longer.

I had an x-ray done earlier that morning, and then went to a different part of the building and waited a long time to get called for my vitals (height, weight, temperature, blood pressure). Then I went back out in the waiting room until they called me to get my blood drawn. Then back out into the waiting room again until I was finally called to see my oncologist. In that room, I waited, and after what seemed like an eternity, my oncologist arrived.

She walked in with a smile. Right away, she said, "I got a chance to check your x-ray out and it looks all clear." Relief washed over us and I turn to smile at my mom. I thought it would go well, but you can never be too sure. I thought to myself, "I'm still in remission, and life is good." My oncologist continued with the appointment, asking how college was and telling me to gain more weight. While I paid attention and responded appropriately, in the back of my mind I reflected on how lucky I was.

> *One of Christa's priorities in practicing autoethnography was to present her experience in as positive a way as possible—certainly a challenge, given her topic. As she said in her interview: "I didn't want to write in a way that made people pity me." It would be easy, maybe, and understandable, certainly, for someone to write to compel sympathy, but Christa's intention was more critically reflexive—to show how she, and others, successfully coped with this disease. For example, instead of beginning her story with her diagnosis, Christa starts with the scene of receiving the happy news of her second remission. Immediately, she demonstrates her reflexivity by framing her account as a survivor's story: "I reflected on how lucky I was."*

The Story

I had cancer. Twice. Hodgkin's Lymphoma both times. As of writing this, I have been in remission for over a year. I go to college, I have friends, I participate in a multitude of activities. You would never know unless you asked, or stalked me on social media. Looking back, even from such a short distance, I have to wonder how I got through it, how I "survived." Surely, I had an "easier" cancer than others in terms of treatment and curability. A study conducted in Poland cited a young age range and good prognosis as reasons for the overall positive attitudes of Hodgkin's Lymphoma patients (Hempel, Politynska, Danilewicz, Sierko, & Wojtukiewicz, 2015). I had both these advantages, and, as I was told by doctors, if you had to get cancer, this was the one to get. Although Hodgkin's is not the worst disease ever, there was so much trauma and hardship during that time that it is difficult to say that I had it easy.

> *In the section "The Story," Christa directly connects her experience with that of others (the Polish study she cites, for example), whether they have had cancer themselves, or know someone else who has, or have simply gone through difficulties that require specific coping mechanisms. We see that Christa's focus is both inwards and outwards, on her self, and on her social/cultural context.*
>
> *We might notice, as well, that Christa displays her dark sense of humor throughout. For example, she recalls: "as I was told by doctors, if you had to get cancer, this was the one to get." These words, morbidly funny, also show Christa's reflexivity, her ability comically to contextualize her own suffering. They demonstrate again her desire not to overwhelm or alienate the reader with complaints—as justifiable as those complaints would be. Rather than dwell on the negative, Christa wants to prioritize the positive aspects of her experience, further evidence of reflexivity.*

Examining my own experience, and how I dealt with all the stresses it caused in my life, I can place it in a broader context of the cancer experience within developed Western cultures like the United States. I can compare the ways in which people cope as well as the contributing factors to how I view my experience. Cancer touches so many lives, even if not directly, and is an issue that not only needs to be addressed medically, but emotionally. I have gone through much of what constitutes the cancer experience, including surgeries, chemotherapy, a bone marrow transplant, radiation, and much more. As a result of these procedures, I needed to deal with fear, anxiety, sadness, and frustration in ways that helped me get through.

Through my autoethnography, I use my experience to provide a true account of what it is like to go through a life-threatening disease and to show both the good and the bad that can come from it, including my life now from the perspective of both an outsider and insider. Exploring my story can help others as well as myself manage feelings surrounding cancer, therapeutically. I hope to answer the following questions: How does cancer affect the individual mentally and emotionally? How can an individual facing cancer effectively cope? What factors make it easier or harder for a patient to cope? How do support systems play a role? How does prognosis and treatment plan make a difference in getting through? What other factors make a difference?...

***

June 20, 2013. The walls were most likely colorful and bright. But whenever my mind remembers that room in the CHOP ER, I always picture it dark and scary. I was sitting up on the bed, the TV was on with the volume low in the background with some cooking show that no one was actually watching. My family surrounded me, sitting in chairs around the room. My mom, my twin sister, my older sister, my dad and my stepmother. They all sat anxiously awaiting the results from my scans. My older sister clutched a yellow bucket in her lap, feeling sick with a migraine from all the stress of the past few hours of uncertainty concerning my health.

> *In the scene portraying her initial diagnosis, Christa again demonstrates her capacity for inward and outward focus. The social/cultural context here—her family—is small in scale, but still significant. A less reflexive writer might concentrate only on her own intense thoughts and emotions, but Christa reflects on her perspective of this excruciating experience while framing it with the feelings and actions of her family. Her concern for her loved ones is evident, maybe most in her sympathetic depiction of her older sister, literally sick with worry.*

In a way, this acted as a distraction from my own stress, if only because it transferred my worries about myself to worrying about her. However, I couldn't keep all of my personal worries away. I tried not to look at the IV in my arm, which scared the hell out of me. I didn't know what was going on, why I had all these tests done, why I was here. But for some reason, I was nervous.

The doctor walked in and closed the curtain over the glass door with a grave expression on her face. She sat down in the chair by the computer, and we all focused on her silently as she spoke: "After a few tests, it looks like Lymphoma." A sharp gasp from my mother quickly indicated to me that this was bad. She came over to me and hugged me tightly. I felt almost numb, but automatically put my arms around her as well. I'm sure the rest of my family had some sort of reaction of distress as well.

The doctor continued, "We're going to have to do a few more tests to be sure, but we wanted to let you know that's what the signs are pointing to. Any questions?"

Before anyone could speak, I blurted out, "What's Lymphoma?"

After 17 years of life, I really didn't know my diseases. I don't remember who told me, but I think it was my mother. She said softly, "It's cancer." I know I should have freaked out, but I didn't feel anything. I didn't know what to think.

> *Despite the severity of the situation, Christa again attempts to lighten the mood with the wry reflection: "After seventeen years of life, I really didn't know my diseases." Having humorously established her then-ignorance, Christa proceeds to inform the reader, as she herself was educated, about the nature of her condition. Having this information helps to situate her experience in medical terms, even if we may not entirely understand it—as she did not.*

The Cancer

> Hodgkin's disease is characterized by the presence of binucleate or multinucleate Sternberg-Reed cells, though the cell of origin of Hodgkin's disease is unknown. The disease predominantly presents as lymph node swellings, which may be isolated or, in more extensive disease, involve multiple lymph node sites, liver, spleen, bone marrow and other organs. Hodgkin's disease is sub-divided according to histological appearance into groups that have differing clinical behavior and prognosis. In the majority of cases Hodgkin's disease is curable with chemotherapy and/or radiotherapy.
>
> Hesketh, 2013, pp. 288-289

I was unaware of the above definition at diagnosis, and even looking at it now, it is difficult to understand my disease described in this way, with the scientific terminology as well as the lack of human presence.

At 17, I was not as exposed to the different types of cancer or the prevalence in my age group. The older a person is, the more likely they are to get cancer (Hesketh, 2013, p. 11). Apparently, 17 years was long enough. Living in the suburbs of Philadelphia most of my life, I did not know anyone my age with cancer. I only thought it was for really young children or the elderly. If someone had cancer in the family, they usually did not talk about it much.

Little did I know that being 17 in Philadelphia was the best thing for me, treatment-wise. I would receive treatment at the best children's hospital, which comparably was a much friendlier environment than an adult hospital would have been. In other hospitals, they focus more on the treatment side of things and less on the patient's health as a whole. At CHOP, I received support from sympathetic nurses, therapists, social workers, music and art therapists, and more. I was also able to attend a good amount of school despite my treatments, which was fortunate for me, as in a Polish study, "every 5th patient had to resign from work and more than half were unable to fully complete their duties" (Hempel et al., 2015, p. 72). The hospital environment and my ability to participate in a good portion of everyday life gave me a greater hope I might not have otherwise had, allowing me to be able to cope easier throughout my treatments.

> *In this section, Christa presents another fascinating example of autoethnographic reflexivity by remarking on specific ways she was fortunate, despite her diagnosis. She shares her privilege, her resources to overcome the obstacles she faced. One of those resources was the simple fact of her location, living close to Children's Hospital of Philadelphia, where she could receive excellent treatment. Geography is an important component of social/cultural context, and Christa notes that not everyone, everywhere would have such advantageous access. She further comments that it was not only the medical care CHOP provided, but the institution's special sensitivity to her age group that made a big difference in her ability to cope.*

June 2013. Following the news of my cancer, I did what any teenage girl would do at this crucial moment: make a post on Facebook. I said, "I'm in the hospital overnight and I need everyone's prayers." People commented on my post, sending me their love and positive thoughts. My mom's post was more explanatory, but came five days later:

> These are the words no parent wants to hear, write or even know they exist. For those who don't already know, my beautiful Christa has been diagnosed with Hodgkin's lymphoma. We've been at CHOP since Thursday and I'm hoping to be home by this weekend. She's a strong girl, a fighter and I know she'll be ok. Thanks so much to friends and family for all your help and prayers. Please keep the positive energy coming. Love you all.

> *Another resource was Christa's support on social media, a major cultural component of modern life. Her account of that support is heartwarming, certainly, but Christa's critical reflexivity is also noteworthy here, in how she positions herself like "any other teenage girl" posting about her experience on Facebook. She recognizes her similarity to others of her community. We also see her social context from the perspective of her mother's Facebook post, giving us insight into that aspect of her experience.*

After four more days, I made a longer post:

> I know a lot of people have been wondering what was going on and I wanted to clear things up. I just got back from a week's stay at the hospital where I was diagnosed with Hodgkin's Lymphoma, a very curable type of cancer. I have to continue with chemo for at least the next few months and hopefully everything goes well. I just wanted to put this out there and let everyone know. Thanks to everyone that sent me their love and support through this difficult time but I am remaining positive!

After four rounds of outpatient chemotherapy, I was declared cancer-free by September 2013, at the start of my senior year of high school....

The Power of Role Models and Community Support

Each time I had cancer, I looked to celebrities that I admire, like Demi Lovato, for inspiration. Early on in my first time with cancer, I read an interview in *Cosmopolitan* that resonated with me. In it, Demi Lovato, who has gone through some rough health issues herself, defined what it meant to her to be a "badass." According to the interview she said, "Being a badass is handling your shit." At that moment, something clicked, and I felt compelled to underline those words, even though I doubted I would ever pick up the magazine again.

Later on in the interview, Lovato explains, "What's badass is when you can sit through your problems and feel emotions when you don't want to have them." Yes, I thought. I wanted to be like Demi Lovato and face my problems to come out stronger. That did not mean holding back tears, putting on a fake smile, and pretending everything is all right. It meant the opposite. Being able to cry and feel the raw emotions when they came, while also knowing things would get better.

Self-reports of adolescent cancer patients suggested that repressors, or patients with "decreased awareness of distress and increased self-restraint," usually report high levels of psychological functioning (Erickson, Gerstle, & Montague, 2008, p. 255). However, this is deceiving, as their "high levels of physiological and behavioral assessments of stress reactivity" contradict their claims of coping well (Erickson et al., 2008, p. 248). Demi Lovato indirectly helped inspire me to be a non-repressor, and deal with my disease and all the emotions that came with it, head on.

> *In her interview, Christa identified a particular moment that perfectly illustrated reflexivity for her. It was like a "light bulb ... a clicking moment ... where I was like, wow, this is really cool that I can connect my personal thoughts and what I get from other people to my research." That moment happened while writing the section "The Power of Role Models and Community Support."*
>
> *In this section, Christa's reflexivity is evident in the way she is able to connect a seemingly small, personal moment of celebrity admiration with scholarly studies on adolescent psychology. Blending her role model Demi Lovato's invocation of "badass ... handling your shit" and psychologists Erickson, Gerstle, and Montague's (2008) theory of "non-repression" is a remarkable instance of Christa's insight into how her own experience was framed by multiple aspects of her social/cultural context.*

Then prom came. My doctors had worked it out so my treatments did not interfere with prom or graduation, and I was overjoyed. Of course, the morning after graduation I would be off to the hospital to spend five more nights of round-four chemotherapy. But nothing could dampen my mood. I attended prom bald, the first time I went anywhere in public without a wig or cap. I knew my name was on the nomination list for Prom Queen, but I did not think I would get it, considering the nomination was surely out of pity. I appreciated it all the same, and voted for myself (of course).

When the time came, just like one of those Disney Channel Original Movies, the announcer pronounced me Prom Queen. As the crowd thundered their applause, one of our class sponsors placed a plastic tiara on my bald head. In that moment, I felt all the love from my peers culminate into one meaningful gesture, no matter how cliché. I recognize that not everyone has such a supportive community, or even the amount of friends and family that always had my back. This may be unique to my experience alone, but that is the thing about cancer. No one person experiences cancer the same way; medically, physically, socially, or mentally....

> *This section also, again, shows how Christa's community supported her through her experience, crowning her Prom Queen, to her astonishment. It is another happy moment, but still not without critical reflexivity, since Christa recognizes how her knowledge of popular media frames the situation: "just like one of those Disney Original Channel Movies ...." Despite (or even because of) the near (or actual) cliché, the experience is personally meaningful, as well as significant in social/cultural terms.*

December 2014. I sat alone at my kitchen table with a peanut butter and jelly sandwich in front of me as I slowly picked at it in between sips of chocolate milk. I pulled my scarf tighter around my bare neck and adjusted the cap over my bald head. It was always so cold up there. Suddenly, my phone rang. It was my doctor and I answered immediately. Unable to sit still during a phone call, I paced the room as I answered, "Hello."

"Christa? It's Dr. R---. We have the results back from your last scan and you're in remission! Congratulations!"

I stopped dead. "Really?" A smile grew on my face as I did my happy dance. I never felt more grateful to be alive then in that moment, all alone in my kitchen.

Conclusion

I went into remission after my bone marrow transplant, and still had to endure four weeks of proton-radiation therapy and many months of isolation (restrictions regarding going out in public, lifting more with every month) until I was completely "free" in the spring. I still need to get checked every few months, which will eventually turn to years unless something new comes up. But as of now, March 2016, I am enjoying my first year of college, previously delayed by my cancer. I find myself appreciating every day just a little more. Every now and then, I walk a little slower and take it all in. What it means to be able to attend class every day. What it means to walk up a staircase without stopping to catch my breath. What it means to sleep in my own bed, and not a hospital bed. What it means to live.

> *In her final short scene and conclusion, Christa explicitly reflects on her overall experience. She retains her dark humor in commenting on how uncomfortable her baldness is: "It was always so cold up there." I also have to laugh, albeit grimly, at her choice of language in "I stopped dead." Whether intentional or not, the irony is exquisite.*
>
> *But Christa also expresses her pure joy at the news of remission, and she articulates her ongoing gratitude for her good health.*
>
> *It is hard for me to imagine more poignant evidence of increased reflexivity.*

References

Adams, T. E., Holman Jones, S., & Ellis, C. (2015). *Autoethnography: Understanding qualitative research*. New York, NY: Oxford University Press.

Delamont, S. (2009). The only honest thing: Autoethnography, reflexivity, and small crises in fieldwork. *Ethnography and Education, 4*(1), 51–63.

Erickson, S. J., Gerstle, M., & Montague, E. Q. (2008). Repressive adaptive style and self-reported psychological functioning in adolescent cancer survivors. *Child Psychiatry & Human Development, 39*(3), 247–260.

Hempel, D., Politynska, B., Danilewicz, A., Sierko, E., & Wojtukiewicz, M. Z. (2015). Psychological, physical, and social situation of patients with Hodgkin lymphoma undergoing radical chemoradiotherapy. *Progress in Health Sciences, 5*(2), 69–76.

Hesketh, R. (2013). *Introduction to cancer biology*. New York, NY: Cambridge University Press.

CHAPTER SIX

Audience Awareness: Improving Writing Skills

> I mean, I know I'm not the best writer but I feel like I did improve a lot. I can give the audience what they want, I guess.
>
> —Kim, Student Autoethnographer

After the last chapter, you may be thinking: "Hang on. Reflexivity is all well and good, but writing teachers are supposed to teach writing. The examination of the self in relation to social/cultural context is not in the job description."

True.

If increased reflexivity were the only outcome of practicing autoethnography, I would not recommend the genre for writing pedagogy. But practicing autoethnography, at least the way it is practiced in my class, requires a lot of writing. My students reported significant improvements in their writing skills, and I saw the outcome myself in the students' written work.

Some of the improvements were relatively common: stronger sense of structure, grammar, conciseness, citation. Christa, whose work I shared in the previous chapter, said in her interview: "I think I just grew as a writer in general." You might reasonably expect this sort of progress in any class that involved plenty of writing instruction and practice. However, some of the specific ways in which my students' writing improved went beyond what I was used to from other classes. In particular, practicing autoethnography made my students much more aware of their audience.

Maybe this should not be surprising, given one of the fundamental reasons to practice autoethnography, according to Adams, Holman Jones, & Ellis (2015):

> Rather than producing esoteric, jargon-laden texts, many autoethnographers recognize a need to speak also to *non*-academic audiences. They satisfy this need by writing and performing in engaging, creative ways. Such techniques make research more *valuable* because more than a select and trained few will read the work. (p. 42)

That is, autoethnography should be accessible and even appealing to any readers, inside or outside of the academy.

Writing in a way that appeals to any audience—academic or otherwise—is hard. Christa said: "At first I felt like, oh, this might be an easy course—just write about yourself, whatever. But it was a lot more difficult." I felt the same way when I wrote my own autoethnography. It was intellectually and emotionally difficult, and because the material was so personal in nature, I cared more than usual about how I represented myself. Writers of autoethnography, who might otherwise not much mind their audience, may suddenly find that their writing matters more than just the grade.

Grades do matter, of course, and my students probably still cared most about the main audience—me. But they also said, and showed, that they cared what others might want to read—even after I told them that further revision would not matter for their grade, or when I told them that they were welcome to disagree with my suggestions for revision, as long as they indicated why. The many peer feedback sessions conducted during the course likely contributed to that audience awareness, as did a simple desire to share their experiences in the most effective way possible.

That desire then also led to another skill evident in my students' work: revision. Compositionists know that writing well is really re-writing better, but teaching revision is hard, especially at the undergraduate level. Before teaching autoethnography, I rarely saw the kind of serious revision I wanted from my students. Without extensive, explicit direction, correcting comma errors and fixing passive voice constituted the majority of their efforts. Even when I provided plenty of detailed feedback, most students appeared to address my comments as minimally as they could.

I didn't fault them at all. I remember how little I revised my own writing as an undergraduate—again, just as much as I thought I needed to get the grade I wanted.

But being aware of readers' needs and wanting to satisfy them means motivation to revise radically. That was the kind of attitude I saw in my students' practice of autoethnography, the kind of attitude that prompted answers to survey questions like this: "I like what I wrote and I can see myself showing it as an example in the future." It's the kind of attitude I saw in students like Edward.

Edward's autoethnography examines issues surrounding family conflict. He writes about a fight he had with his father about Edward's first girlfriend, culminating in an extended period of strained, but ultimately productive silence between father and son. Edward discovered the sociological theory of separation-individuation during his research, and he uses it to comment on dramatic scenes of tension and confrontation.

I suspect that Edward's (and other students') audience awareness and enthusiasm for revision came from a desire to tell a good story, an essential aspect of autoethnography. Whereas conventional academic writing doesn't require—and seems, perversely and often bafflingly, to avoid—any artistic flair, narrative needs to be engaging.

That necessity can be exciting, and intimidating. I remember sitting with Edward after a class as he expressed anxiety about telling a story that could engage readers. He had never written narrative before, and he was nervous. I assured him it was natural to feel that way—writing stories can be hard. I also reassured him that he would do just fine.

He did.

Edward—"Adolescent Separation-Individuation"

May 17, 2011: It's a mess on the floor: the wreckage of my cell phone, the broken broomstick, and bolsters fallen from the couch. The sound of our fight spreads from the living room to the whole building; I bet the old meddlesome woman from the second floor is listening intently, curious about what is happening here.

I watch his eyes growing increasingly red, and I see her face turning increasingly alarmed. I cannot see what I look like at that time, but certainly, I look extremely emotional and I cannot stop wrinkling my nose. I feel hurt, both physically and psychologically. I sense the little shiver of my arm, feeling small blood vein under the skin bursting; also, I sense the "tart," as I would put it in Chinese, stemmed from my heart. Why? Why would he do this to me?

According to Daniels (1990):

> normal adolescent development involves learning to be psychologically independent of one's parents, developing relationships outside the home and family structure, and seeking one's own identity. These achievements, however, cannot be accomplished if adolescents continue childhood-like attachments to their parents. (p. 105)

Instead, as Daniels (1990) points out: "the transition to mature self-reliance is a process of individuation" (p. 105). According to Blos (1962): "these tasks are accomplished through successful separation-individuation" (cited in Daniels, 1990, p. 105). I will present a stage of my adolescence, where I had a typical parent-adolescent conflict with my father and where I experienced separation-individuation for almost a year....

> *Edward showed himself a natural at writing narrative. In his interview, he said one of his favorite parts of the course was writing description and dialogue. Both are in abundance in his autoethnography.*
>
> *Look at Edward's first paragraphs, the description of the aftermath from his fight with his father. The scene Edward sets is vivid. He evokes several senses—sight, sound, touch—and captures the reader's attention with his own attention to detail. I especially enjoy his imagination of the nosy neighbor "listening intently." Even the deliberately vague pronoun references to "his eyes" and "her face" create curiosity—we may suspect whose is "our fight," but we will need to keep reading to know for sure.*

February to May 2011: My first relationship with Helen makes everyday life different to me. I no longer loathe getting up early, eating breakfast on my bike, and climbing up the cliffy bridge sitting just in front of my school gate. Instead, I greet life everyday with passion and expectancy. I am just like anyone else who is experiencing his or her first relationship—never getting tired of spending time with my girlfriend....

I did not drink much, but my grade certainly has suffered a dramatic dropping: I fell from top 200 to top 600 of my class in the mid-term exam. My parents, who never worried about my grade before, are starting to push me, regulating my use of cellphone and time of playing video games, whereas I do not care about my grade anymore. The main focus of my life has already shifted from the tedious academic world to a romantic wonderland.

May 16, 2011: "Wait for me, sweety. I'll be right back."

I mistakenly sent this text message to my father, right after I finished homework late at night and had the chance to grab my cell phone. As soon as my father's cell phone rings, I know I am finished.

"Who are you sending the message to?" Dad scowls.

"I didn't send this." I try to act as calm as possible, "It must be China Mobile's mistake. It's from someone else."

He stares at me, "How could it be? The contact shown here is you. I'll ask you once more. Who are you sending the message to?"

"It's not me."

"Are you playing me as a fool?" He is getting angry. "Bring me your cellphone."

Thank god I am smart enough to have the message deleted as soon as I realized my fault. "Check it yourself, I didn't."

> *For evidence of Edward's skill with dialogue, look at the scenes of the conflict between him and his father. From Edward's affectionate text to his girlfriend through the fraught conversation with his father, we hear the growing tension. Yet there is no melodrama—I admire the naturalness of this exchange. Even Edward's choice not to use speech tags for every line contributes, at that moment, to the atmosphere. There is an ironic rhythm to the quick denial of "It's not me," so obviously Edward, in every sense.*
>
> *It's worth noting also that Edward is translating the dialogue from the original Chinese. For multilingual writers, the challenge of portraying credible and engaging dialogue may be especially difficult, but Edward's work is evidence that it is entirely possible.*

He takes the phone, taps the screen for a while, and then just looks straight into my eye, trying to see through me. I hate that feeling of being examined. "I'll go take a shower, it's already late." I know it is not possible to have my phone back tonight. I wait and see if I can get it back tomorrow.

It is an extremely long night. I toss and turn in bed, meditating. Having been secretly hiding this relationship for three months, I do not want it to be discovered now. I need to come up with more excuses later and inform Helen tomorrow. We'd better stop contacting each other after school for a while, just to eliminate my parents' suspicion.

May 17, 2011: Dad visited China Mobile and checked my texting history. Now he is certain that I sent that message. Back home the first question he asks me is, "Who's Helen?" Apparently he went through my contact list, and found the number I've been texting for over three months.

"She's just a friend."

Now I cannot look directly into his eyes. He seems to already know everything: the name of my girlfriend, the reason of my poor grade, and most importantly, that I am experiencing a puppy love. Awkward, I think it is better to change subjects now.

"Can I have my phone back now?"

"No," he responds plainly. He takes off his shoes, puts my cellphone on the desk, and sits on the couch.

"Why?!" Standing in front of him, I ask. I hate his tone whenever he just says "no" to me, without any reason to explain his decision. It makes me feel like he just unfairly has the power to decide every aspect of my own life. According to Canary and Canary (2013), "Adolescents tended to become more self-directed than parent-directed due to their growing desire for autonomy" (p. 90). What I thirst for now is autonomy, the freedom of making decisions for my own life. He should treat me as an adult, instead of still considering me as an ignorant kid. However, "Chinese families have been traditionally characterized as emphasizing absolute parental authority" (Xia et al., 2004, p. 125). I do not have the freedom.

> *Notice another small but remarkable detail: Edward's description of his father taking off his shoes. It is not a vital part of the story—not as important, say, as where the cellphone goes—but it adds texture to the scene.*
>
> *Furthermore, Edward is not limited to narrative writing. Throughout the essay, he includes analysis of his experience, using reference to multiple sources from his research. For example, right in the middle of the scene of conflict with his father, Edward refers to two sources (Canary & Canary, 2013 and Xia et al., 2004) to analyze the experience. Though the research, Edward said, was not his favorite part of the process, still he included important social/cultural context to the story of his own experience.*

I need to use my cell phone to connect with my friends, to use my social networking software, and most importantly, I need my cell phone to keep connection with Helen at night.

"There's no reason. You don't necessarily need a cell phone. And you should focus on your school work." The insistence in his voice tells me he is not going to budge on this. And he still uses that tone of "I'm the one in charge."

I am frustrated and angry about his tone and proclamation. "No! I need my cell phone." I yell at him. He does not realize how much it means to deprive me of my cell phone. As a teenager who is trying to get more control of his own life and expect his parents to treat him as an adult (Daniels, 1990), I cannot accept his seemingly easy decision. Does he know by making that decision, without affecting him in any way, my life would totally change? Can he imagine living without his own cell phone? How inconvenient is that?

He is offended by my yelling. "I said no, then it is a no. You want that cell phone so bad? I will smash it if you keep going." His dominant tone becomes even more decisive now. Perhaps he already foresees the upcoming huge fight and thinks by making this threat, I will stop asking.

But I don't. "Smash this, smash that. Since I was a kid, you've been smashing my toys as long as you are unhappy. So now what? You are going to smash the cell phone?" Somehow, we do not talk about my puppy love at all. It seems that we just need a reason to start a fight, no matter why.

"老子!" He turns furious, rises up from the couch and fetches my cell phone.

> *Edward said an important part of practicing autoethnography was getting feedback, both from his peers, and from me. We spent considerable time discussing one moment in particular: the moment in which his father, angry at Edward, crushes the young man's cell phone underfoot.*
>
> *In the first draft, while not ineffective, I felt the moment was not fully successful:*
>
> "老子!" He turns furious, gets up from the couch and fetches my cell phone.
>
> HE SMASHES IT!
>
> How could he!
>
> *In my feedback, I suggested that the all-caps and the exclamation point overemphasized the action, actually undercutting its significance and making it melodramatic instead. I encouraged Edward to try something else, perhaps simply an empty space. He followed my advice, marking the moment with an absence:*
>
> "老子!" He turns furious, gets up from the couch and fetches my cell phone.
>
>
> How could he!
>
> *While I preferred Edward's revision to his first draft, I still wasn't totally satisfied. I told Edward he didn't need to make any changes to this moment to affect his grade, but I also said I would be happy to see another version, though I didn't make any specific suggestions this time. His third and final draft was different again, as you can see.*
>
> *Opinions may vary on which version works best, but the point is that Edward kept working, trying to improve, to refine his words. He revised because he cared about his audience.*

Before I have time to react, I hear the sound, the sound of my phone cracking. I lose it. In that moment, I lose the phone and the connection to Helen and to my friends, along with my head....

Shek (2002) introduces the commonly known traditional belief of Chinese family: "children were socialized to be submissive to the parents," and "parent-adolescent conflict was basically regarded as an unfilial act" (p. 193). My action is considered as unfilial. I somehow broke the traditional Chinese parenting rule. Perhaps I should not have argued back with my dad; instead I should follow his word and be a good Chinese kid as my dad requires me to be. He would always say, "Children should obey their parents' words and behave, regardless." But parents' words can be wrong, and his demand, like depriving and smashing my phone without any explanation, is unreasonable, isn't it?...

Extremely furious, I did not want to resolve the conflict at all. I preferred both of us to calm down and live our own lives for a while. Only never did I expect that this time, it was a much longer while, and during this long while, I started my process of *separation-individuation*....

July 2011: We have not talked to each other for three months. Still living under the same roof, we are having totally irrelevant lives. It is awkward when mom asks both of us to prepare for having dinner. Before our fight, one of us fetch the chopsticks and bowls, while the other take over the bowl and fill it with rice for three of us. Now, we do it separately. After hearing mom's call, one of us will get our own pieces of cutlery while the other one wait until mom calls the second time, "Dishes are getting cold!" That is when the other one of us, whether in our own rooms or in the living room, gets informed that we would not collide in the kitchen room.

I am still angry with him....

Daniels (1990) states that adolescents who are given new freedoms and adult responsibilities establish their own values and beliefs. After the fight, what I am trying is to achieve the stage where I can both be entertaining and serious about academic work. I'd like to have a romantic relationship and a full enjoyment of all kind of social events, as well as keeping a decent grade.

However, I am starting to get a little tired of keeping myself regulated, without anyone pushing me. Since there were so many changes and excitements in my past, perhaps now I have been relieved from the fight. When I think of my dad, instead of feeling angry, I feel rather strange. In my home, whenever I pass the living room and have a glimpse on him on the couch, I feel distant to him. He seems like a stranger to me, whom I never had any contact before. Perhaps I was too emotional before to realize the impact of the sudden disappearance of a man who used to be in every day of my life.

Grandma often says, "You have no idea how much he loves you. When you were just born, he held you like treasure, and I never saw him that excited."

Mom often says, "It's certainly your fault to fight your dad. You just can't. I can't see if there's any meaning of you two's cold war. You should make peace with him."

> In this section, Edward's occasional grammatical error, odd diction, or unconventional stylistic choices might distract some readers. However, they may also reinforce his authentic, multilingual voice. Increasingly, accented "natural" English—written or spoken—is acceptable, or even preferable to adherence to some supposedly perfect "native" standardization.
>
> For example, the absence of the article in Edward's grandmother's memory of his father holding him "like treasure," while not technically incorrect, might sound awkward to some, like a multilingual writer not thoroughly in command of English. Actually, I find the phrasing poignant, more moving than the more conventional "a treasure."

I wouldn't. My first reaction right after hearing mom's advice is that I would not do that. My pride does not allow me to conduct such behavior that can be regarded as confession. But she does not know the second thought that goes through my mind: I would not reject his peace offer, if he would make the offer.

After all, he is my dad and I miss him. When I think of him, my mind is not restricted to the conflict anymore; I recall more delighted memories: He taught me how to ride a bike holding my back steadily, he took me to the most palatable cheap restaurant secretly without mom knowing, and he bought me the cutting-edge toys from America whenever he has a business trip there...

At noon, February 23, 2012: It is the first day of Chinese Spring Festival. The refreshing air brings out all the birds settled in my home district and warm Sunshine beams into the house. Mom goes to grandma's home to help her clean the house for the upcoming new year. Dad and I are left in the house. I lock myself in my own room, just as the way I've been doing for nine months, to avoid contact with him. There is a usual long period of silence, until a sudden hollow echo of knuckles rapping on the door.

Dad knocks my door, "come, I made you dinner."

CODA

Now I can answer my mom's words. There definitely are some meanings of our fight and the cold war. I thought I was the one who employed the "no-resolution" style (Canary & Canary, 2013, p. 99). However, after years passed, when I asked my father why he did not make peace with me earlier, it turned out that he'd like to have me separated and individuated from the family. He believed the separation and individuation allowed me to change my lifestyle, no longer depending on them so much on everything, to realize without parents' help, which I should cherish, how different it would be for me to live my life, and to have my own thoughts and solutions when confronting any obstacles in my life....

January 28, 2016: When I first begin to think of a topic of my autoethnography, this conflict with Dad comes to my mind right away....

I immediately call my dad.

"Dad, I am considering writing our conflict and cold war as my first piece of autoethnography. What do you think? Are you ok with this?"

"What is an autoethnography?" Instead of answering, he asks.

"Well, autoethnography..."

After explaining it to him, he responds happily, "Why not? I am pretty proud of that experience."

References

Adams, T. E., Holman Jones, S., & Ellis, C. (2015). *Autoethnography: Understanding qualitative research*. New York, NY: Oxford University Press.

Canary, H. E., & Canary, D. J. (2013). *Family conflict*. Cambridge, UK: Polity Press.

Daniels, J. A. (1990). Adolescent separation-individuation and family transitions. *Adolescence, 25*(97), 105–116.

Shek, D. T. L. (2002). Parenting characteristics and parent-adolescent conflict. *Journal of Family Issues, 23*(2), 189–208.

Xia, Y. R., Xie, X., Zhou, Z., Defrain, J., Defrain, J., & Combs, R. (2004). Chinese adolescents' decision-making, parent-adolescent communication and relationships. *Marriage & Family Review, 36*(1–2), 119–145.

CHAPTER SEVEN

Relevant References: Improving Research Skills

> Not only did it help me become a better writer but also allowed me to do some engaging research.
> —Anonymous Student Survey

> I really liked the research aspect because it gave a lot of validity to what I was feeling.
> —Emily, Student Autoethnographer

In addition to writing, compositionists are often responsible for teaching basic research skills. John Bean (2011) emphasizes the importance of undergraduate research instruction: "Research assignments flow from our desire that students become self-directed inquirers who can bring their own critical thinking to bear on interesting problems" (p. 224). We want to cultivate curiosity in our students and provide them with the skills to find, process, and present useful information, preparing them for other academic work, as well as better equipping them for their personal and professional lives.

But Bean (2011) also acknowledges that our ideal often does not match our students' reality:

> We all know students' tendency to manufacture a term paper by patching together passages closely paraphrased from their sources. There is something mechanistic about

> the way many of our students produce research papers, something disturbingly unlike the motivated inquiry and analysis that we value. (p. 224)

In Bean's description, I certainly recognize my own experience, both as teacher and as student. Especially as an undergraduate, I often felt frustrated by assigned topics and uninterested in doing more than the bare minimum, and I have seen the same thing in my own students. Simply put, the motivation is lacking.

Practicing autoethnography can supply that motivation. The genre provides an opportunity for students to, as Bean (2011) puts it, "become invested in academic inquiry, doing real undergraduate research" (p. 225). Because the topics are personal, students are more likely to care about the research process. They are also more likely to produce valuable results. This is a chance to make a genuine contribution to a field of knowledge in which the student is—if not yet an expert—at least experienced. How often do undergraduates, especially in their first year, get to participate in a scholarly conversation like that?

As I mentioned in Chapter Two, not all autoethnographers agree on the necessity of consulting outside sources. Some might say the story is sufficient (Boylorn & Orbe, 2014). I disagree. To me, research is a crucial component of the genre, and my course requires substantial research. It is unsurprising, then, that all students' interviews and essays evidenced this outcome, though some of the improvement was, apparently, less than pleasantly achieved.

Several participants said the research was what they liked least about practicing autoethnography, though they affirmed its value, nonetheless. Edward, for example, who enjoyed the story-writing portion of autoethnography more than expected, couldn't say the same for the research: "That's suffering," he recalled in his interview, laughing ruefully as he recalled trying to find and process sources.

He hastened to point out the many ways in which the research process was useful, even if it wasn't much fun. After practicing autoethnography, he felt more confident in using specific search terms and in skimming sources quickly to determine whether or not they would be relevant. Still, he laughed again: "it's so tiring."

Many others echoed Edward, both in his frustration and in his appreciation for the value of the research. One student survey reported: "Not really my style of research [but] I like that I was able to write about my experience." Another mentioned appreciating the help finding and preparing "solid evidence and citations." But of all the students who found the research worthwhile, Betty stands out as someone who also genuinely enjoyed the research process.

Betty began her research feeling much like Edward, but she found herself caught up in the process with an enthusiasm she had not anticipated. In her autoethnography, Betty describes her experience during a religious riot in her home country, Myanmar. She shows how disturbing it was to witness this violence, especially given her Buddhist beliefs—beliefs shared by many participants in the riot. Betty draws on a wealth of external resources, as well as her own memories, to demonstrate the devastation resulting from this conflict.

Betty—"On the Meiktila Riot: A Story of Destructed Coexistence"

March 20, 2013. I was happily watching a movie together with my family—my parents and my younger brother. The unfolded curtains prevented the sunshine from entering into our room. The yellow, dim light was on; the room was pleasant and quiet except for the sounds in the movie and our occasional conversations. Unexpectedly, the silence of the room was interrupted by a rather loud knock on the room. It was one of my parents' employees....

My memory limited me from recalling her exact words but not their tension and the consequence. We quickly got off the bed, pulled the curtain and looked out from the window. The main road at the front of our compound was filled with a furious mass of people holding weapons in their hands. The more than 50-yard distance between our house and the road could no longer cut off the angry shouts and noises. My parents quickly went downstairs, out of the house and instructed the employees to shut the main door.

***

> *Betty said in her interview:* "Previously, I was mainly interested in fictions, and I wasn't interested in non-fictions, especially reference books. But then while I researched about my country and about Buddhism in the reference [workshop], I found myself deeply engaged in it. And I spent a lot of time at the library."
>
> *Betty described one occasion on which she spent an entire afternoon in the library, immersed in finding background information for her topic, something she said she never would have expected to do before practicing autoethnography.*
>
> *The reason for Betty's enthusiasm was the relevance of her research to her personal experience. Rather than merely trying to support an abstract, academic point, she was genuinely curious about her topic:* "we are not just looking for something that will be useful for our argument, but we're open to every resource. So I can actually look for every resource about Buddhism, about my country and also because I feel emotional connection to my country, I'm particularly interested in it."

> *Betty drew on a wide variety of kinds of sources, from* New York Times *stories, to religious studies scholarship, to presidential proclamations. In her interview, she mentioned an online video about the riot that she found during her research. She didn't end up using this video in her essay, but it helped frame her further exploration because, as she said, "it made me feel closer to the residents of my hometown." This emotional connection motivated her while continuing the research process.*

According to a *New York Times* article by Win (2013), the chaotic riot resulted from a trivial brawl over a broken gold clip between a Muslim jeweler and Buddhist customer at a gold shop in the market that morning. The brawl left an old lady, the Buddhist customer, with an injury to the head. Obviously unsatisfied with the Muslim jeweler's action, the angry Buddhists came back in the afternoon and destroyed the gold shop....

While the brawl happened, I, together with a bunch of friends, was celebrating our final day of the matriculation exam, ignorant of the outside world. I felt sorry to later hear about the unfortunate news of the brawl, but it did not alarm me. I was not anticipating more violence.

In fact, the heated tension erupted that afternoon as the local Muslims, in revenge, stabbed a monk to death while he was travelling from a nearby village (Win, 2013). The infuriated Buddhist mobs then gathered in the evening with various kinds of weapons and sought for the ugly, historic, deadly revenge that lasted for three consecutive days....

> *One noteworthy aspect of Betty's autoethnography is the way she structures her narrative alongside her research. The counterpoint she creates between the two serves to strengthen the overall impression of each. In her first scene, for example, she presents her memory of her first encounter with the riot, then supplements that memory with the* New York Times *report on the riot's inciting incident. This juxtaposition reinforces the factual impact of her own memory while adding emotional resonances to the* Times *report.*

Pre-riot: Background Information

Meiktila is a small city in the central part of Myanmar, a predominantly Buddhist country. Surrounded by several armies, it was a peaceful town with diverse groups of Buddhists, Hindus, Muslims and Sikhs (Physicians for Human Rights [PHR],

2013, p. 4). Muslim *Bamars*—roughly one-third of the town's population—form the second major group to Buddhist *Bamars* and play a considerable role in the town's commerce (PHR, 2013, p. 4).

The long-term tranquility of the town was taken away as an unprecedented communal violence rose between Buddhists and Muslims on the 20th of March 2013. Serious violence and massive destructions lasted for three days until the martial law was proclaimed. Properties were destroyed; many precious lives were lost; the long-established relationship between the two groups was broken. Ironically, the pleasant town famous for its graceful lake became notorious for the immense burnings and terrorized actions.

Widespread throughout Meiktila, the violence was nonetheless heavily concentrated near Thiri Mingalar Ward, an area densely populated by Muslims. Starting as a small quarrel between the two communities, the violence later resulted in the vicious killings of Muslims by a group of furious Buddhists. As Buddhist outliers residing in Yan Myo Aung Ward, close to Thiri Mingalar, our family witnessed the traumatic violence....

During the Riot: A Long, Dark Night

"It's gonna end soon," rather (too) optimistically we hoped, albeit knowing that it, in fact, was just an empty wish....

Around 7 p.m., most employees scattered in groups at our front yard and stared outside with dead silences. I joined them and gawked at the direction they were looking; I saw the darkness and the fire angrily and massively rolling in the air up to the open sky. The relatively low brick walls of our compound had no capacity to hide the scene from us. I highly doubted even high walls could hide....

I looked at the other direction. Behind our closed main entrance door was the angry mob, predominantly males and monks, with weapons. Unfortunately, the dark night did not fail to single out the monks, ironically wearing their saffron robes and carrying weapons.

***

PHR (2013) identifies the three waves of religious violence between Buddhist and Muslim communities from June 2012 to April 2013 (p. 4). The first two waves happened between Rakhine (*Bamar*) and Muslim (Rohingya) communities.... the third wave took place between Buddhists and Muslims, both of whom had co-existed as fellow citizens for long. More sadly to me is that it was in Meiktila that the third wave of violence originated (PHR, 2013)....

***

> *Another important element of Betty's essay is the way she comments on the religious significance of the riot. As the* Times *reported, the riot began as a market brawl between Buddhists and Muslims, but as PHR reported, the ensuing violence tended to target Muslims more.*
>
> *Betty comments on the sad irony of seeing monks carrying weapons. As a Buddhist herself, Betty struggled to reconcile her own non-violent beliefs, the beliefs she associated with Buddhism, and the violence perpetrated by other Buddhists during the riot.*

While we were trapped in our own house with little chance to escape, Muslim students and teachers from the Madrassa were hiding, splitting into smaller groups, out in the field of Wat Hlan Taw with no chance to escape (PHR, 2013). According to PHR (2013), "this boggy area, measuring 95 by 80 meters ... overgrown with a variety of vegetation, including tall grasses" (p. 10) was their only protection.

The hiding students consistently and distinctly heard the threatening shouts "Kill the Kalars!" (PHR, 2013, p. 10) "Kalar" is a derogatory term which, according to Zin (2015), is used as a racial epithet for Muslims (p. 379). "Kalar" originally means "foreigners."

The open field as well as the air was cruel enough to serve as a medium for easy transmissions of these sounds. Their lives were in jeopardy. Despite my own experience, I will not completely comprehend what these students had gone through that night; theirs is far out of my understanding....

During the Riot: Stories of Survivorship

March 21, 2013. I woke up to the warm morning sunbeam penetrating into our room. The sun shone brightly as if nothing had happened, giving us the illusionary hope that it would be a beautiful day. I was a bit perplexed and thankful that we were still safely in our bed....

As the chaos of the night seemed to have adjourned (sadly, "adjourned" was a more appropriate word choice than "stopped"), my parents and I walked out of the compound and looked around our neighborhood. We saw burned or destructed houses—broken doors, empty windows, or half-burned brick walls. Some destructed family utensils left in the heap of the remains were the only indicators of families residing peacefully in these homes until the night before. Now, these homes were abandoned; so were sweet family moments....

RELEVANT REFERENCES: IMPROVING RESEARCH SKILLS | 75

The student survivors had no choice but to witness the sufferings of their fellow students and the residents. According to PHR (2013), an Oat Kyin resident witnessed the death of a student:

> another man took a horizontal swing at the boy with a long knife, first slicing into his neck. The second blow came down vertically on top of the boy's skull, at the frontal bone, and passed through the jaw. ... the boy's entire face was sliced off and he fell to the ground. (p. 14)

> *In her interview, Betty emphasized that autoethnography requires rigorous research, though she also noted that "it doesn't necessarily include a lot of resources, but the resources that fit your autoethnography." Prioritizing quality over quantity is admirable, but Betty didn't exactly skimp on quantity either. The minimum number of sources required for the final draft was six. Betty's final references list contains 14 sources.*
>
> *And these sources were thoroughly discussed. The minimum requirement for references to each source was three quotations or paraphrases. Betty's most frequently referenced source is the report by the Physicians for Human Rights (PHR), which she quotes or paraphrases more than twenty times.*
>
> *The PHR report collects testimonies from witnesses, participants, and victims. Some of these testimonies are difficult to read, brutally vivid accounts of the atrocities committed and suffered. Even just the clinical list of injuries one student survived is sobering, as are the memories of psychological trauma suffered. All these voices contribute to the impact of Betty's research.*

During the Riot: A Crack of Light

I am glad to notice certain beautiful acts of humanity in the midst of darkness during the Meiktila riot. According to PHR (2013), a Muslim woman resident narrated how a Buddhist man saved her, her brother and their neighbor who was carrying a baby: "I don't want to hit you and the baby. Come with me," the man mentioned (p. 14). At his house, they saw about 15 other Muslim women and girls hiding (PHR, 2013).

Also, some monks around Myanmar strongly stood to protect Muslims. Walton and Hayward (2014) highlight that the monk U Withuta in Meiktila provided safe sanctuary to hundreds of Muslims; he faced the madding Buddhist crowd and claimed that they needed to kill him first to get to the Muslims inside (p. 32). They further mention U Withuta's comment that "[he] was only doing it in accordance with Buddha's teachings" (Walton & Hayward, 2014, p. 32): he also added that "It would be best if we could steer clear of all the violence instigated by people abusing religion for nefarious means" (Walton & Hayward, 2014, p. 32).

***

U Withuta's responses reverberate with Omer (2010)'s mention of religious teachings and narratives: "Indeed, religious vocabularies, narratives, and claims have been associated with violent conflicts around the world. Yet, religious teachings and religious authorities and individuals have constituted a central, although overlooked, aspect of the practice of peacebuilding and conflict transformation" (Omer, 2010, p. 530). They further emphasize the role of religious narratives in violence and conflicts: "Religions are often invoked to justify acts of violence and protest between and within nation-states"; religion is also evident in generating and challenging the conceptions of common identity, such as nationalism (Omer, 2010, p. 513). The latter mention directly resonates with the Buddhist nationalist movements, interchangeably used as anti–Muslim movements, which Abdelkader (2014) mentions as "nationalist–Buddhist extremism" (p. 515)….

Understanding the Riot: Buddhist Narratives

… Arai (2015) traced fear—specifically the fear of losing Myanmar's Buddhist heritage—as a justification for structural violence: "We are organizing a national Buddhist movement in order to protect our nation and our religion," mentions one Buddhist interviewee (p. 48). Such views might somehow explain some Buddhists' hostility toward Muslims, including in Meiktila….

> *Betty uses religious studies and legal scholars to make some sense of her position in relation to that of her community. For example, Arai (2015) and Walton and Hayward (2014) comment on the fear that Buddhists would lose their heritage—a sadly common cause of conflict. These scholars helped Betty to understand, if not to justify, the reasons for the riot.*
>
> *She also found some comfort in accounts both by the PHR and by Walton and Hayward of Buddhists risking their own lives to protect their Muslim neighbors.*

Walton and Hayward (2014) confirm that fear is reflected in the rumors of Buddhists that the country is under the threat of being taken over by Muslims (p. 17). They also highlight that some Buddhists in Rakhine not only believe the Muslims' potential dominance but are also frustrated "that the global community is

demonizing Buddhism and is only acknowledging Muslim grievances" (p. 19)....
I imagine, like in Rakhine, there will be also certain Buddhists in Meiktila who perceive themselves as groups who actually "suffer" due to Muslims....

Post-riot Impacts: The Students' Narratives

Several massacre survivors were severely attacked during the riot. PHR (2013) spotlights the medical examination of a student consecutively beaten with swords or knives:

(1) A 5-cm laceration running from the thenar eminence around the base of the thumb onto the dorsal aspect of the hand;
(2) A 2-cm straight laceration on the left forearm;
(3) Three small lacerations on the back of the right hand, forming a slight arc measuring about 5 cm total; and
(4) Four lacerations at various angles on his back. Two lacerations measured approximately 10 cm, one measured approximately 16 cm and one measured 20 cm. (p. 19)

The student interviewees also reported some psychological distress, particularly nightmares: "nightmares in which he sees the conflagration of the school, and people from his neighborhood fleeing the scene and screaming. He cries 'almost every day' and feels very fearful about the future" (p. 19).

The students survived and struggled to confront with their tough witnesses of collapses of their significant others; I survived and struggled to confront with my witness of the collapse of my beloved hometown in the three days.

We survived, but we were wounded inside-out.

Post-riot: Deflated "Official" Figures

According to PHR (2013), official figures claimed the lives of 44 people, 86 to 93 injuries ... (p. 4). Unverified estimates, nonetheless, predict 148 deaths, and 3,000 more displaced people awaiting assessment (PHR, 2013, p. 4).

To me, to us residents who experienced the riot, the figures, whether inflated or deflated, do not matter anymore. This is not because we do not care about the death of our fellow residents. This is because the deflated "official figures" will not heal our wounded hearts. To us, 148 or 44 deaths, or even one single death, matters. It matters because it is our fellow resident; because it is so hard to believe that Buddhists, generally known to be kind, gentle and peaceful, can commit such terror; because the rest of us are struggling to accept the term "Buddhist Terrorists."

I am disheartened that the officials seem to assume 44 deaths to be acceptable while 148 is not.

Even one bloodshed, one death awfully matters, screamed our wounded hearts.

***

> *Maybe the most moving combination of research and personal perspective is when Betty cites sources on the numbers of deaths caused by the riot. These sources disagree, some generalizing, some more specific.*
>
> *Betty simply rebukes the quantification of suffering altogether, insisting in a passionate passage that any life lost is just too much.*

January 2016. As I attended a Muslim family's wedding with our guests, they noticed a Buddhist attendee heartily chatting with the Muslim hosts. Their observation made me think of the past three years. Almost three years ago, an exuberant Muslim wedding in Meiktila, and a tensionless chat between a Muslim and a Buddhist would have been an odd phenomenon. Now, it might still be odd to some residents and strangers; but, to certain residents, it is not, anymore. Reflecting so, I felt pleased with our relational development.

David Weaver-Hightower (2012) mentions in his autoethnography: "Grief may abate, but it does not end" (p. 485). I would like to respectfully invert Weaver-Hightower's statement: To us, grief might not end, but it will abate. We have struggled through the harsh reality of the communal violence: the collapse of our once beautiful town as well as our long-built relationships. We are now struggling to fight against the apparent oddness of our re-existence: We will continue our struggle to liberate from unpleasant past memories and vengeance, and rebuild a peaceful coexistence. Our journey ahead is not easy, but I am optimistic that we will move on.

> *Earlier I mentioned the potential that autoethnography offers students, even first-year undergraduates, to participate meaningfully in a scholarly conversation. These opportunities are unusual for students so early in their learning, but in this genre it is possible because their topics are personal, and their data come from their own experiences.*
>
> *Betty was one student who seized the opportunity, submitting her work for presentation at the International Congress of Qualitative Inquiry. Her submission was accepted, and she was able to travel to Chicago and share her research with other scholars—again, a remarkable rarity for a first-year undergraduate student.*

References

Abdelkader, E. (2014). Myanmar's democracy struggle: The impact of communal violence upon Rohingya women and youth. *Pacific Rim Law & Policy Journal, 23*(3), 511–541.

Arai, T. (2015). Toward a Buddhist theory of structural peace: Lessons from Myanmar in transition. *Peace and Conflict Studies Journal, 22*(1), 34–59.

Bean, J. C. (2011). *Engaging ideas: The professor's guide to integrating writing, critical thinking, and active learning in the classroom* (2nd ed.). San Francisco, CA: Wiley.

Boylorn, R. M., & Orbe, M. P. (2014). Introduction: Critical autoethnography as a method of choice. In R. M. Boylorn & M. P. Orbe (Eds.), *Critical autoethnography: Intersecting cultural identities in everyday life* (pp. 13–32). Walnut Creek, CA: Left Coast Press.

Omer, A. (2010). Conflict and peacebuilding. In R. D. Hecht & V. F. Biondo (Eds.), *Religion and everyday life and culture* (pp. 513–548). Santa Barbara, CA: Praeger.

Physicians for Human Rights. (2013). *Massacre in Central Burma: Muslim students terrorized and killed in Meiktila*. Washington, DC: PHR.

Walton, M. J., & Hayward, S. (2014). *Contesting Buddhist narratives: Democratization, nationalism and communal violence in Myanmar*. Honolulu, HI: East-West Center.

Weaver-Hightower, M. B. (2012). Waltzing Matilda: An autoethnography of a father's stillbirth. *Journal of Contemporary Ethnography, 41*(4), 462–491.

Win, S. (2013). Kristallnacht in Myanmar. *The New York Times*. Retrieved from https://latitude.blogs.nytimes.com/2013/03/29/violence-against-muslims-in-meiktila-myanmar/

Zin, M. (2015). Anti-Muslim violence in Burma: Why now? *Social Research: An International Quarterly*, 82(2), 375–397.

CHAPTER EIGHT

Writing Rightly: Ethical Consideration

> I need to be courteous and respectful of others in my own writing ... I think not just autoethnography but in any type of work that you know is going to be put out there ... even pictures on social media, things that are out to the public ... I'm definitely happy I learned about this as of right now because there are a lot of things that can go wrong with assuming people's consent.
> —Spencer, Student Autoethnographer

As I mentioned in Chapter Two, one of the strongest criticisms of autoethnography is that practitioners tread dangerously close to the edge of ethical research (Delamont, 2009; Tolich, 2010). The genre involves writing about others—friends, family, rivals, enemies—who might not like the way they are represented, or who may not want to be represented at all. These others can be considered research subjects, and thus, the depiction of their experiences may be protected by research codes of ethics. Often it is difficult or impossible to follow the kinds of ethical procedures required by more traditional research, like obtaining informed consent from all subjects prior to beginning research.

While I acknowledge those challenges and the risks inherent in this kind of research, I prefer the perspective that practicing autoethnography offers an opportunity for researchers to consider seriously the ethical implications of their work and to make the appropriate decisions (Ellis, 2007; Tullis, 2013). Adams, Holman

Jones, and Ellis (2015) claim one of autoethnographers' core ideals is "attending to the ethical implications of their work for themselves, their participants, and their readers'" (p. 25). Ethical consideration, then, is fundamental to autoethnography *because* of the challenges involved, not despite them.

More than adhering to any single set of rules, autoethnographers must think seriously about the ethical issues their research raises and demonstrate how they have addressed these issues. Whatever decisions they have made about obtaining consent or protecting identity, they should show, explicitly, how they arrived at those decisions. So, for example, if an autoethnographer cannot obtain informed consent from a subject, they might instead protect that subject's privacy by giving them a pseudonym and disguising their identity through other means.

There may be many ways to address ethical issues, then, and autoethnographic ethics may depend more on the depth of consideration of appropriate action than on strictly following any precise guidelines. This is a principle I try to impart to my students. During the course, we spend substantial time discussing the ethical implications involved in practicing autoethnography. We devote much of two weeks of the semester to this aspect of the genre, followed by a formal writing assignment comparing the ethics of two autoethnographies (see Appendix C).

Also, several in-class exercises prompt students to consider the ethical implications of their own projects, and describing the ethical considerations of each individual project is a requirement of the final assignment. That portion of the prompt reads: "Do you explicitly consider any ethical issues and resolve them appropriately, referring to sources to support your position?" Despite these direct instructions, some students omit this consideration from the first draft, and so need to be reminded of its necessity for subsequent drafts. By the final draft, however, all students, without exception, meet the expectation. Many exceed it, crafting thorough and eloquent discourses on their ethical deliberations.

In his critique of autoethnographic practice, Martin Tolich (2010) asserts: "Telling undergraduates to think deeply about the ethical implications is not useful advice" (p. 1605). That statement has always sounded slightly condescending to me. I suspect Tolich means that *only* advising undergraduates to think deeply about ethical implications is insufficient, and I would agree that providing students with specific tools to make ethical decisions is also important. But if Tolich means to suggest that undergraduates are not capable of making responsible choices regarding ethical research, he's just wrong.

In interviews, most of my students mentioned an increased awareness of ethics as an outcome of practicing autoethnography. Some students emphasized that ethics are among the most important elements of autoethnography. For example, when defining autoethnography, Betty said: "it's a discipline that allows us flexibility that at the same time demands honesty and certain standards, especially ethical standards." When I asked her what was the most important aspect of practicing autoethnography, Betty said, without pausing: "To me, ethics."

Like Betty, Kaitlyn's consideration of ethics stands out. Kaitlyn's autoethnography is an exploration of her Asian American identity, specifically concentrating on sensitive aspects of that identity, including race and privilege. Beyond even the explicit attention Kaitlyn pays to the ethical issues of consent and protection of privacy, the way she critically reflects on her own biases and behaviors shows that undergraduates are completely capable of serious ethical consideration and action.

Kaitlyn—"Somewhere in Between"

I chose to use autoethnography for its ability to capture the breadth of experience, explore multifaceted aspects of humanity and facilitate invaluable amounts of understanding of culture and society. I intend to present "my story" in a way that reveals how my Asian American identity has influenced my perspective on myself as well as the community in which I live. Using its creative and analytics techniques, I want to reveal, analyze and explicate my inner conflict between wanting the "white experience" that my peers had and my inescapable Asian heritage. I hope to bring insight to the pressures to succeed and assimilate and the inner identity conflicts that may characterize many minorities' experience....

Ethical standards in autoethnography serve as guidelines to help the autoethnographer avoid harming the subjects through his or her subjective narrative. Therefore, this approach requires careful consideration of the subjects' needs to limit "the vulnerability [that] topics might generate" (Tolich, 2010, p. 1605). I have received verbal consent from each of the "characters" mentioned in "Somewhere in Between." I have also changed their names to protect their identity and integrity....

> *Early in her essay, Kaitlyn makes a statement about the importance of ethical consideration "to help the autoethnographer avoid harming the subjects." In particular, Kaitlyn cared a lot about consent. In her interview, she commented on the applicability of ethical consideration, and specifically the issue of consent, to more than autoethnography: "I think consent is a concept that society still struggles with and that the guidelines are really blurred, and I felt that it was really important to discuss it in class because the discussion directly transferred outside of the classroom."*
>
> *Additionally, Kaitlyn notes, it is crucial to protect individual's identities, especially when writing about those individuals in less than flattering ways.*

> *Kaitlyn wanted to represent her friends and family fairly, but without skirting the critique of some of the ideological positions she found problematic. The nature of these relationships made it hard for Kaitlyn to request consent, as she said in her interview: "I didn't want to text my old teammates that I hadn't talked to since graduation." Still, she knew it was important to do so.*

A Twinkie? (August 2014)

I sit down next to the bleachers, pull up my kneepads, tighten my laces and wait for volleyball practice to start. As the rest of my teammates finally trickle into the hot gym, I look at the freshmen and new students who are trying out for the team. I mentally sigh upon seeing them walk in as a group. Each girl wore Nike athletic spandex, Lululemon headbands and some sort of fitted tank top. They all had their long blonde or brunette hair tied up in sleek ponytails, an iPhone in one hand and some sort of lanyard swinging in the other. The uniformity still amazes me. It was almost as if they had all coordinated their outfits before practice.

During my time on this volleyball team, there has only been three Asian girls, including myself, on the team at the same time. Although I know better than to blame the volleyball program itself for the lack of diversity, I often find myself thinking about what it would be like if the team had more people of different racial and socioeconomic backgrounds.... I guess I should not be surprised that all the new players were white since Asian athletes were relatively uncommon on the Main Line.

My thoughts are interrupted as my friend Ashley, the only biracial player on the team, tapped my head to get my attention.

"Damn, I wonder why there aren't any Asians or blacks who try out for volleyball," she whispered in my ear.

I cringed at her tone but sympathized with how she was feeling. "I know, right," I agreed.

Ashley continues, "It's like ... I like this team and all but I get tired of being the *only* black girl on this team. I guess that sounds kinda harsh but this team is just SO white." I hear the guilt in her voice as she concludes, "I don't even know if I'm making any sense, Kaitlyn."

"No it makes sense," I reassure her, "... I guess a part of being on a team is learning from each other ... and this lack of diversity inhibits that or even skews it."

> *In "A Twinkie?" Kaitlyn comments on the issue of race, recalling a problematic interaction with her teammates. The scene begins with Kaitlyn's reflection on how few Asian athletes there were at her school, an observation she finds both amazing and not surprising at all. Kaitlyn's acknowledgment of the paradox primes the reader for the tensions inherent in this issue.*
>
> *The scene continues in a whispered conversation with the only other non-white athlete on the team: "Ashley." Ashley also finds the lack of diversity troubling, and while Kaitlyn cringes at her teammate's bluntness, she shares the feeling. The frankly confessional reflection shows Kaitlyn's self-awareness, and her ability to be self-critical, not only critical of others.*

I genuinely believed that our volleyball team could benefit from more diversity. It lengthens "the extent that they identify themselves with a particular group and remain separate from others" (Segal, 2002, p. 181). The whole team basically consists of white players of the same upper to upper-middle class background. Consequently, the team's lack of overall diversity inhibits exposure to different cultural and economic background, thus preventing any type of exchange or learning.

Molly, another senior sits down next to us and asks what we were whispering about. I hesitate before answering, unsure if she would understand my and Ashley's conversation because she essentially epitomizes the "upper-middle class white girl" stereotype. Maybe I fear some sort of reprimand for admitting that this team is not as seamless as the rest of the girls think it is.

Ashley gave me a soft, reassuring smile, as if acknowledging that she understood the brief, inner turmoil I had just experienced. "We were just wondering why we're the only minorities who've tried out for volleyball....Like I'm one of the only Asians," I calmly respond and bite my tongue waiting for her response.

"Oh, well it's because you're different Kaitlyn. You're like....like a Twinkie."

Wow. There it is again. I have had heard this term a few times before in middle school and am surprised it's followed me up into my senior year of high school. Asians who strayed from the Asian stereotype by participating in "white" activities, like sports or non-orchestral instruments, were labeled as Twinkies. I try to remain calm and keep a neutral expression. I want to see how Molly will elaborate.

> *Then the conversation is interrupted by another student, who uses a racial slur. The term seems well intended—not as an insult, certainly. The ellipsis in "You're like … like a Twinkie" suggests a pause before using the term. Clearly, Kaitlyn wanted to convey her teammate's hesitance, however that pause may have been heard.*

> *The need for care in presenting this scene is obvious. While it would be impossible to represent "Molly" in a fully favorable way, Kaitlyn takes pains to show her as not maliciously racist. She also depicts Molly with few identifying details. It would be hard, if not impossible, from her description, to know who Molly actually is.*

Confused by the expression on my face, Molly looks over to Ashley for reassurance. However, Ashley seems just as concerned as I am. Molly continues, "You know what I'm talking about right? It's like, you're Asian, like yellow, on the outside but white on the inside….Like you're Asian but you're white on the inside because you act white."

"The issue of identity has always occupied a central place" in my mind (Zhau, 2000, p. 21). Even when I was young I wondered: Am I "acting" in a certain way? And if I was, exactly how and why would I? What does "acting white" even mean?

"What the hell does that even mean?" I act surprised and then add a slight chuckle to hide my vexation. Molly elaborates, "Well, you're really athletic … for an Asian you know? Even in middle school you were a good player and now you're a senior captain! Like, you put your time into sports rather than playing the violin or studying math or whatever."

Is that how she really saw the Asian community—as high achieving robots who do not care for a well-rounded education? Is that how white people see us? I cringe at the thought of a whole race having their culture labeled and stripped of any dimension. However, I also feel a slight sense of validation that Molly had essentially praised my athleticism. Is it wrong to feel this way? To feel even the slightest sense of satisfaction with her "compliment," even if it is in an elitist way. Then almost immediately I feel guilt for not being completely insulted by her reasoning. This isn't right.

I often "hesitate to call myself American because as I [perceive] it, American [means] all the beautiful Anglo children in my classes" (Zhau, 2000, p. 23). On the other hand, I feel a disconnect when I call myself Vietnamese because I have not visited the country or speak the language. Being called a "Twinkie" makes it seem as though I am purposely going against or distancing myself from my Asian culture, almost implying a sense of shame from being associated with my heritage. Playing sports does not mean I am ashamed of my culture, devalue my heritage or change who I am on the "inside." Enjoying what makes me happy does not make me any different from that of my Asian peers. I am who I am.

Molly and Ashley are staring back at me, curious to how I will react to Molly's rather derogatory generalization. "Hmm, I don't really see it. I guess so," I respond as to not challenge her rationale.

I'm angered that I do not have the courage to challenge Molly's reasoning for labeling me as a "Twinkie." A part of me knows that no matter how much I assimilate to "white" culture, I will never fully be on the "inside" because of my appearance. I was born with "almond-shaped eyes, straight black hair, and a yellow complexion" and therefore "[I am] a foreigner by default" (Zhau, 2000, p. 21). Oddly enough, a part of me still wants to attempt to assimilate, to see how close to the "inside" I can get. Or better yet, reach the "inside" and bask in the glory of surpassing the invisible criteria. I have been caught in this "insider/outsider" divide where the only way to get on the "inside" is to conform to the dominant culture and distance myself from my own heritage (Zhau, 2000, p. 21).

I cannot bring myself to tell Molly that I am not trying to "be white" and that I am just doing what makes me happy. I guess I'm just not courageous enough to speak out. I'm not strong enough to take up the challenge to fix this judgmental ideology so I let the unjust stereotyping persist. Or maybe I can't bring myself to speak out because, deep down, I'm still deciding in my own head if I take being called a "Twinkie" as a compliment or an insult.…

> *Kaitlyn also admits, subsequently, that her own response to Molly may leave much to be desired. We see her confusion, and the tension between feeling offended, but also guilty at not being "completely insulted," and even a bit proud about being accepted by her peer. Kaitlyn articulates some disagreement with Molly's reasoning, but she doesn't really reject the thinking, or the term.*
>
> *Kaitlyn admits she is angry with herself—maybe more than with Molly—that she does not express more, and she wonders if it's because she herself has tried to assimilate, wanting to appear as similar to her surroundings as possible. In this scene, as throughout the essay, Kaitlyn is as critical of herself as she is of her peers.*

Just Enough (April 2016)

I remember how some of my high school classmates had warned me that the college I had chosen to go to—a small, private liberal arts college in Pennsylvania—was "full of rich, white prep school kids, just like those on the Main Line." Even my cousin had snickered when I told him I was going to join the rowing team. He laughed, "way to choose a hella white college and join the whitest sport possible."

I knew that they were just teasing me and were not trying to hurt my feelings or insult the college itself. However, when I got to campus I noticed that their comments did turn out to hold some truth. Many of my peers are from the wealthier parts of Connecticut, New York and Massachusetts, or went to private boarding schools. In addition, the majority of my rowing teammates were also white, as are many of the other athletic teams on campus.

Thinking back, I ask myself: If I feel resentment towards the Main Line, why did I choose to go to a college where the majority of the students come from the same upper to upper-middle class economic background? If I complained about not having enough diversity on my volleyball team, why didn't I choose to go to a larger university in a diverse city?…

My decision to choose this college stripped me of the opportunity to escape these thematic social and cultural pressures. So I guess the question is: Why didn't I take that chance?

My thoughts are interrupted by the smell of food overwhelming my senses. Like a stampede of animals, my teammates and I storm in, mouths salivating, eager for food. There must be nothing more intimidating than fifty rowers coming in for dinner after practice. Just as I was about to take my first bite of my dinner, I heard raised voices yelling. Tommy and Sophie, sitting across from me, were arguing over who went to a more diverse high school. Oh gosh, how did they even get to this topic?

"No way! My high school was only 20% white people. TWENTY!" Sophie exclaims. Tommy counteracts, "that's nothing! Mine was 9% white, 10% Asians, like 6% Mexican and the rest was other or whatever!"

"We'll you're from Atlanta," Sophie argues back, "aren't there supposed to be lots of minorities down there? I'm talking like 'Asian-Asians'… Not like Kaitlyn." She nudges my shoulder and I roll my eyes.

Tommy asks, "Soph, what do you mean 'like Kaitlyn?'" I knew exactly what she meant. Tommy answers his own question before I can even respond, "OHHH!! She's talking about 'FOBs.' Like 'Fresh-Off-the-Boat Asians'… like straight from like China or whatever."

Sophie adds in, "Yeah, like Kaitlyn was born and raised here. The ones at my school came straight from a foreign country."

Although, it makes me uneasy hearing Tommy and Sophie, two close friends, using a derogatory acronym to describe Asian immigrants, I must acknowledge that the essence of what they're trying to say is true. Second generation immigrants and immigrants who have recently moved to the United States should definitely not be generalized together. They are two completely different groups with completely different experiences. Although both terms unjustly label groups of human beings, the term "FOB," surprisingly, does not insult me as much as "Twinkie" does.

I see "FOB" as an insensitive acronym that refers to a group of immigrants in a particular situation. "FOB" can definitely be used in a very negative way but the essence and purpose of the term is simply to differentiate groups. On the other hand, being called a "Twinkie" implies that one is acting a certain way in order to break away from their Asian culture and heritage. Witnessing this conversation made me realize that, even though I am really close to Tommy and Sophie, they still see my race as a distinguishing trait of who I am.

Tommy and Sophie notice my quiet contemplation. "Hey Kaitlyn … you okay?" Sophie asks.

"Yeah, I'm fine" I quickly respond. I wasn't lying. I actually was "fine." This conversation provided me with an answer to the question simmering in my subconscious. Now I know why I did not choose to go to a school that removed me from the overwhelming presence of privilege, unjust stereotyping and pressures to succeed.

The answer is simply that I've gotten used to this because this is all that I've ever known. I am used to being around this privilege. I am used to the pressures to succeed. That is why I feel comfortable around my white teammates, even if I'm one of the few minorities on the team. That is exactly why I have chosen to attend such a predominately white college, because I've gotten used to the fact that my race will always be the first thing others notice. Or the fact that no matter how much I integrate and assimilate to the majority that surrounds me, I will never be whole heartedly accepted. I am comfortable with the alternating feelings of integration and ostracism.

I am comfortable with fitting in "just enough."

In her concluding scene, "Just Enough," Kaitlyn continues to question the extent to which she truly wishes to adapt to her social/cultural context. She has chosen to attend a college with predominantly white (and wealthy) demographics, and when a new friend uses another slur—FOB—Kaitlyn is again confronted with the casual, perhaps unintentional racism around her, but also with her own complacency and complicity.

She insists she's "fine," and she realizes that she's telling the truth, and that she's grown comfortable with always being different, as long as she is "fitting in 'just enough.'"

When combined with her prioritization of consent, as well as her efforts to disguise the identity of her research subjects, Kaitlyn's self-criticism here, as throughout the essay, provides ample evidence of ethical consideration.

References

Adams, T. E., Holman Jones, S., & Ellis, C. (2015). *Autoethnography: Understanding qualitative research*. New York, NY: Oxford University Press.

Delamont, S. (2009). The only honest thing: Autoethnography, reflexivity, and small crises in fieldwork. *Ethnography and Education*, *4*(1), 51–63.

Ellis, C. (2007). "I just want to tell my story": Mentoring students about relational ethics in writing about intimate others. In N. K. Denzin & M. D. Giardina (Eds.), *Ethical futures in qualitative research* (pp. 209–227). Walnut Creek, CA: Left Coast Press.

Segal, U. (2002). *A Framework for immigration*. New York, NY: Columbia University Press.

Tolich, M. (2010). A critique of current practice: Ten foundational guidelines for autoethnographers. *Qualitative Health Research*, *20*(12), 1599–1610.

Tullis, J. A. (2013). Self and others: Ethics in autoethnographic research. In S. Holman Jones, T. E. Adams, & C. Ellis (Eds.), *Handbook of autoethnography* (pp. 244–261). Walnut Creek, CA: Left Coast Press.

Zhau, M. (2000). Identity, emerging ethnicity, and the assimilation problem. In Gatewood, J., & Zhou, M. (Eds.), *Contemporary Asian America: A multidisciplinary reader* (pp. 21–31). New York: New York University Press.

CHAPTER NINE

Writing Wrongs: Critical Empowerment

The public should know and be exposed to these things.
—Allison, Student Autoethnographer

It also helped me become more aware of problems today and how people felt about them.
—Anonymous Student Survey

Contrary to the criticism of autoethnographers being self-indulgent navel-gazers, the genre requires both the inward examination of the self and the outward exploration of the self's social/cultural context, which can result in increased awareness of contextual problems, and a desire to affect change. Adams, Holman Jones, and Ellis (2015), for example, insist that the genre "strives for social justice and to make life better" (p. 3). For some practitioners, this critical empowerment is autoethnography's most important goal.

I recognize and admire autoethnography's potential to challenge and change the status-quo, even if this critical capacity is not the foremost focus of my teaching. Naturally, the subject comes up in discussions of core texts (Adams, Holman Jones, & Ellis, 2015; Ellis, Adams, & Bochner, 2011), and near the end of the course, we spend several class periods discussing examples of critical autoethnographies relating to gender and sexuality, race and ethnicity—aspects of life that are rife with social inequality.

Though it is not a top priority in my teaching, many of my students indicated that practicing autoethnography led to feelings of critical empowerment. For example, in her interview, Kaitlyn said: "I felt like I was writing something that actually had purpose … that was bigger than myself …. I felt like I needed to write this in order to do some good." Her purpose was to challenge a narrative of ethnic stereotyping, and her essay provided plenty of opportunities to confront problematic aspects of identity. She said: "It kind of shifted my focus from being in the college bubble as a student to a broader person … by writing autoethnography, I felt like I was writing something that could contribute to something bigger."

Another student for whom critical empowerment was both a powerful motivator and a remarkable outcome was Tania, who shared the deeply personal and difficult experience of domestic violence. She showed scenes of conflict from her family life framed by research on the social/cultural factors—such as ethnicity and gender—that contributed to the conflicted dynamic.

Tania—"A Bengali-American Perspective: On Opposing Cultural Definitions of Patriarchy"

Scene 1

It was the first snow day that winter. While most seven-year-old kids felt excited to play in the snow, I dreaded it. I lacked the appropriate clothing for the weather, and it made me extremely uncomfortable. I wanted to make the request for new shoes and possibly a coat, but I was afraid. Would I be asking for too much? Would dad get mad at me for asking?

As my mother dressed me in layers of sweaters and long sleeve shirts, I wondered if I could make the request for winter clothing. "I want a jacket, mommy. And shoes because my toes turn purple in the cold." I whispered to my mom. I couldn't bear the humiliation of wearing sandals in the winter anymore. I was hoping she would make the request for me. We both avoided the conversation for weeks because we knew how angry dad got at us when we asked for anything.

He had the money, and he knew we needed it. Asking him for money added to his feeling of control over us. He used it to his advantage, to feel more powerful…. His sense of control over us fueled his ego. He needed a constant reminder that we needed him. Because my mother was unemployed, we had no choice than to ask him and he used it to belittle us….

The use of money as being a mode of gaining control over the abuser's victims is more common than I thought. As I was conducting research, I learned of an Indian woman, Prema, a domestic abuse survivor who gained more control over her life after she began working: "In 1980, I started taking control, slowly. I started taking control of the money … He lost control over the kids, over the money, over me" (Abraham, 2000, p. 150). I was amazed by how much power money had over our relationships. It saddens me to know something materialistic could be the force that causes destruction in a family, but could also heal it. I wonder what my family would be like if my mother own her own money. Would we have left him? Would my father still feel entitled to his authority?

"Hey, Tania needs a new jacket. Winter's here I think the kids should go shopping," my brave mother said as she zipped my hot pink sweater.

"What else does she want? I don't have a single person in this world to purchase anything for me, and she expects me to shop for her?"

My mother and I were silent. How could I be so greedy? It was true, my father didn't have anyone to take care of him. I lacked the resources in order to provide for him, and I hated myself for it. That day I decided when I grew up I would give my dad everything he wanted.

"It's okay then, I'll just layer." I felt pity for myself.

"I feed you, I give you a home, I take care of you. What else do you want?"

He kept going but I wish he would stop. I became distracted by the cereal at the table and hopped into my seat to eat my breakfast. Before I could grab the spoon the bowl went flying across the table and crashed into pieces on the ground.

"Your mother taught you right? To destroy my life? She teaches you all evil. I paid for that food. If you were my daughter you could've ate that. But you're her daughter. So go ask your mother to get a job and feed you."

My father did this often. He blamed my mother for things that often had nothing to do with her. He was convinced my mother was the root of all of his problems. This is a common trait in abusive fathers: "Children are also frequently told by abusive fathers that their families would be together were it not for their mother's behavior, thus attempting to put pressure on the mother through the children to return to him or driving a wedge between the mother and her children" (Edelson, 1997, p. 3). Edelson's attempt to understand the reasoning behind this tactic seems appropriate to my situation. Abusive fathers often attempt to turn the children against the mother. My father had tried to convince us why my mother was a failure in all aspects and the cause behind his unhappiness. We never believed him.

I can't remember what my mother's response was to his decision to throw the food onto the ground, but whatever it was it made him angrier. He grabbed the glass filter on the table and threw it against the wall. The crack is still there today....

> *In her interview, Tania was explicit about her goals for her work, commenting on her autoethnography's potential value to others like her:*
>
> *Bengali-American youth specifically needs to understand the situation they're in. It's not a coincidence or just by chance. There are social structures sort of set up for them to face those limitations, specifically women.... we need more Bengali writers. More Bengali narratives. And I think Bengali youth needs to read it.*

Scene 3

"I'm gonna write about it mom" my voice trembled as I held my cell phone close to my ear. Silence followed. I didn't have to explain "it" for her to know what exactly I was talking about. My mother knew it was only a matter of time before her only outspoken and shameless daughter would expose the family secret.

"For what?"

"For class. I'm going to use the words 'domestic violence' because that's what it was mom. And I want to understand why you didn't." My words were aggressive. I regretted it immediately. Was I practicing power over my mother? I tried to gulp down the sense of guilt that was now stuck in my throat. The tone in my voice surprised me, but also reminded me of how angry I still was at my mother for not yet admitting to her abusive marriage. However, I didn't want to accuse her of more than my father already had.

"Who will read it?"

"My professor, and anyone else I want to share it with" I responded as I scribbled down the English translations of our conversation to include in my autoethnography....

"Do it. I trust you"

"Thanks mom. I love you."

"Your father is not a bad man, Tania. He loves you so much"

"I love him more."

I hung up and giggled. Being reminded of his love for me couldn't make me forget the pain he's inflicted on us....

> *Maybe more even than the possible value to her classmates or to other Bengali young people, Tania imagined a benefit to someone more immediately connected with her. In her interview, when I asked Tania what moments she most remembered from practicing autoethnography, she said:*
>
> The first one would be when I called my mom to ask her for consent. Because it was a little weird to voice something that we don't really talk about in the house often. And I felt a part of me was giving her back that sense of power and control. So it was a little bit empowering for the both of us.

Scene 5

"I want to be a makeup artist and a model!" I enthusiastically told my mother one day as she chopped vegetables in the kitchen.

"Oh, how will I get this girl married to a good Muslim man?"

"That's not funny mom, why does everything I want to do have to do with whether or not it will make me a good wife?"

"You always get so upset when we speak of marriage; it's a beautiful thing."

"No it's not. I would hate to have a husband like dad." I intended for that to be offensive. I wanted her to know her marriage was destructive.

"Why? What's wrong with your father?"

I stared at the ground. Did she not know or did she just want to hear it from me?

"He fights with you a lot." I didn't know how else to say it.

"A strong woman has patience. The kind of patience men don't have."

It blew my mind that she viewed staying in this marriage as a positive thing. Was I a weak woman then if I chose to leave an abusive marriage? For so long, I held in so much anger toward her for being submissive. For not standing up for herself and protecting her children. My sisters and I spend countless hours wondering if dad would be different if mom had not allowed him to get his way early in their marriage. I'm not sure my mother would even describe her husband as being abusive.

Shamita Dasgupta conducts a research study on the effect of domestic violence on South Asian women and reports, "The interviews indicate that South Asian women are more likely to mobilize more familiar forms of discourse as cultural and pragmatic, rather than that of mental and emotional health and suffering to discuss their abuse experiences" (Dasgupta, 2007, p. 81). Did my mother not see a problem in his behavior at all? Did she accept that her husband's volatile nature was acceptable by culture? Did this acceptance take away from the effect the abuse had on her?

I can't be sure if a Bengali definition exists for marital abuse or domestic violence, but I wanted to explain it to her. I also wanted her to know that for her American children, we understood his violent outbursts as traumatic. I lacked the Bengali vocabulary in order to explain this to her, and I felt too embarrassed to use the words I did know. A part of me didn't want to see her confront these ideas in front of me. She's tried to hide so much of her abuse to protect me, I think I would rather pretend as if it didn't exist. One day, one day I will try to explain it to her....

> *Tania also hoped that her autoethnography could help distinguish her broader cultural background from the specifics of her religion, to push back against the stereotype of, as she put it: "Muslim women who need saving and all of that." Instead, she wanted to emphasize that her situation was characteristic of a different context: "This is the patriarchy in Bangladesh." She knew this distinction would be a challenge: "It's just easy to get it confused, especially with a culture that is so different from American culture."*
>
> *I asked if she thought she had succeeded. She said: "I did do my best, but I think I could have done a better job." I told her, for whatever it was worth, I thought she had done very well, and she nodded and said: "I just realized it was so different. I was so ... my story was so different. But in a good way. I think that a lot of students find it hard to believe that there were parents who didn't want their kids to go to school."*

Scene 7

I sat down on the couch as I massaged my father's broad, muscular shoulders.

"Harder." He said as he dropped his head into his chest.

I was never doing it right, But I had to do it anyway.

"Dad," I whispered

"Hmm," he responded.

"I visited Franklin and Marshall, daddy. I fell in love, I think I want to apply early decision."

"Where's that?"

"Lancaster, Pennsylvania. Only a three-hour drive, daddy, you could see me anytime."

I could feel my heart beating fast. Bengali girls never left home. Not unless they were married. But I knew I couldn't accept the expectations assigned to me as a Bengali woman: "South Asian culture mainly constructs women as submissive, self-sacrificing, inferior, nurturing, of high moral values, docile, socially dependent, and modest" (Mahapatra, 2008, p. 24). What made up the ideal Bengali women according to Bengali society made me feel malleable. I know if I continue to live here with him he will continue to encourage these expectations from me. I have been building the courage to share with him my consideration in applying to a residential college for months now.

"Why do you care so much?"

I wasn't sure what he was asking. "About?"

"College. Just go help your mother in the kitchen. You'd be more useful."

I stopped rubbing his shoulders. I couldn't believe what I was hearing. "Dad, I can't believe you just said that."

"Bengali girls don't need college. You need to learn how to be a good wife."

I was taken back. Disgusted even. My father was telling me my service to a man is more relevant than my education. I had always viewed my adult self as a professional, using her skills and education to help people in her community. My father, however, never imagined a different future for me other than to be a housewife.

I felt so attacked by his words I walked away. Could he be the reason behind why my sister chose to be married at a young age? Would they try to get me married if I stay here? I've seen it happen. Girls who were forced into marriage at a young age, forced out of school, and forced out of the workforce to be a housewife....

Was it men like my father that kept women from achieving excellence? If I stay home will he stop me from achieving my goals? If I got accepted to Franklin and Marshall, I was going to go.

Here I'm going to encroach a bit into next chapter's territory; in her autoethnography's introduction, Tania refers, albeit indirectly, to the genre's therapeutic potential: "For some authors, autoethnographies have been a way for them to make sense of their experiences." While there may be no way to completely resolve the complicated feelings coming from such experiences, still Tania said in her interview that she had indeed made some sense of her situation: "I also learned that once I confronted how unique it was, I realized it wasn't the norm. What I had made the norm in my head so long was actually not the norm."

And at an even more personal level, she also realized:

Somebody can only love you the best way they know how. And so once I understood the culture, and I understood the limitations it had in terms of gender and things like that, I felt less angry, less confused. Because you can't offer me knowledge and care and nurture if you never had it yourself. If you've never been taught yourself.

> *Confronting and understanding the social/cultural context of her experience, especially the expectations and limitations due to gender, Tania understood her father better. Tania was even able to replace the anger and confusion with more positive feelings: "I don't know if this is what you're looking for in this answer, but I kind of learned that I love my dad very much."*

References

Abraham, M. (2000). *Speaking the unspeakable*. New Brunswick, NJ: Rutgers University Press.

Adams, T. E., Holman Jones, S., & Ellis, C. (2015). *Autoethnography: Understanding qualitative research*. New York, NY: Oxford University Press.

Dasgupta, D. S. (2007). *In body evidence: Intimate violence against South Asian women in America*. New Brunswick, NJ: Rutgers University Press.

Edelson, J. (1997). *Children's witnessing of adult domestic violence* [PDF file]. Retrieved from http://citeseerx.ist.psu.edu/viewdoc/download?doi=10.1.1.308.1330&rep=rep1&type=pdf

Ellis, C., Adams, T. E., & Bochner, A. P. (2011). Autoethnography: An overview. *Forum: Qualitative Social Research, 12*(1).

Mahapatra, N. (2008). *South Asian women and domestic violence: Incidence and informal and formal help seeking* [PDF file]. Retrieved from https://pdfs.semanticscholar.org/a472/a9026b64e466382afa6e264c6d1ac936a0d1.pdf?_ga=2.239222531.1091745484.1569436789-1905196380.1569436789

CHAPTER TEN

Creative Catharsis: Therapeutic Potential

It's therapeutic and helped me find closure of that part of my life ... I felt like I didn't know if that was missing, but I feel like there was an end to that chapter of my life. It's over now, this is me, I'm healthy.
—Christa, Student Autoethnographer

Practicing autoethnography can produce feelings of mental and emotional healing. Ellis, Adams, and Bochner (2011) emphasize this aspect of the genre: "Writing personal stories can be therapeutic for authors as we write to make sense of ourselves and our experiences" (p. 25). Researching and writing about difficult past experiences can lead to a better understanding of those experiences, and a sense of catharsis.

The therapeutic potential of writing in general is not news (Pennebaker, 2004, 2010), but in the context of a first-year undergraduate writing class, it can be controversial. I recognize that this outcome is problematic. As a compositionist, my job is to teach my students to write, not to address their psychological health. I have none of the requisite qualifications for counseling of that kind. There are professionals trained and tasked to do that work. Also, I cannot judge if what my students reported as therapeutic was genuinely so.

However, they did report that, overwhelmingly, in both interviews and in their essays. Tania talked about how practicing autoethnography helped her come to terms with her troubled family life. Kaitlyn said that her research and writing were cathartic: "I was finally saying all the things I wanted to but didn't have the chance to, didn't have the courage to." Betty was able to mourn the violence in her community, while Edward appreciated reconnecting with his father about their past shared conflict. Even one end-of-the-semester surveys mentioned this outcome: "Writing the autoethnography was an incredible experience. Not only did it hone my writing skills, but it was an introspective journey and proved very therapeutic."

I must stress that I do not foreground autoethnography's therapeutic potential in teaching my course. It emerges, necessarily, in discussions of core texts (Adams, Holman Jones, & Ellis, 2015; Ellis, Adams, & Bochner, 2011), and I acknowledge it, but I repeatedly emphasize that there is no guarantee of this outcome, and it will not be the focus of students' work in the class.

That warning does not negate my responsibility for my students' psychological well-being. As I will discuss further in Chapter Twelve, I have conversations with students who choose emotionally difficult topics, like the loss of loved ones, or troubled home environments. In those conversations, I urge students, if they feel emotional distress, to seek the support of the appropriate professionals.

Some writing teachers may be reluctant to engage with any emotionally difficult material produced by students, and that is fair. I would have to caution these teachers against adopting autoethnography into their pedagogy, since it is likely that at least some students will choose those tough topics.

However, like other compositionists who have considered similar challenges (Burdick, 2009; Lucas, 2007), I would encourage even wary teachers at least to consider the potential benefits of students confronting such topics. Those benefits were powerfully evident in many of my students, especially Elizabeth, who processed the death of a beloved family member in her autoethnography.

Elizabeth—"The Loss of a Grandmother, Mother, and Friend to Idiopathic Pulmonary Fibrosis"

I was on top of the world on that mountain in Alta, Utah, eight hours by plane away from all of my problems and not a care in the world. Gazing over the wide expanse of blue sky and jagged peaks cutting into the clouds like daggers, I was at peace with myself, engaged in the one activity that my family and I loved more than any other; skiing. It was our first time back out west for years, and we were loving every minute of it. There is nothing like the feeling of freedom gained from flying down a slope with two feet of fresh powder, the crisp cold air only intensifying the excitement of cutting between trees down miles of slopes only to ride back up on the chilly lift, bundled together, to do it all over again....

We were having the time of our lives; waking up to hit the slopes, coming back tired and relaxing and laughing together, snacking on junk food, watching Christmas movies, as it was the season, enjoying the hot tub, and attending fancy dinners that came with our trip at the lodge every night, ordering whatever we liked (even though my youngest brother insisted on getting chicken fingers for every meal). We were in a dream world it seemed, too perfect to be real, when it all came crashing down around us.

> *In her interview, Elizabeth admitted that at first she had been skeptical about autoethnography's therapeutic potential: "I didn't think that was going to happen, but then later on, you could actually feel the effects—like, wow this is great to write it all down." The abstract of her autoethnography confirms those effects as well: "Retelling these memories has been therapeutic for me."*
>
> *The memories begin pleasantly, idyllically even, as Elizabeth recalls the happy time of a family vacation, and a series of pleasant activities. Of course, the positive feelings she evokes must change, as her essay's title foreshadows.*

One evening after a few days of skiing, my brothers and I relaxed in our room at The Goldminer's Daughter lodge until a panic in my parent's voices told us to pack our things as they quickly tried to find a flight home. They had gotten a call, and even though we all knew it was coming, we didn't want to believe that she was really dying. That plane ride home will always be the worst time of my life. We were being ripped apart by the fear that we wouldn't make it back in time. That eight dreaded hours was spent listening to sad music, trying not to cry and imagining life without my best friend, my second mother, and my role model.

My Grandma.

What if I couldn't even say goodbye....

This journey began many months before this moment, when my Grandma was diagnosed with chronic obstructive pulmonary disease (COPD), and sometime after with Idiopathic Pulmonary Fibrosis. I vaguely remember my parents telling my two brothers and I in 2013 about both of her diagnoses. At first, I remember it not really phasing anyone, as she still seemed almost perfectly healthy....

> *Elizabeth carefully researched her grandmother's condition and presented her findings with clinical attention to detail. It cannot have been easy, emotionally, to explore the disease that took her grandmother's life, but Elizabeth did not balk from depicting the grim specifics in these medically-focused passages that punctuate the overall narrative.*

At this point when she was first diagnosed, her body was only beginning to show symptoms of the two diseases. Chronic obstructive pulmonary disease, commonly called COPD, is one of the most prominent diseases in the elderly and is expected to be the third leading cause of death in the year 2020 (Pistelli et al., 2011, p. S43). … It is developed through the alveolar regions of the lung which consist of two types of epithelial cells which communicate with one another. This communication is broken down with the development of the disease, leading to unchecked and unregulated matrix producing cells, which trigger the disease, subsequently scarring lung tissue (Barkauskas & Noble, 2014).

I still remember, when I was quite young, how my parents used to take me to my Grandparents' house for sleepovers, when they were both alive and lived about an hour away. After losing my Grandpa, who had always been my "buddy," around the age of three, it became just a girl's sleepover with me and my Grandma. I remember exploring the house my dad grew up in and sleeping in his old bedroom, even though late at night I would always crawl into bed with Grandma.

I remember exploring her large jewelry box with her, as she explained what each sparkling piece was to a younger me, who tried on everything. She would jokingly play along and allow me to dress myself with as much as I could fit on my tiny body and run around the house laughing with her.

I remember one ring in particular, that she said she wanted me to have someday when it fit. It was gold with a ruby that always reminded my young self of an apple. Every time I visited, she would let me try it on, both of us hoping it would fit, even though it never did.…

> *Elizabeth's love for her grandmother is plain throughout her essay. She writes about their shared experiences with palpable, albeit bittersweet joy, establishing the nature of their close relationship before the incursion of illness.*

The beginning of my junior year in the fall was when her symptoms became much worse. She could no longer leave the house on her own, but, being her, she still found a way to have her favorite hairdresser come dye her hair. I remember visiting her alone and going through a lot of her life's treasures she had decided to keep, collectibles passed down or found through her travels of the world. Each one had its own story, more fascinating than the last, and I sat while she told me all about it for hours....

Eventually her condition required her to move into hospice care. She was there for nine months. We visited as much as we could, but it was never enough. Sometimes when we visited we would take funny pictures together or I would bring her gifts or food, but most of the time we would all exchange stories of each other's lives, keeping her updated while she listened attentively. She would tell us stories of her life too, past or present.

Soon enough she had been there for months, and it was Christmas time. Our family had been planning a ski trip out west to Alta, Utah for a long time now. Even though she was getting much worse, she did not want to stop us from going. We all needed an escape.

At this point, the myofibroblast cells were becoming much more prominent and taking over from the pulmonary fibrosis side of things, they could not be held back anymore (Barkauskas & Noble, 2014). They were helping the COPD with its inflammation process, and she was having a harder and harder time breathing, even with her oxygen levels all the way up on her breathing tube. At this point, there was absolutely no going back, it was only a matter of time and how strong she was. She had already lasted much longer than the doctors had predicted; she did not have much time.

> *Elizabeth began college intending to become a pediatrician. In her interview, she described how, after practicing autoethnography, she had a summer internship working with seniors, many of them suffering from the same or similar conditions as her grandmother.*
>
> *Elizabeth said her autoethnographic research helped her connect with these individuals in a powerful way: "I knew what people were going through." She also said that now she might want to redirect her medical path towards working with an older population.*

As soon as our plane touched back down in Pittsburgh, PA, very late on the night of December 26, 2013, the day after Christmas, my family and I rushed back to see her. When we got back and saw her, I barely believed she was still alive.

She was completely color stricken. Her once always bright red hair had become white. Her face was gaunt and almost transparent. Her eyes were closed and multiple tubes were strapped to her body including one on her face that was giving her air to breathe and keeping her alive.

    We stayed for a while, and eventually it got late and my parents decided some of us needed to go home. My father and I both had no intention of leaving her side. I remember falling asleep on a chair next to her bedside, using a blanket and pillows the nurses had kindly brought us. I woke up on multiple occasions to hold her hand in the middle of the night, just to make sure she was still with me. My dad didn't seem to sleep at all. The next morning my mom and brothers returned, and told me she would be here a little while longer and I needed to go home and get clean....

    That afternoon we went back to the hospice care center where my Grandma had been moved once again into a room that was too small to fit us all at once. I remember staying in there with her for a while, holding her hand, hoping that she could sense my presence, but with no way to know. Eventually, I couldn't stand being in there anymore. Me and my brothers left to sit in the lounge, where I remember *The Little Mermaid* was playing and sufficiently distracting us.

> Until a nurse came running.
> Until she told us it was time.
> Until I got light-headed and couldn't run fast enough back to the room with her.
> Until I got there and saw her.
> Struggling to breathe.
> Racing to her side,
> Crying,
> Not wanting her to be gone yet,
> Wishing for more time,
> Wishing for a word,
> Wishing her eyes would open and see that we were all there with her, and that she wasn't alone.
> It was quick.
> Her breaths faltered.
> I remember hearing her last one and screaming along with the monitor that traced her heartbeat.

My family held each other and cried for a long time. My mom and I kissed her forehead, and I gently closed her eyes, as they had opened one last time. I hugged my mom, dad, brothers.

    I like to think that she died peacefully, but researching her dying process proved me wrong: She likely died in pain. I now understand exactly what was going on in her body and it could not have been pleasant to constantly struggle to breath.

> *Describing her grandmother's last night must have been hard for Elizabeth. It was hard for me even to read sentences like this one: "I like to think that she died peacefully, but researching her dying process proved me wrong, she likely died in pain." I remember thinking and feeling exactly the same thing about my own grandparents' passing; it hurt me to see them suffering, just as it did Elizabeth.*

Even though it must have been painful, she never let it show. She always had a brave face and a beaming smile for us every time we visited. But she was with family in her final moments, so I like to believe this somewhat softened her pains, as being together through our period of bereavement helped us survive the loss of someone so important to each of us. As my mother put it when I asked her what it was like going through this experience for her: "If it hadn't happened like it did, we all wouldn't have been set on the same course." Losing her united us more in many ways, but it also destroyed a part of us individually.

Upon losing a family member, the family experiences both turmoil and cohesion, or fighting and bonding (Baum, Revenson, & Singer, 2012, p. 496). This means that there will be both good and bad times when someone is lost, as each person copes differently, perhaps rubbing each other the wrong way…. which seems to be exactly what my family and I did….

We, as a family, held the funeral, as Christians do, a few days after her death, to pay our respects and grieve with friends and family….

Even though I just wanted to get it over with, I also wanted it to be special, for her. I helped my mom set up a table with pictures and memories with her. I remember helping my mom pick out what she would wear, as it was open casket, one last time before she was cremated. We picked her favorite cozy blue sweater that my mom got specially for her from Nordstrom. I helped remember what rings she always wore, recalling the many times as a child sitting next to her in church and asking to play with them as at least one changed every week. My mom picked a gold necklace and her classic gold earrings.

The funeral ceremony occurred at the church, I remember my pastor speaking very fondly of her, as he visited her often during her nine months in hospice….

Others spoke a few words.

I did not. I could not.

> *Often the aftermath of losing a loved one is the hardest aspect of the experience. Elizabeth describes the challenges she and her family faced, as well as the ways they coped, individually and as a group. Everyone grieves differently, but at the time, Elizabeth found comfort in her religious beliefs, and also in the personal, material possessions her grandmother had left behind. In looking back, Elizabeth seemed to appreciate that other individuals and families had processed their own losses similarly to her own.*

Many people offered their condolences and told me and my family how amazing she was. Surprisingly, my family and I held our ground. There were tears, of course, but overall, we stuck together, with my mom and dad occasionally hugging us each for comfort. The viewing was the next day. So many faces came and went, blurring together, talking to me and my brothers, and saying their own goodbyes. The room was full of flowers sent by dozens of people. One large basket of white roses held a larger beautiful glass cross that now sits on the shelf above my bed at school as a remembrance.

Eventually we had to say goodbye. Seeing her in a casket up close was something I had been avoiding, waiting until no one else was there but family. She didn't look like herself. Her makeup was done in a way she never wore it. So was her hair. I think that helped. We each said our individual goodbyes. All in tears now. I kissed her forehead, following my mom, and gave her hand a squeeze. She was so cold and stiff. This wasn't her.

We all avoided going through her possessions. None of us were ready to really accept it. Eventually, my mom gave me a few large boxes for me and my brothers to someday have and allowed me to go through trinkets from all over the world that my Grandma had shown me before. I didn't want to get rid of anything, so I barely did. My mom wasn't happy, but I protested and she let it go. I didn't want any memory of her to be lost....

She isn't gone from our lives in the slightest. She is with us every time something reminds us of her and she is with us when I drive her gold 2010 Toyota Camry.... She is with us through her jewelry that my mom and I now wear. She is also with us with the wisdom and the things she left behind including a book to her three grandchildren, explaining how to live life in its fullest, that will forever be my most treasured possession. Though I have only been able to read it once, as it is very emotional for me, I know that I can always turn to it in times of need. I brought it with me to college and I plan on taking it with me everywhere for the rest of my life. The ending is the most emotional for me as she speaks about the things she will miss out on, but to know that she is still here with us, watching over us. This again goes back to how we, as Christians, don't believe we are fully separated.

She is with me in my thoughts every day, wondering what she would think of me now. She is with me in her Snoopy slippers that I now wear. She is with me when I wear her signature red nail polish, or when I drive by her old condo. She is with me through her undying love for "her girl." She is with me in the gold ring with a single ruby and two small diamonds that she hoped I would one day grow into. I finally have.

> *Most of all, Elizabeth's words memorialize her grandmother, a testament to the love the two shared. Here Elizabeth honors her grandmother's legacy, especially the gift of the gold ring. Her use of repetition—"She is with me"—is a tribute, an almost ritualistic reaffirmation of her grandmother's ongoing presence, despite her death, in Elizabeth's life.*

References

Adams, T. E., Holman Jones, S., & Ellis, C. (2015). *Autoethnography: Understanding qualitative research*. New York, NY: Oxford University Press.

Baum, A., Revenson, T. A., & Singer, J. E. (2012). *Handbook of health psychology* (2nd ed.). New York, NY: Psychology Press.

Barkauskas, C. E., & Noble, P. (2014). Cellular mechanisms of tissue fibrosis. 7. New insights into the cellular mechanisms of pulmonary fibrosis. *American Journal of Physiology: Cell Physiology, 306*(11), C987–C996.

Burdick, M. (2009). Grading the war story. *Teaching English in the Two-Year College, 36*(4), 353–354.

Ellis, C., Adams, T. E., & Bochner, A. P. (2011). Autoethnography: An overview. *Forum: Qualitative Social Research, 12*(1).

Lucas, J. (2007). Getting personal: Responding to student self-disclosure. *Teaching English in the Two-Year College, 34*(4), 367–379.

Pennebaker, J. W. (2004). *Writing to heal: A guided journal for recovering from trauma and emotional upheaval*. Oakland, CA: New Harbinger Publications.

Pennebaker, J. W. (2010). Expressive writing in a clinical setting. *The Independent Practitioner, 30*, 23–25.

Pistelli, R., Ferrara, L., Miscuraca, C., & Bustacchini, S. (2011). Practical management problems of stable chronic obstructive pulmonary disease in the elderly. *Current Opinion in Pulmonary Medicine, 17*(1), S43–S48.

CHAPTER ELEVEN

Enjoyment and a Sense of Community

It was something huge that I really wanted to work on, and I was excited about.
—Kaitlyn, Student Autoethnographer

I felt extremely safe to share my thoughts and my experiences.
—Selena, Student Autoethnographer

Two outcomes of practicing autoethnography that surprised me were the sense of community that developed amongst the students in the courses, and the enjoyment the students expressed. One always hopes for a healthy, positive class dynamic, and I had suspected that the personal nature of the genre might help. However, I knew it might just as easily go the other way and generate an awkward atmosphere of tension. I also hoped students would genuinely enjoy practicing autoethnography, but I knew that they might well find it just another chore—and an uncomfortable, intrusive one, at that.

Any group of classmates has the capacity to develop a sense of community. However, in my experience, even in small classes, the strength of camaraderie—of trust and respect—that seems evident in the students who practice autoethnography is unusual, if not unique. When individuals share aspects of their personal lives, I think they tend to take seriously the respect and trust that they wish to be shown, and which they in turn show others.

There is no guarantee, of course, of this mutual respect and trust, and there will always be the risk of apathy or antagonism. But so far that has not been my experience, even when opinions and values have differed, sometimes starkly. Several of my students have presented autoethnographies that were, ideologically, diametrically opposed, but what I witnessed was neither aggressive dispute, nor passively ignoring the difference. Instead, the students with opposing positions acknowledged their differences and indicated appreciation for being exposed to the conflicting perspective.

I suspect this attitude is less likely in a course in which students discuss and present texts abstractly, rather than personally. To intellectually distance oneself from a subject may be useful in some circumstances, but it can limit the level of investment. As one student wrote in a survey: "In so many courses we never get to make a connection to our personal lives." Autoethnography, of course, requires that connection.

As with some of the other outcomes, I recognize that the development of a sense of community is not really in a writing teacher's job description. But if this benefit comes as an extension, rather than at the expense of more conventional and occupationally expected results like improved writing and research skills, why not?

Regarding enjoyment, during my time as a teacher, I have been fortunate to have many students express (often surprised) enjoyment of my courses. However, both from explicit reports, in interviews and in surveys, as well as my impressions of class atmosphere, I have not experienced such strength of enthusiasm for a course as when my students practiced autoethnography.

Students often do not care for composition courses—or writing-intensive seminar equivalents—which are usually required, and not unusually remedial in nature. Perhaps students see themselves as already sufficiently skilled, or maybe they feel inadequate as writers, or they do not have a choice of topic, or they do not like the choices they have, or they are impatient to get on with their "real" studies, or extra-curricular activities. Any number of factors can interfere with any possible pleasure.

Those factors do not appear to interfere as much with my students' enjoyment of practicing autoethnography, as one student wrote in a survey: "I loved everything about this course. I loved learning a completely new genre, and eventually writing my own. I have never learned so much from one course."

Once more, as with other outcomes, I believe the personal nature of practicing autoethnography just makes it more fun. Once more, as with other outcomes, I do not believe that writing instructors should feel obligated to make their courses more fun, but I don't know why they wouldn't want to, if they could.

Many students commented explicitly and enthusiastically on how much they enjoyed practicing autoethnography, and how it helped develop a special kind of community in the classroom. Those outcomes are evident in Sophie's interview, as I will show. First, however, I want to share Sophie's autoethnography, an intelligent and moving account of the way she used exercise to process the death of a close friend. Her essay contains examples of each of the outcomes discussed thus far and can serve as a reminder of each.

Sophie—"Grief, and Other Things: Dreams, Words, and Running Away"

I cried on my graduation day.

It was a hot Saturday in June, and sweat streamed down the faces of devoted family members and relatives as they sat in the bubble of heat that was the Dean Smith Center. The ceremony was typical—predictable even—and featured many cliché messages of new adventures, fresh beginnings, and "the first day of the rest of our lives." But amongst the happy tears of proud parents and excited peers, my tears were melancholy.

I always assumed that she would be there. She was, of course—she was there in the flowers that adorned her empty chair, in the wristbands that bore her name, and in the moment of silence led by our school principal. She was there, just not in the way that I had imagined.

Just days after ringing in the New Year of 2016, a very close friend of mine passed away in a plane crash in the mountains of Wyoming. From the time we were young, Kenzie had a vibrant personality and a unique energy that contributed to her constant enthusiasm and positive attitude. She smiled relentlessly, and with a joke forever stored in her back pocket, her laugh was contagious. She sought adventure in the skies in the cockpit of her family's small plane, and adventures on the ground through her passions in sports, the outdoors, and her family and friends.

I miss her every day.

> *Sophie's essay begins with a paradox of mourning in the midst of celebration. Her sense of loss at this moment of accomplishment is palpable.*
>
> *Probably predictably, Sophie's autoethnography could serve as evidence of the genre's therapeutic capacity and its potential for critical empowerment. However, neither was the focus of Sophie's work, as she explicitly indicates—though both were welcome outcomes.*

Autoethnography

The genre of autoethnography is distinctly personal, as is the story of grief that I seek to share. Shaped by a synthesis of academic research and personal narrative, autoethnography uses the analysis of experience as a means to a better understanding of a larger cultural phenomenon (Ellis, Adams, & Bochner, 2011, p. 1). Offering "stories rather than theories," autoethnography is unique in providing accessibility and reach that traditional academic writing often lacks (Ellis, et al., 2011, p. 1). The genre of autoethnography is an appropriate forum for the topic of grief because grief is inherently personal. An examination of grief through traditional academic writing might come across as cold or clinical, alienating readers who would be more likely to connect with the personal narratives that autoethnography presents.

One important aspect of autoethnography is found in the therapeutic value that it imparts on the writer. Through the process of composing a personal narrative, autoethnographers are faced with numerous opportunities for introspection, coping, and an exploration of self. Therefore, as explained in Ellis et al. (2011), "autoethnography is both [a] process and a product" (p.1). Therapy is found in the *process* of composing the work, and the final *product* allows for connection with society.

The promise of healing did not draw me to autoethnography, per se, but instead shepherded me towards sharing my story through writing. I hoped to tell the story of my own experience, not necessarily for others, but for myself. Upon further examination, I came to realize that the lens of autoethnography would enrich my story and add a larger societal significance. The study of my grief, while already tightly enmeshed in the experience of those within the story, was also easily woven into the "phenomena" of grief itself, offering connections to readers who may have found themselves bereaved at one time or another. Though I initially began to write for the sole purpose of myself, I ultimately found that the process of composing this piece was therapeutic in the introspection that it introduced as well as the opportunities for connection that it fostered.

> *Sophie's essay could also serve as evidence of the outcome of ethical consideration. She carefully addresses the implications of her research and writing, emphasizing that while her focus is on her own experience, it must also include the experience of others.*

In maintaining such a strong basis in personal experience, the narrative of autoethnography often tells the stories of others, and therefore "the narrative is rarely entirely one's own" (Tolich, 2010, p. 1602). It is important to consider the ethical implications of autoethnography because the story that one spins almost always has the potential to impact the lives or reputations of those who are involved. Ethics is of paramount importance when presenting the stories of others in a manner that is accurate, balanced, and objective. In composing this piece, I fully recognize the fact that much of this story is not my own. The narrative centers on the passing of a close friend, so her life clearly plays a key role in defining the topic. However, the grief was my own, so I have made a conscious effort to focus more on my personal experiences than on telling the story of Kenzie....

Shock

I wake to the sound of my mother's footsteps on the stairs. It is a Tuesday morning, a detail that will soon become insignificant and meaningless. When she walks into the room with tears in her eyes, I know—even through the grogginess of sleep—that something is wrong. My mind travels to my aging grandparents and relatives, but I am not prepared for what she says next. The words that she speaks hold meaning, but the weight of the situation is too much to fully comprehend at the time.

She softly explains to me that during the late afternoon of the previous day, Kenzie's plane went down near her family's vacation home in Wyoming. There is not much information available at the time, only that both lives—that of the pilot of the Yak 52, a family friend, and Kenzie—were lost on impact. She was 17 years old, just one day shy of her 18th birthday.

I do not react at first. There are no tears, no dramatic appeals of "why" or "how:" just silence.

> *There is also substantial research in the autoethnography. Sophie uses scholarly sources like Reed (1998) and Dyregrov and Dyregrov (2008) to frame her own experience of sudden loss and the consequent sense of shock. I specifically remember talking with Sophie about the necessity of finding reputable sources in her research, and she did so.*

Tragedy is impossible to predict or prepare for, so when hit with a sudden loss, one is obviously shaken (Reed, 1998). When I was notified of Kenzie's passing, there was naturally intense shock and significant disbelief. After all, no one expects loss at such a young age. While grief is complex in and of itself, more complex still is the concept of grief following sudden or unexpected death. In a study conducted through analysis of feedback from those who have experienced sudden loss, Reed (1998) explores how "sudden bereavement leads to more immediate and long-term coping problems than deaths that are anticipated." This study examines grief symptomology by considering aspects of loss such as mode of death, personality characteristics of surviving loved ones, and social support structures available during the grieving period. For me, the experience of sudden loss has presented unique challenges throughout the grieving process because there have been limited opportunities for closure that lacked the "goodbye" moment that one might encounter with an aging or ill relative (a more "expected" death).

The jarring nature of sudden loss also contributed to the immense shock experienced by grieving loved ones. In their book on grief and bereavement support, behavioral scientists Kari and Atle Dyregrov explore how, when emotionally unprepared for loss, shock is magnified and grieving individuals may experience the sensation of "time standing still" (Dyregrov & Dyregrov, 2008, p. 27). During the moments and days immediately following the news of Kenzie's passing, things like the date and time became blurry and insignificant.

Time stood still because quite simply, shock consumed me and nothing else seemed to matter. The unusual alteration of the seemingly concrete measure of time represents the idea that "the shock becomes so intense that the bereaved cannot absorb everything that has happened at once" (Dyregrov & Dyregrov, 2008, p. 27). The emotions came in waves—they still do—because everything was too much to take in at one time....

Coping

Several weeks have passed since the funeral, and winter has finally reared its ugly head.

There is snow on the ground as I run down the train tracks. To my right, an asphalt bike path snakes through the trees, but today it remains icy and treacherous from a recent—yet rare—snowstorm. The snow blankets the railroad ties too, gently muffling the sound as my footsteps disturb the pristine powder.

The sounds of the world are distant, imparting a feeling of intense tranquility, and I am left alone with my thoughts. I run away from it all: away from the countless tears, away from the endless condolences, and away from the sadness.

I'll be the first to admit that I run from my problems. In the traditional sense, this might refer to various techniques of avoidance, but in the context of my own life, I—quite literally—lace up my sneakers and seek answers through exercise. For me, running has always served as a coping mechanism, among other things. I find comfort in the even, measured breaths, the rhythmic footsteps on the pavement, and the ability to escape into nature for an hour or so. When faced with Kenzie's passing, I naturally turned to running to process my grief.

> *Earlier passages also demonstrate reflexivity, the connection of the personal experience with a larger social/cultural context. However, reflexivity is even more directly displayed in this passage, where Sophie reveals the core of her autoethnography, how her exercise helped her cope with loss, and how her experience is similar to that of others', as demonstrated in studies by Hale and Raglin (2001) and Mishra (2015).*

While copious anecdotal evidence supports the idea of running as therapeutic, the same conclusion is also backed by several clinical studies. Hale and Raglin (2001) present a study on the impact of aerobic exercise on healthy college students. Over an eight-week period, researchers measured state anxiety following 50-minute exercise sessions. Findings show that aerobic exercise has "consistently been found to reduce stated anxiety" for an extended period of time following the activity (Hale & Raglin, 2001, p. 108). Grief is often associated with feelings of anxiety and stress, so the anxiety reduction established by this study can easily be translated to the symptoms that grieving individuals may experience. In this respect, my experiences with running as therapeutic may hold true to the experiences of others.

Additionally, running provides therapy in natural stress relief by causing the body to release endorphins—feel-good chemicals—that boost mood and impart a cathartic, calming effect on the runner. In a study conducted on the benefits of running, Dr. Suresh Mishra (2015) finds that the endorphins released through running "act as a natural 'drug' that make a person more energetic, more awake, and yes, happier" (p. 59). Consistent with my own experiences, Mishra (2015) concludes that "almost every runner experiences an elevated mood after running" (Mishra, 2015, p. 59).

Quite simply, I feel better after running. My mood improves, my stress levels lessen, and I feel somewhat renewed. By providing these positive effects, running has acted as a coping mechanism through times of distress. During the grieving process, frequent runs offered a chance to process my thoughts and to ride out the ever-changing waves of emotion....

Remembrance

We run in a pack as our footsteps trace ovals around the red rubber track. The team becomes one in our shared exertion, with our heavy breaths matching one another and our strides working in harmony. The heat of the late summer evening is testing, and I begin to feel discouraged as the fatigue sets in. I look towards the horizon, straining to distract myself from the exhaustion that threatens to take over my tired body, when I see a plane passing gracefully across the sunset sky.

I think of Kenzie—her enduring work ethic, passionate spirit, and tireless determination—and push through the final laps of the workout inspired by all that she accomplished and all that she stood for.

This one's for you, Kenz.

As coincidence would have it, my team practices at a track that is located roughly six miles away from a small airport. Kenzie's passion for aviation was strong, having recently fulfilled the dream of earning her private pilot's license. Planes remind me of her, not only because of her fascination with flight, but also because of her endless pursuit of sky-high goals. Whenever a plane graces the horizon, I am reminded to lead a life of vigor, to live to the fullest, and to relentlessly chase after my dreams.

> *Maybe most of all, this essay showcases Sophie's writing skills. I have observed how students practicing autoethnography demonstrate unusual audience awareness and an almost unique motivation to revise their work. Sophie was no exception, but one section of her essay particularly and ironically illustrates how this genre not only allows but compels students to take responsibility for their writing decisions.*
>
> *Near the end of her autoethnography, Sophie wrote this reflection on running near an airport. Given the way her friend died—in an airplane accident—my feedback to Sophie included advice to adjust her original draft of this section, which did not comment on the implicit irony of her reflection. I thought maybe she should make more of this connection, and I told her to consider revising—not for a grade, since I assured her that was already set, but for the quality of her final product.*
>
> *Sophie considered my suggestion, and decided against.*
>
> *The more I reread this paragraph, the more I am convinced she made the right choice.*

When those we love have passed, their absence is noticed but their presence is still very much felt. Corr, Corr, and Nabe (1999) deftly observe that "death ends a life, but it does not end a relationship" (p. 256). This idea rings true in the everlasting remembrance of those who we have lost. While they may not be a physical presence, they are with us in daydreams, in memories, and in moments of peace and beauty. Our loved ones "remain a transformed or changed but ongoing presence" in our lives, and in the all of the lives of those who loved them (Corr et al., 1999, p. 256). In many ways, we live on in their honor, and they live on in our hearts.

Conclusion

Naturally, things are different now. Visits to my hometown include flowers placed at the cemetery, melancholy reminiscence of shared laughter and fond memories, and admittedly, a tear from time to time. But little by little, the memories have come to inspire more happiness than heartache.

I used to worry that I would forget—that the vivid memories might lose their luster—but I am constantly reminded that grief has no end. While overwhelming at first, grief gradually becomes a changed form that persists in small reminders, moments of reflection, and ongoing empathy for others who experience loss. In many ways, I cherish the permanence of grief as a reminder that I will never forget the strong friendship that we shared and the memories that I forever hold dear.

No matter how much time has passed, I remember Kenzie as if it were yesterday. I remember the way that her bright smile lit up her face, the way that she laughed at her own jokes, and the way that her happy-go-lucky nature brought joy to all those around her.

I still miss her every day.

****

Now, how did Sophie's experience of practicing autoethnography illustrate the outcomes of enjoyment and the development of community?

In her interview, Sophie told me that she initially thought the idea of autoethnography was "kind of silly," and she "didn't see how it fit into academics." Sophie was far from alone in this opinion. Recall, for example, the reaction of my respected graduate school professor to the apparently oxymoronic term. Other students, too, expressed skepticism. Elizabeth was surprised that she found herself enjoying the class. When it began, she confessed, she doubted she would be much engaged: "But then every story had some sort of relatable aspects, or at least it was an interesting new idea, and it was really actually fun to read."

Sophie also told me that she was not a naturally open person, emotionally speaking. She said that sharing personal experiences, especially one as emotional as the topic she chose, was difficult. By the end of the course, however, she had overcome those obstacles and benefited greatly from the practice of autoethnography: "Ultimately I was able to find a lot of personal growth."

Regarding the sharing, while the peer feedback sessions were, at first, "awkward," and Sophie had anxiety about the final presentation—"nobody wants to be judged"—the end results were worth it. Specifically, she said, the impact of her peers' presentations shocked her: "It was amazing for me to be allowed into their personal lives that they wouldn't have shared with me otherwise. I learned that sometimes I can judge people too much ... perceptions are often quite wrong." This was something she knew at some level before, but it "resonated much more" because "I saw 15 examples of where I got it wrong." That is, her classmates' presentations changed how Sophie perceived them and helped her connect with their shared experiences.

Emily, one of her classmates, echoed Sophie's feelings, noting how "really potent" the presentations were, and how her assumptions about her peers "immediately went in the trash." Sam, another classmate, said the presentations helped make "more intimate connections between people," even the ones she already knew, since the autoethnographies involved "making yourself vulnerable while everybody else is too."

Sophie said that practicing autoethnography helped her realize that "people will accept you ... including the sad parts, without judgment." That word, "judgment," which Sophie repeated several times, had also come up in Tania's interview a year earlier: "That was one of the concerns that I had—that I would be judged personally, but that wasn't the case." Given the gravity of her topic, Tania's anxiety about presenting was entirely understandable. We spoke several times beforehand about how she wanted to handle the presentation—what, specifically, she wanted to share. Afterwards, she reflected on how positive the experience had been: "I think that we were all really respectful to each other and gave each other really warm feedback."

Elizabeth had also been nervous to present, especially considering the emotional intensity of her topic: "But then everyone was so open in general with theirs ... it kind of motivated me to be, like, oh, it's okay. I can say these things." Elizabeth believed that reassurance came from the sense of community built during the semester: "These people are a close, tight-knit group."

Though Sophie was not part of either Tania's or Elizabeth's class, her reflections on the presentations matched both theirs and others'. I asked Sophie why she felt the class was such a "very supportive environment," in her words. Sophie thought carefully and answered that perhaps it was because *everyone* was sharing, everyone was making themselves vulnerable, "everyone was going out on a limb ... doing that together fostered a sense of trust."

That answer reminded me of Elizabeth's response to a similar question: "Because we were writing about difficult things ... it was nice to be leaning on each other." Taylor, too, had talked about how the course content affected the sense of support: "Our class was pretty close. Sharing that information, I thought was really special." She recognized: "You need to be able to trust the people in your class." Betty believed the process provided a natural path to community: "By writing autoethnography and by being exposed to others' autoethnography as well, I think we can respect the other person really, really deep inside."

That sense of community even lasted beyond the class. Elizabeth observed: "Every single person in that class, if I see them, we say hi! How are you doing, how is your summer?" When I asked Elizabeth if this outcome was unusual or unique to autoethnography, she said yes. While one might connect with classmates in other courses, the likelihood to form such strong connections in, say, chemistry (her example), was not as high:

> I probably wouldn't have bonded with some of those people, and now one of them is my roommate. And we had a discussion the other day, and I was like, oh yeah, you wrote about that [in your autoethnography], and she was, like, yeah, yeah.

For Sophie, even if she didn't get a roommate out of the experience, what she did gain was a profound awareness of her classmates' lives. Practicing autoethnography, she said, "allowed me to realize the struggles and challenges that other people face … everyone is struggling with something." In each of these accounts of anxiety allayed by warmth, openness, and mutual support, we see direct evidence of the development of a sense of community.

But practicing autoethnography wasn't all solemn, according to Sophie: "On a happier note, I found that I really enjoyed writing it." She said it was the first time she found herself "looking at writing [academically] as something fun." She was surprised to find herself "excited to engage in revision."

Again, she was not the only one. Taylor found that writing the autoethnography actually distracted her from her other work. She recalled: "I was in the library and I [thought] I should probably put this before all my other work, because I wanted to make sure it was a really well-written piece." She emphasized her enjoyment: "It was fun for me to research the culture and discover new things."

Like Taylor, Haley found herself wanting to spend much more time on the autoethnography than on other coursework. "Passion" was a word she used repeatedly in her interview: "It was something I was passionate about," she said, as compared to, say, an essay on nineteenth-century history. Researching and writing about her learning difference excited Haley more than an arbitrarily assigned topic. Her enthusiasm was palpable, and she followed up our interview with an email offering to contribute more to the project.

For many other students, while they might not deny the seriousness of many of the presentations, the overall impression left by practicing autoethnography was one of profound pleasure. Christa said: "I enjoyed writing my autoethnography cause it gave me a chance to tell my story, and I think a lot of people like talking about themselves." Spencer said: "I enjoyed the opportunity to tell my story and speak a lot of things that I'm very proud of." Even Tania, for all the weight of her topic, insisted: "I really enjoyed confronting it and discussing it. I think it was important for me to recognize and just write everything down and just analyze how maybe some of those things made me who I am."

Enjoyment was also evident throughout the surveys, most of all in answers to the final question: "What did you like most about this course? What suggestions do you have for improving it?" Answering these questions almost required an expression of enjoyment, but while many indicated a solid appreciation for practicing the genre—"I liked the autoethnography we were required to write"—the intensity of that enjoyment stood out in some answers.

Several used the word "loved" rather than "liked." Others indicated they wanted to continue the practice: "I hope to apply [autoethnography] in my writing during my free time" and "I want to publish my autoethnography & write others." One suggested: "Instead of writing about autoethnography for the first essays, I think it would've been more interesting making multiple autoethnographies." And one wrote that the autoethnography was "one of the best assignments I have done ever."

In her interview, Sophie neatly summed up her experience of practicing autoethnography: "I came in with a closed mind, thinking I wouldn't get anything out of it … and in the end it was a really rewarding experience."

References

Corr, C. A., Cor, D. M., & Nabe, C. M. (1999). *Death and dying: Life and living*. Belmont, CA: Wadsworth Publishing.

Dyregrov, A., & Dyregrov, K. (2008). *Effective grief and bereavement support: The role of family, friends, colleagues, schools and support professionals*. London: Jessica Kingsley.

Ellis, C., Adams, T. E., & Bochner, A. P. (2011). Autoethnography: An Overview. *Forum: Qualitative Social Research*, *12*(1).

Hale, B. S., & Raglin, J. S. (2001). State anxiety responses to acute resistance training and step aerobics across 8-weeks of training. *Journal of Sports Medicine and Physical Fitness*, *42*(1), 108–112.

Mishra, S. C. (2015). Reasons running is good for you. *Deliberative Research*, *26*(1).

Reed, M. D. (1998). Predicting grief symptomatology among the suddenly bereaved. *Suicide and Life-Threatening Behavior*, *28*(3), 285–301.

Tolich, M. (2010). A critique of current practice: Ten foundational guidelines for autoethnographers. *Qualitative Health Research*, *20*(12), 1599–1610.

CHAPTER TWELVE

"What Could Go Wrong?" Critique and Concern

It is crucial to address not only the positive outcomes of practicing autoethnography, but also any critiques of the genre that students might make, and any concerns it might cause. In Chapter Two, I mentioned several serious critiques of the genre, including the consideration of ethical issues, academic rigor, and assessment.

Chapter Nine demonstrates that one of the outcomes of practicing autoethnography is actually an increased ethical awareness, and Chapter Eight shows how rigorously students research their topics. I feel no need to expand on those discussions.

However, the critique most urgent to writing teachers might be the issue of assessment. How does one evaluate this kind of work? I will address this question below, along with other matters of concern arising from student interviews and surveys.

****

Regarding assessment, I readily acknowledge the difficulty in establishing evaluative criteria for such a genre. Some autoethnographers rebel against the idea of criteria altogether (Bochner, 2000); others offer varieties of standards (Tracy, 2010). I am happy to share how I have handled the challenge of assessment.

As you can see from my syllabus (available in Appendix B), the autoethnographic essay is worth 40% of the final grade, broken into several portions. The research proposal is worth 3%; each of the three research memos is worth 3%; the first draft is worth 6%; the final draft is worth 12%; the presentation is worth 10%. These values have fluctuated slightly, semester to semester, but not much.

Generally, students do very well with this assignment. I usually give full credit—or close to it—for the proposal. I deduct points from the memos for incorrect citations, inadequate annotations, or the wrong kind of sources, but students usually only lose 1–3% on all the memos combined.

For the first draft, I tell the students that as long as they meet the bare minimum requirements of the assignment (available in Appendix C), they will receive some form of B or A. For the final draft, as long as they address the feedback provided by their peer and myself, they will receive the same. For the presentation, as long as they stay within the time limits and address both their personal experience and their research, they will receive the same. I rarely give lower than a B– on the first or final drafts, or lower than an A– on the presentation. Final grades for the overall project tend to stay in that same range.

Students seem satisfied, even pleased with these results. Sometimes I think, perhaps, I should be more demanding. But given how hard practicing autoethnography is, how personal the process is, and how flexible the professional expectations for the genre are, I am comfortable with the standards I set.

****

Because of their anonymity, end-of-semester teaching evaluation surveys may be an especially useful source for identifying critiques and concerns. The survey answers include what I've come to expect: the usual complaints about too much work and too harsh grading. One unimpressed student wrote: "kinda boring. But it's a writing class." Fair enough.

However, there were some comments that related more directly to practicing autoethnography. Some were mild expressions of boredom: "readings could have been more interesting" and "I am not particularly interested in the topic." Others were stronger assertions about the genre: "The field is not very intellectually significant" and "I learned about autoethnography but I don't see that being helpful later in life." Some did not much like autoethnography, despite enjoying the course overall: "was not a huge fan of the genre but the course itself was thought-provoking" and "Still not interested in the field [though] I enjoyed class discussions and I did improve my writing."

There were also more ambiguous or ambivalent responses. I wasn't sure how to interpret the comment "strange writing style," which accompanied a numerical rating in the exact middle of the five-point Likert scale. But it's safe to assume "strange" was not meant as a compliment. Another tough one to parse: "I excelled in this one particular field." One wonders whether or not that student felt pleased with the excelling or frustrated that the excelling might not extend to other fields. Or both.

Maybe most severe, some students indicated that practicing autoethnography was neither unusual nor unique. When asked "To what extent were writing assignments helpful," they answered: "No more so than any other writing assignment" and "felt like writing for anything else." Thankfully, these kinds of comments were rare, and their contraries common.

Though in the interviews I explicitly asked students which parts of practicing autoethnography they found difficult or distasteful, few offered many, if any, critiques or concerns. Perhaps they felt uncomfortable expressing those issues, despite my encouragement for them to do so. But there were several issues raised.

First, practicing autoethnography is hard. It may seem easy, but it isn't. I have already discussed some students' feelings about the difficulty of the writing and, more so, the research component of the practice, and I will not revisit those issues here.

Other participants commented on the specific difficulty of recalling the events about which they wrote in sufficient detail. In her interview, Betty said: "Trying to remember everything, that's very challenging." In her autoethnography, Kaitlyn wrote: "I must disclose the fact that these scenes are grounded in my memory. My recollection is nowhere near perfect but I've tried to depict these experiences as accurately as I can remember." Christa said she had to call her mother and ask if she remembered whether the walls of the hospital room were yellow or not.

****

There is another, more important way in which practicing autoethnography raises concerns. The genre not only requires writing and research, it also requires a commitment to introspection and a willingness to open oneself to others' scrutiny, which can be daunting and difficult. In her interview, Kim noted that practicing autoethnography may not be realistic for everyone: "some people may not take it as seriously as they should … So it really depends on what kind of crowd you get." Caroline was more specific still, saying she thought that while autoethnography was well suited to students who did not already have a firm foundation in writing and research, it might not be as interesting for those who have already developed those academic skills. On the other hand, Sophie said: "Autoethnography is a higher level" of research and writing, so if one were starting college at a basic level, "it might be too much." Haley put it more bluntly: "You can't just—not to be crude—half ass it," she said.

Then there was Spencer, who articulated the most direct critique of the course, despite his own enthusiasm for practicing autoethnography. Spencer said that while he believed autoethnography was a useful genre for undergraduates to practice, courses should carry a caution about the potential for discomfort. In his interview, he insisted: "People with shy personalities might not be too in love with the idea of expressing themselves in that way." He imagined an uncomfortable interior monologue:

> Okay, I'm in a class with students that I've never really seen before. Will they care about what I have to say? Will I embarrass myself in front of them? Will they tell anybody about me? What are the repercussions of sharing this stuff?

Spencer also pointed out the possibility of students feeling especially pressured to reveal personal information in the context of a heavily assessed assignment. This is certainly a potential problem.

Spencer felt the pressure of making himself vulnerable in his autoethnography, "Avoiding Temptations: My Journey Through Adolescence," in which he presents his decision to resist peer pressure and refrain from alcohol and drugs. Throughout this account, he emphasizes his desire to stand out from the crowd around him: "Something inside of me admittedly hates conformity. I perceive drinking as a practice that resembles such behavior. Though those who choose not to, like myself, will ultimately feel left out." In this case, autoethnographic practice results in identifying *against* a dominant social/cultural context, rather than in synch with it.

But Spencer also admits that his desire to be different—and the way he went about it—can clash with the basic human need for companionship. In a scene of striking vulnerability—a characteristic Spencer repeatedly insisted during his interview is crucial for autoethnography—he illustrates his social isolation as he finds himself alone on yet another weekend night:

> Due to the fact that I was known as a non-drinker, I was not invited to a single party where alcohol was present during high school. My social life took a prodigious hit. There were days when I would come home from track meets, still excited by my races. I would ask my buddies if they wanted to hang out later. They were busy or had other plans. I never bothered to ask what they had going on—I could take a wild guess.
>
> As night would roll around, I sat on my couch, switching between watching baseball highlights and drowning in self-pity. I had to feel bad for myself because nobody else did. Nobody else understood....
>
> My mom would make the trip upstairs to see how I was doing. She would ask how I thought my races went, what I was feeling physically, and then jump to the elephant in the room.
>
> "Have you talked to your friends? What are they up to tonight?"

"Yeah I texted them. They had plans."

"All of them?"

"Yes, all of them. But I'm fine chilling here. It's probably best for me to relax."

She always gave me a slight look of doubt before she left. Mom had caught on, given how many times this routine had played out. Knowing me as well as anyone, she could tell that I was uncomfortable. I could no longer hide my tension. Nonetheless, she would leave me with a little smile and my independence. I appreciated her concern, but I had done this to myself.

Reflecting on these moments, Spencer realized: "I did crave fitting in at times."

In his interview, Spencer said that writing this scene was the hardest thing about practicing autoethnography: "facing the truth that I did struggle mildly with accepting who I am .... Laying out that personal discomfort that I'd refrained from telling people beforehand was really tough." But Spencer also found embracing this kind of vulnerability the most valuable outcome of practicing autoethnography: "I was able to look back at hard times to say, 'Yes, this happened, yes I admit it was a very hard time, but at the same time here I am today, and I don't experience these feelings anymore.'"

Sharing his vulnerability in class helped Spencer reaffirm his satisfaction with his choices: "I think I came out with a better understanding of myself, and I came out a better person for it. I realized that I have the resiliency and strength to stick with what I believe in." He also found the response of his peers encouraging. He had been nervous about their reactions to his presentation: "You don't know how it's going to be thought of.... You really have no control." But Spencer's classmates conveyed their admiration for his passion and dedication. Even if they didn't share his specific resolution, they praised his resolve.

****

Other participants also indicated they had felt anxious about this aspect of practicing autoethnography. For example, when defining autoethnography in her interview, Lynne said: "vulnerability is a huge aspect." Her topic, growing up in a rural area, might not seem especially sensitive, but Lynne felt extremely nervous sharing her experience with the class, even classmates who were already friends. She was glad she did so, since autoethnography prompts "identifying the roots of your life that make you you." Lynne said practicing autoethnography "helped me realize more who I was." But it was not easy.

Tania struggled with anxiety as well. Because of the nature of her topic, she and I had had several conversations about how to handle the process, or even if she should pick another topic entirely. I did not want her to feel unnecessary stress in revisiting a difficult experience. But Tania decided to continue, and in her interview, she reaffirmed that decision: "I wanted to talk about it. I wanted to write it."

Tania's is not the most controversial topic my students have chosen. It is not unusual, when the time for picking topics arrives, to have a student ask, hesitantly, if they are allowed to write about anything … pause … illegal. At that point, I remind them of my Title IX obligation to report any kind of sexual misconduct. I also note that while I would feel obligated to report actions of a serious criminal nature, I am not in the business of, say, narking on underage drinkers. That usually gets a laugh.

But what if someone did write about something more serious? There is always the possibility that a student will push the boundaries of what I would feel comfortable allowing as a topic.

Indeed, every time I have taught the course, I have had students who have picked topics that are obviously emotionally fraught. Avoiding such topics entirely is not possible, and the potential and actual emotional vulnerability coming from producing personal work for assessment is obviously problematic.

Compositionists have been critical of putting students in this position through genres other than autoethnography. One such compositionist complained to me that we—teachers of writing, that is—have no business working with such emotionally charged material as might arise from practicing autoethnography—we are not therapists, and we should leave such tasks to the appropriate professionals.

While I respect the point and recognize the risk, I simply disagree that we should stay away from personal experience—even difficult experience—as a writing topic. The therapeutic benefit of writing in general has been well established (Pennebaker, 2004, 2010), and it seems unnecessarily chary to avoid a genre simply because it might prove emotionally challenging, especially when it might also prove emotionally beneficial.

Furthermore, practicing autoethnography does not necessarily require confronting difficult experiences. Art Bochner (2013) calls for more examination and expression of joyful experiences, and there are examples of these (e.g., Blinne, 2012; Sturm, 2015). Some of my students write about less stressful—even happier—topics, such as involvement with sports and positive interactions with family members.

However, the fact is that most autoethnographies are about experiences that are not particularly pleasant, and my students' work has been no exception. I have had and will continue to have conversations with students about how to handle emotionally challenging subjects. I believe these conversation help, but are they enough?

In his interview, Spencer urged an upfront description about what would be expected in the course. This would allow students to withdraw if they felt fundamentally uncomfortable with sharing aspects of their personal lives.

Spencer is right, and, at the same time, his suggestion may not be enough. I followed his advice, and I do my best to inform students of the nature of the work at the beginning of the course, from the very first class. Occasionally I have had students withdraw, and a few have told me they appreciated the warning, and that they didn't think autoethnography was for them. I am certainly glad to spare anyone any undue anxiety or discomfort. But I suspect it might never be possible for students to understand fully what practicing autoethnography involves until they are in the midst of the process.

Even if students cannot be wholly adequately warned ahead of time, they can and should be accommodated and supported throughout the process as much as is possible. In my syllabus (under a section of "Course Procedures," which I did not include in Appendix B), in addition to the Title IX-required language informing students of my status as a mandated reporter of sexual misconduct, should they consider examining such a subject in their autoethnographies—which no one has—I also provide the following passage:

> Autoethnography sometimes results in individuals confronting difficult or even traumatic events or circumstances from their lives. However, no-one in this class is required to share anything they do not wish to share, and I hope everyone will respect the space of the class as safe and confidential. If at any time you feel uncomfortable for any reason, feel free to excuse yourself. Please feel free to come to me with anything you wish to discuss, but do not feel obliged to do so. Counseling services are always available for further support at #.

I read this passage aloud on the first day of class, and I return to it periodically during the semester, reminding students to do what they need to take care of themselves.

Beyond this kind of caution, finally, it must be the students' responsibility to make choices to take care of themselves, as in any adult life situation. I have found no indication that my students have not taken care of themselves, and plenty of evidence that they have.

It is worth noting that, unlike in the interviews, no survey answers gave any indication of emotional discomfort as a result of the personal nature of practicing autoethnography. Especially given the anonymity of these surveys, the absence of any such critique or concern is significant.

****

In addition to the student experience, I should mention my own concern that compositionists who decide to teach autoethnography may make themselves professionally vulnerable. Though autoethnography is an established academic genre and is respected and admired by many, there are also plenty who do not appreciate its blend of personal and scholarly research and writing.

At least one autoethnographer (Poulos, 2010) has documented his struggle to receive tenure based on the unconventionality of his research. Eventually he was successful, but only after an appeal of the initial rejection.

Quite apart from tenure or promotion, since writing teachers frequently already occupy relatively vulnerable (i.e., adjunct, and/or otherwise contingent) positions, they may find themselves wondering whether using this still relatively new genre in their pedagogy is wise, from an employment standpoint.

I have certainly wondered that.

I have had several conversations with colleagues skeptical or even outright critical of the value of autoethnography. In one particularly unpleasant interaction, a senior faculty member scolded me for exposing my students to the genre. I was told I was undermining my colleagues' work in more serious fields of study, since, apparently, my students were bringing their experience of autoethnography into other classes and raising objections about more traditional methods of research and writing; these students preferred to continue practicing autoethnography, instead. That was unacceptable, I was told.

I did my best, diplomatically, to justify my pedagogy, the genre itself, and my students' enthusiasm for it. I assured my colleague that I had never and would never discourage students from pursuing more traditional methods of research. I had distinguished and would continue to distinguish autoethnography from those methods as something neither better nor worse, but substantially *different*.

Since then, from the very beginning of each course, I (over)emphasize that while autoethnographers have drawn on disciplines like anthropology and sociology and their ethnographic methodologies, *autoethnography is not ethnography*, but something different. While some social scientists might appreciate and practice autoethnography, others may be ambivalent or even antagonistic towards it. I urge students not to bring autoethnography into their other courses, unless they are confident that their professors approve.

My institution guarantees my academic freedom to teach what and how I want—within reason—but without a tenure track position, I can't say I feel any *more* secure in my job than I did when I taught more traditional topics. Others with less academic freedom—and less supportive institutions—might feel even more vulnerable, and while I do encourage compositionists to consider teaching autoethnography, I also exhort them to consider their contexts carefully.

****

Finally, I must also mention the limitations of my own experience teaching autoethnography and studying its outcomes. The evidence I have presented here is from a limited population and a specific demographic. Most—though not all—students at Franklin & Marshall College come from privileged backgrounds, so many of them have strong educational foundations, with considerable resources dedicated to their success. After a semester already spent at F&M, they also should have received instruction in basic writing and research skills from their Connections 1 courses. As well, they have the advantage of being able to choose my course from amongst many other options.

My point is that many of my students come to my course with a level of intellectual development and agency of which many other students could not boast. It seems important to ask, would practicing autoethnography be as successful in a school where students might be less likely to come from such a high level of privilege? I would be happy for the opportunity to study outcomes of students practicing autoethnography in a wide variety of other educational contexts. I would also be happy for the outcomes of practicing autoethnography to be studied by someone(s) with less personal investment in the outcomes than I. Of course, I was hoping for, and even teaching for, many of the outcomes I observed. No wonder they were there, right?

Still, despite these limitations; despite the valid critiques of autoethnography in terms of ethics, academic rigor, and assessment; despite the serious potential emotional concerns; and despite the professional risks and costs of teaching this genre, I do not doubt for an instant that it has been worth it, for me, as for my students.

References

Bochner, A. P. (2000). Criteria against ourselves. *Qualitative Inquiry, 6*(2), 266–272.
Bochner, A. P. (2013). Putting meanings into motion: Autoethnograpy's existential calling. In S. Holman Jones, T. E. Adams, & C. Ellis (Eds.), *Handbook of autoethnography* (pp. 50–56). Walnut Creek, CA: Left Coast Press.
Blinne, K. C. (2012). Auto(erotic)ethnography. *Sexualities, 15*(8), 953–977.
Delamont, S. (2009). The only honest thing: Autoethnography, reflexivity, and small crises in fieldwork. *Ethnography and Education, 4*(1), 51–63.
Pennebaker, J. W. (2004). *Writing to heal: A guided journal for recovering from trauma and emotional upheaval.* Oakland, CA: New Harbinger Publications.
Pennebaker, J. W. (2010). Expressive writing in a clinical setting. *The Independent Practitioner, 30,* 23–25.

Poulos, C. N. (2010). Transgressions. *International Review of Qualitative Research*, *3*(1), 67–88.

Sturm, D. (2015). Playing with the autoethnographical: Performing and re-presenting the fan's voice. *Cultural Studies⇔ Critical Methodologies*, *15*(3), 213–223.

Tracy, S. J. (2010). Qualitative quality: Eight "big-tent" criteria for excellent qualitative research. *Qualitative Inquiry*, *16*(10), 837–851.

CHAPTER THIRTEEN

Conclusion

The question that prompted this project in the first place was whether or not autoethnography could or should be practiced at the undergraduate level, especially during the first year. At the end of each interview, I directly asked each student this question. I'll share their answers here.

Most said yes without hesitation, many indicating that not only is practicing autoethnography useful, but it is an unusual, or even unique experience. Betty said practicing autoethnography can have an impact beyond just the development of academic skills, opening up students' perspectives to intellectual possibilities previously unconsidered: "We might be thinking about our majors and what our further directions will be. And by writing the autoethnography, and by reflecting about ourselves, maybe we can understand about ourselves more."

Tania also talked about how practicing autoethnography was particularly appropriate for first-year undergraduate students:

> And I also think that this is the time to reflect and understand yourself ... thinking about separating yourself physically and looking back at the community you're coming from and how that culture and society might have shaped you. And specifically recognizing how that sets you apart from the rest of the group. I think this is a good time to do it, so that we can grow from here.

Selena said:

Writing an autoethnography helps us define who we are as people and what matters to us and can sometimes put into perspective what you want to do with your life, and what subjects stick out the most ... That's really, really important for first-years.

Haley would have liked to have practiced autoethnography even earlier: "I wish I had been able to write this in eighth grade."

Several students qualified their reply. For example, Edward said practicing autoethnography is less stressful than other academic work—he indicated that it is "somewhat stressful, but not a lot."

Similarly, Spencer said yes, "but only if students are made aware of the implications of autoethnographic writing beforehand." He emphasized his own satisfaction with the experience: "I got to create and achieve a goal, which was, I thought, revolutionary for any sort of academic work."

Elizabeth echoed Spencer's concerns about the implications of practicing autoethnography for assessment, especially as a part of the general education curriculum: "Maybe [it should] not necessarily [be] required because some people aren't interested in that sort of thing." But she also affirmed her experience: "It wasn't just like some class assignment."

When I asked students if they would consider writing another autoethnography, most said yes. A few said only for another class assignment, but many others had ideas in mind and indicated they would enjoy exploring them through this genre. Several survey responses echoed these interview answers. One mused: "Maybe one day I'll write another autoethnography." Others were more confident: "I am actually considering taking further steps to being an autoethnographer. I want to get published within the field" and "I want to publish my autoethnography & write others."

****

Now, obviously, students may not be the best people to make curricular or pedagogical decisions.

On the other hand, I don't know why they shouldn't be consulted. After all, even if they lack teaching expertise, students have plenty of experience of being taught, and they may have a strong sense of what in their education has worked, and what hasn't, and why.

Moreover, when we look to what the experts do advise about teaching writing, we can see autoethnographic principles and practices in that advice. In Chapter Two, I showed how compositionists from David Bartholomae (1993) to Suresh Canagarajah (2020) have already considered teaching or have actually taught autoethnography, but another, earlier example comes to mind. While literary scholars and social scientists were experimenting with autoethnography in the early 1990s, some compositionists were already calling for what sounded an awful lot like the genre.

Maxine Hairston (1992), critiquing the (over)politicization of writing pedagogy at that time, proposed an alternative. Instead of requiring students to write about issues that mattered more to the teacher than to students, "we can create a culturally inclusive curriculum in our writing classes by focusing on the experiences of our students" (Hairston, 1992, p. 31). This suggestion fits neatly with autoethnography's foundational principle of "foreground[ing] personal experience in research and writing" (Adams, Holman Jones, & Ellis, 2015, p. 26).

Additionally, the hypothetical examples Hairston provides of her "culturally inclusive" pedagogy contain characteristics of autoethnography. The student from Malawi writing about his tribal traditions could frame his personal experience with more formal anthropological research and analysis of those traditions. The Vietnamese-American man might include historical accounts of the Vietnam War alongside his own narrative. The Greek woman's reflection on sexism in religion could be complemented by reference to sociological studies on similar issues. And so on.

Hairston (1992) wrote: "The strength of all the themes I've mentioned is that they're both individual and communal, giving the students the opportunity to write something unique to them as individuals yet something that will resonate with others in their writing community" (p. 33). Such blending of individual and communal are, of course, fundamental to autoethnography. One of the reasons I assert autoethnography would work well in undergraduate composition courses is that many of the most common subjects of autoethnography—injury, illness, family, race, ethnicity, gender, and sexuality—would probably resonate with many, if not most students.

Furthermore, in July 2014—coincidentally at the same time as I was first encountering autoethnography—the Council of Writing Program Administrators (WPA) published a statement on the desired outcomes for first-year undergraduate composition. These outcomes are arranged in several categories: rhetorical knowledge; critical thinking, reading, and composing; processes; and knowledge of conventions. Many of the components of these categories seem strikingly similar to the outcomes of practicing autoethnography.

For example, from the first category—rhetorical knowledge—the WPA's goal for students to read and write "in several genres" and to "develop facility in responding to a variety of situations and contexts calling for purposeful shifts in voice, tone, level of formality, design, medium, and/or structure" seems ideally suited to the practice of autoethnography. One of the explicit goals of autoethnographers is to make scholarship more accessible to more people, which fits perfectly with the WPA's goal for students to "address a range of audiences."

Critical thinking, reading, and composing are certainly not unique to autoethnography, but I would suggest the genre is well suited to meet the goals in this second category of the WPA's statement. In particular, practicing autoethnography requires students to "use strategies—such as interpretation, synthesis, response, critique, and design/redesign—to compose texts that integrate the writer's ideas with those from the appropriate sources" (WPA).

Likewise, students can learn process writing through almost any kind of assignment, but autoethnography lends itself especially well to some of the WPA's goals in this section. For example, my students' enthusiasm for revision is evidence that they were indeed able to "develop a writing project through multiple drafts" (WPA). Their enthusiasm for giving and receiving peer feedback and presenting their autoethnographies is evidence that they could "experience the collaborative and social aspects of writing processes" and "learn to give and act on productive feedback to works in progress" (WPA). The reflexivity evident in my students' interviews and essays also shows that they were able to "use composing processes and tools as a means to discover and reconsider ideas" (WPA).

Finally, practicing autoethnography may not be ideal for teaching the knowledge of certain conventions such as "grammar, punctuation, and spelling" because the genre does not necessarily prioritize these kinds of conventions, though there is no reason students can't punctuate and spell correctly in these essays. Furthermore, some of the WPA's other goals in this section do match autoethnographic outcomes. For example: "Gain experience negotiating variations in genre conventions." Also, at least as far as my assignments were concerned, autoethnography was a perfect opportunity to "practice applying citation conventions systematically" (WPA).

Again, many of these outcomes could be achieved through other assignments, other genres of writing. But the fact that autoethnography meets so many of these goals impresses me. At a time when compositionists are struggling to define and sustain their positions in the academy, when they are grappling with a multitude of theoretical and practical concerns like transfer, translingualism, and myriad issues of privilege and access, it is refreshing—inspiring, even—to find a genre that simply but strongly motivates students to do meaningful research writing.

Indeed, I propose practicing autoethnography can produce what David Hanauer (2012) calls *meaningful literacy*: humanistic and holistic engagement with language in ways that "make meaning of the world we live in" (p. 107). I believe the concept of meaningful literacy aptly captures the overall potential outcome of practicing autoethnography. Actually, meaningful literacy shares its foundations with autoethnography: the social and cultural context of the individual, personal expression of experience, and "an interaction with everything that makes up the experience and understanding of the learner, including issues of identity and self-perception" (Hanauer, 2012, p. 108). This is a lofty goal, for sure, but not beyond reach.

****

I know autoethnography may not be immediately appealing to all. Let me return for a moment to Emily, the exemplary student I introduced in Chapter One, and have mentioned elsewhere. In her inteview, Emily admitted she was one of the students who was "definitely not excited" at the beginning of the course. She did not understand the genre, and she was nervous about the prospect of sharing personal experiences with the class.

But, like many others, Emily changed her mind. She found that the best part of practicing autoethnography was the aspect of discovery, of "letting it be powerful for you and letting yourself see what you find out" even if that wasn't "what you expected." Emily said that she thought autoethnography was a genre especially appropriate for first-year undergraduates because they often "don't know where they stand," and the research and writing process gives them "a chance to figure it out and settle." In her essay, Emily eloquently expressed this settling:

> Writing this autoethnography has given me a more concrete understanding of my dreaming experiences and how they connect with film and other media. I doubt I'll stop watching horror fiction anytime soon, as I continued to view them throughout this writing experience and plan on viewing more in the future. Perhaps they are to blame, as some of my nightmare experiences would indicate, but I cannot give up the sense of safety and excitement they bring to fear. I still experience regular dreams and nightmares, and while they may lessen with time, I am prepared for them to stay.

I spoke with Emily two years after she was in my class. The frequency of her dreams had indeed lessened. Of course, there's no way to know to what extent—if at all—practicing autoethnography was responsible. But I suspect—as did she—it had helped.

****

Before submitting my manuscript for publication, I sent a draft to all of the students who contributed to my research. I asked them to confirm their continued participation in the project, and whether they had any suggestions for changes to the draft. In the email, I also asked students several questions:

- Has your opinion about practicing autoethnography changed at all since our interview, and if so, how?
- What did you decide to major in, and what are you planning to do after graduation, and do you think autoethnography had any influence on those decisions?

Only a few students answered these questions, but it's worth sharing their answers.

Most said their opinions had not changed. Edward responded that he still thinks "autoethnography is a great way to reflect on my past experiences, learn from them, and store them as a different form of memories."

Several indicated they appreciated autoethnography even more in retrospect. Sophie wrote:

> More and more, I've realized that the course on autoethnography is one that I value the most. So if anything, my opinion about practicing autoethnography has only risen. I remain proud of the piece that I wrote, and strive to find as much meaning in my other courses .... I'm not sure if I'll ever succeed.

For Hannah, reflecting on her experience reinforced the idea that "autoethnography is not a 'once and done' action. It is quite literally a practice, one that has to be continued and done multiple times ... each following practice does not erase the previous, but only adds on to each previous practice."

Emily wrote:

> I am still surprised that a writing style that seems so obviously perfect for so many topics remains a secret to most. We don't think in the binary of scientific literature or personal writing, but a mix of all of our memories, opinions, facts we've memorized, and emotions we tow. Our thoughts are not confined, so why is our writing?

Though none of the students intended to practice autoethnography as professional scholars, several said that the experience had influenced their choices of major and their post-graduation plans. Christa, for example, had begun a major in creative writing, and even though she had switched to the literature track, autoethnography "fueled a love for writing narrative prose, whether that be nonfiction or fiction, and writing (and reading) as a way of empathizing with 'characters' and understanding their experiences." Hannah, too, had felt the impact of practicing autoethnography when it came to her choice of major:

> I began my studies to major in SPM (Studies of the Scientific/Philosophical Mind) with the goal of becoming a speech-language pathologist. I am now double majoring in English literature and Spanish, without any goals after graduation other than wanting to help others tell their stories. I'm not sure what path that will take at the moment, but I think that practicing autoethnography made me recognize I had wanted to hear stories all along, and that I should study my interest, instead of choosing a more secure or "fail-safe" career path.

Edward also believed that his experience practicing autoethnography "directly influenced" his decision to major in psychology. Taylor said that though autoethnography didn't influence her choice of major, it did affect her overall motivation for research: "I found an interest in understanding how people understand the world and interpret meanings." And though Sophie was hoping to work in advertising after graduation, she affirmed that practicing autoethnography had "helped me to discover a love for writing that has continued to shape my life."

It's a small sample size, certainly, but these students went out of their way to reaffirm their enthusiasm, even passion for practicing autoethnography, and to articulate the genre's significant impact on their lives.

****

I'll end with a quote from a student. That's against my own frequent advice to my students to finish their work with their own words. But since this work is built so much on others' words, it feels somehow appropriate.

In the last moments of the last interview of the first half of my study, Lydia asked me why I had thought of creating the course. My answer was long(-winded) and repeats much of what I've written already, but I'll quote myself anyway because the full effect of Lydia's response requires the extended set-up:

> I took an autoethnography course myself as a graduate student a couple of years— few years ago now. I wrote my own [autoethnography], of course, and I found it very, very meaningful for me on a lot of different levels, and as I was thinking about it, it made a lot of sense that this sort of writing would be a kind of a perfect transition or bridge from high school writing into college writing. A kind of a really nice, comfortable, but challenging exposure to research skills.
>
> I think because, as you probably know, most research projects at this level … you'll get assigned a topic or maybe you'll get a slight choice in a topic, but it's probably not something that you're terribly interested in, and you're just kind of going through the motions of the exercise.
>
> Not all. There are some that don't, but I thought this was a chance for students to pick something that they are really interested in, and they already know quite a bit about, at least from their own perspective, and complement that with research. I thought that would be a really nice sort of package. And it's been done, of course, a lot at the graduate level, but I wasn't sure how undergraduates would respond to it, especially students earlier in their experience—if they would find it just too weird or too uncomfortable.
>
> So, that was kind of the big question I had going into teaching the course, and while there were definitely moments that were difficult and challenging for everybody, it seems like for the most part that people enjoyed it and were motivated and enthusiastic about doing the writing and the research.

Lydia paused, and nodded, saying: "Yeah. 100%. I agree with that, actually."

References

Adams, T. E., Holman Jones, S., & Ellis, C. (2015). *Autoethnography: Understanding qualitative research*. New York, NY: Oxford University Press.

Bartholomae, D. (1993). The tidy house: Basic writing in the American curriculum. *Journal of Basic Writing, 12*(1), 4–21.

Canagarajah, S. (2020). *Transnational literacy autobiographies as translingual writing*. New York, NY: Routledge.

Council of Writing Program Administrators. (2014). WPA outcomes statement for First-Year Composition (3.0), approved July 17, 2014. Retrieved from http://wpacouncil.org/aws/CWPA/pt/sd/news_article/243055/_PARENT/layout_details/false

Hairston, M. (1992). Diversity, ideology, and teaching writing. *College Composition and Communication, 43*, 179–193.

Hanauer, D. I. (2012). Meaningful literacy: Writing poetry in the language classroom. *Language Teaching, 45*(1), 105–115.

APPENDIX A

Invitation to Interview and Interview Questions

Greetings, student.

I am contacting you (and all of your classmates) to invite you to participate in a study I am conducting as a part of an ongoing research project. The study examines the outcomes of practicing autoethnography in the context of an undergraduate writing course, which, of course, you completed. Specifically, I am looking for support for or against including autoethnography as an assignment in future writing courses.

Here is how I would like you to be involved. First, I would like to analyze the autoethnographic essay you completed for my course and present my perception of its outcomes. If you feel at all uncomfortable in having your personal information analyzed and presented in my research, I would be happy to identify you by a pseudonym (either of your choosing, if you prefer, or mine, if not). Second, I would like to interview you about your experiences in the course you completed this semester. I would ask you about what you feel you learned and whether or not you enjoyed and benefitted from the course. The specific questions I would ask are included below. I would interview you either in person, if you are still on campus, or, if you are not, by telephone or Skype. The interview should not take longer than 45 minutes.

It is important when inviting someone to participate in research to identify the potential risks and benefits. Benefits could include contribution to a better understanding of autoethnography, especially as it might be practiced in future undergraduate writing courses. You might also benefit from reflecting on your experience in the course, gaining new insights into what you learned (or didn't). On the other hand, risks include, as indicated above, the possibility of feeling uncomfortable about having your personal information presented. As indicated, you will have the option to be identified by a pseudonym. However, as we discussed in class, even pseudonyms may not necessarily completely disguise individuals, especially given the personally revelatory nature of autoethnographic writing. As an added attempt to protect your privacy and comfort, after I analyze your autoethnography, I will share my representation with you and offer you the option to suggest further changes. In no way do I want you to feel uncomfortable by participating in this project.

It is also important to point out that because the course is complete, and your grade is recorded, I hope you will not feel undue pressure to participate in this research study. Participation would be completely voluntary.

One final but important note: for legal reasons, I cannot invite minors to participate in the study. If you are not 18 years of age at the time of receiving this email, I am afraid I cannot include you in the project.

I hope you will consider participating in this study. I believe your contribution would be extremely valuable, and I would very much enjoy hearing your reflections on the course. If you have any questions or concerns, please don't hesitate to let me know.

If you do choose to participate, please send me an email indicating your decision and your availability for an interview.

I look forward to hearing from you.

Interview Questions

[Before beginning to ask interview questions, I ask students to take a few moments to think about their experience of practicing autoethnography. I prompt them to think of and to list specific moments in class and in their own writing that strike them as meaningful.]

- Could you describe each moment you listed for me?
(*about each moment*)
- What was so meaningful about this moment?
- Why do you think you remember this moment?
- Is there anything else you would like to tell me about this moment?
(*moving to main questions*)

- How would you define autoethnography?
- What do you believe are the most important aspects of practicing autoethnography?
- What did you enjoy (or not) about practicing autoethnography?
- What was the hardest part about practicing autoethnography?
- What do you believe you learned about yourself from practicing autoethnography?
- What do you believe you learned about the world from practicing autoethnography?
- What academic skills do you believe you learned from practicing autoethnography?
- How was practicing autoethnography different from other academic assignments?
- How was practicing autoethnography similar to other academic assignments?
- Can you recall what your initial impression(s) of autoethnography was/were? How did your impression(s) change?
- Would you write another autoethnography? If so, why, and what would you write about? If not, why not?
- Do you believe autoethnography should be included in undergraduate writing courses? If so, why? If not, why not?
- What changes would you suggest making to the course you took?

Appendix B

Sample Course Syllabus

Connections 2: The Story of You: Autoethnography in Action

Course Goals

Autoethnography is a multi-disciplinary genre of research writing that draws on anthropology, sociology, psychology, and creative writing to combine reflection on personal experience with analysis of that experience in a cultural context. Students will strengthen critical thinking, communication, and information literacy skills through readings, class discussions and presentations, and a series of essays exploring this unique form of qualitative inquiry. That exploration will culminate in students producing their own autoethnographic projects, examining facets of their lives in relation to broader cultural phenomena.

As a Connections 2 course, The Story of You aims to help you develop certain skills. These include the following:

- Reading
- Speaking
- Writing
- Critical Thinking
- Research/Information Literacy

Course Schedule

Week 1:	*Introduction to autoethnography*
Tuesday	Introduction
Thursday	Read and discuss (R&D): Ellis et al. (2011), Hanauer (2012)
Week 2:	*Basics of autoethnography*
*Tuesday	R&D: Adams et al. (2015) Chapter 1&2, Dowling (2012)
Thursday	R&D: Sturm (2015)
Week 3:	*Basics of autoethnography continued*
*Tuesday	R&D: Adams et al. (2015) Chapter 3, Sparkes (1996)
Thursday	R&D: Ellingson (1998)
Sunday	**Due:** Essay 1 Draft 1
Week 4:	*Critiques of autoethnography*
*Tuesday	R&D: Delamont (2009), Ellis (2009)
Thursday	R&D: Tullis Owen et al. (2009)
Sunday	**Due:** Research Project Proposal
Week 5:	*Ethics of autoethnography*
*Tuesday	R&D: Tolich (2010), Medford (2006)
Thursday	R&D: Jago (2011a)
Sunday	**Due:** Essay 1 Draft 2
Week 6:	*Autoethnographic research*
*Tuesday	R&D: Bochner (2000), Tracy (2010) Library Workshop 1
Thursday	Jago (2011b)
Sunday	**Due:** Essay 2 Draft 1
Week 7:	*Autoethnographic representation*
Tuesday	R&D: Adams et al. (2015) Chapters 4 & 5 **Due:** Memo 1
Thursday	Library Workshop 2
Week 8:	*Autoethnographies about parents*
*Tuesday	R&D: Bochner (1997), Ellis (2001)
Thursday	**Due:** Memo 2
Week 9:	*Autoethnographies about children*
*Tuesday	R&D: Yang (2012), Martinez & Andreatta (2015)
Thursday	R&D: Weaver-Hightower (2012)

Sunday	**Due:** Essay 2 Draft 2
Week 10:	*Autoethnographies about gender and sexuality*
*Tuesday	Adams (2014), Berry (2007)
Thursday	Drafting workshop
	Due: Memo 3
Sunday	**Due:** Essay 3 Draft 1 (Autoethnography)
Week 11:	*Autoethnographies about race and ethnicity*
*Tuesday	R&D: Boylorn (2014), Martinez & Merlino (2014)
Thursday	Peer feedback workshop
Week 12:	*Wrapping up*
Tuesday	R&D: Hopkins (2015)
Thursday	Revision workshop
Week 13:	*Presentations*
*Tuesday	Individual presentations
Thursday	Individual presentations
Week 14:	*Presentations*
Tuesday	Individual presentations
Thursday	Individual presentations
Sunday	**Due:** Essay 3 Draft 2

Course Assessment

- Essay 1: 10%
- Essay 2: 15%
- Essay 3: 40%
    - o Proposal: 3%
    - o Memo 1: 3%
    - o Memo 2: 3%
    - o Memo 3: 3%
    - o Draft 1: 6%
    - o Draft 2: 12%
    - o Presentation: 10%
- Journals (10 entries, due on dates marked*): 10%
- Participation: 25%

Course Texts

Adams, T. E. (2014). Post-coming out complications. In R. M. Boylorn & M. P. Orbe (Eds.), *Critical autoethnography: Intersecting cultural identities in everyday life* (pp. 62–74). Walnut Creek, CA: Left Coast Press.

Adams, T. E., Holman Jones, S., & Ellis, C. (2015). *Autoethnography: Understanding qualitative research*. New York, NY: Oxford University Press.

Berry, K. (2007). Embracing the catastrophe: Gay body seeks acceptance. *Qualitative Inquiry, 13*(2), 259–281.

Bochner, A. P. (1997). It's about time: Narrative and the divided self. *Qualitative Inquiry, 3*(4), 418–438.

Bochner, A. P. (2000). Criteria against ourselves. *Qualitative Inquiry, 6*(2), 266–272.

Boylorn, R. M. (2014). A story & a stereotype: An angry and strong auto/ethnography of race, class, and gender. In R. M. Boylorn & M. P. Orbe (Eds.), *Critical autoethnography: Intersecting cultural identities in everyday life* (pp. 129–143). Walnut Creek, CA: Left Coast Press.

Delamont, S. (2009). The only honest thing: Autoethnography, reflexivity, and small crises in fieldwork. *Ethnography and Education, 4*(1), 51–63.

Dowling, E. (2012). The waitress: On affect, method, and (re)presentation. *Cultural Studies⇔ Critical Methodologies, 12*(2), 109–117.

Ellingson, L. L. (1998). "Then you know how I feel": Empathy, identification, and reflexivity in fieldwork. *Qualitative Inquiry, 4*(4), 492–514.

Ellis, C. (2001). With mother/with child: A true story. *Qualitative Inquiry, 7*(5), 598–616.

Ellis, C. (2009). Fighting back or moving on: An autoethnographc response to critics. *International Review of Qualitative Research, 2*(3), 371–378.

Ellis, C., Adams, T. E., & Bochner, A. P. (2011). Autoethnography: An overview. *Forum: Qualitative Social Research, 12*(1).

Hanauer, D. I. (2012). Growing up in the unseen shadow of the Kindertransport: A poetic-narrative autoethnography. *Qualitative Inquiry, 18*(10), 845–851.

Hopkins, J. B. (2015). Coming "home": An autoethnographic exploration of Third Culture Kid transition. *Qualitative Inquiry, 21*(19), 812–820.

Jago, B. J. (2011a). Chasing Laurie: An autoethnographic short story. *Qualitative Inquiry, 17*(9), 780–786.

Jago, B. J. (2011b). Shacking up: An autoethnographic tale of cohabitation. *Qualitative Inquiry, 17*(2), 204–219.

Martinez, A., & Andreatta, M. M. (2015). "It's my body and my life": A dialogued collaborative autoethnography. *Cultural Studies⇔ Critical Methodologies, 15*(3), 224–232.

Martinez, A., & Merlino, A. (2014). I don't want to die before visiting Graceland: A collaborative autoethnography. *Qualitative Inquiry, 20*(8), 990–997.

Medford, K. (2006). Caught with a fake ID: Ethical questions about slippage in autoethnography. *Qualitative Inquiry, 12*(5), 853–864.

Sparkes, A. C. (1996). The fatal flaw: A narrative of the fragile body-self. *Qualitative Inquiry, 2*(4), 463–594.

Sturm, D. (2015). Playing with the autoethnographical: Performing and re-presenting the fan's voice. *Cultural Studies⇔ Critical Methodologies, 15*(3), 213–223.

Tolich, M. (2010). A critique of current practice: Ten foundational guidelines for autoethnographers. *Qualitative Health Research, 20*(12), 1599–1610.

Tracy, S. J. (2010). Qualitative quality: Eight "big-tent" criteria for excellent qualitative research. *Qualitative Inquiry, 16*(10), 837–851.

Tullis Owen, J. A., McRae, C., Adams, T. E., & Vitale, A. (2009). truth troubles. *Qualitative Inquiry, 15*(1), 178–200.

Weaver-Hightower, M. B. (2012). Waltzing Matilda: An autoethnography of a father's stillbirth. *Journal of Contemporary Ethnography, 41*(4), 462–491.

Yang, S. (2012). An autoethnography of a childless woman in Korea. *Affilia: Journal of Women and Social Work, 27*(4), 371–380.

Appendix C

Sample Course Assignments

Essay 1

Assignment

Referring substantively to *either* Adams et al. (2015) *or* Ellis et al. (2011) *and* at least two of the autoethnographies we've read thus far, answer these questions:

> *What are the most important aspects of autoethnography, and what are the reasons for or against practicing it?*

Refer to at least two but no more than four aspects of autoethnography.

Audience

A scholar unfamiliar with autoethnography

Length

900 words

Essay 2

Assignment

Pick one of the autoethnographies we have read thus far. Referring substantively to Tolich (2010), compare your pick with Jago (2011), answering the following questions:

> Which of these autoethnographies is more ethically responsible, and why?

In your essay, you *must* consider and counter at least one opposing perspective.

Audience

A scholar familiar with autoethnography

Length

1,200 words

Essay 3

Assignment

Write an autoethnography. In your autoethnography, answer the following question:

> How does my personal experience connect with a larger social/cultural context?

I will direct your research process by a series of assignments throughout the semester. During two classes, we will meet with a librarian for instruction on how to find and assess sources, and there will be an in-class workshop explaining how to use those sources. You will submit three memos describing your progress, which should help you shape your essay as you go along.

Proposal

Pick a topic for your autoethnography. Write a 300-word description of what you intend to research and why. Include some initial description of your experience and

some potential social/cultural connections, as well as at least two specific questions you hope to answer.
Library Workshop 1

Research Memo 1

Find and read three sources (at least one reference book and two other scholarly books). For each source, write a 150-word annotation. Include a summary of the source's content, an explanation of how you expect to use the source in your essay, and an APA-style citation of the source for your References page.
Library Workshop 2

Research Memo 2

Find and read three more sources (all scholarly articles). For each source, write another annotation according to the description above.

Research Memo 3

Find and read three more sources (of any kind). For each source, write another annotation according to the description above.
Essay 3 Draft 1
Essay 3 Draft 2
In-class Presentations

Length

Essay 3 must be at least 2,700 words, though you *may* write more, as much as you want.

In addition to writing an essay, you will prepare an oral presentation of your work. Your presentation must be eight minutes (+/- 10%) and must include *substantial* references to *both* your personal experience *and* your research of the cultural connection.

Assessment

The Research Project is 40% of your final grade. Refer to the syllabus for what each part of the project is worth. Because I believe writing is a holistic endeavor,

I do not like to provide a piecemeal rubric breaking down the value of each part of the process/product. However, I do offer a checklist (below) of elements you are required to include in your essay.

Topic:	Do you answer the prompt question?
Research/Analysis:	Do you substantially analyze your sources? This involves the following: *a bare minimum* of three quotations and/or paraphrases of *at least* three scholarly articles, three scholarly book sections, and three additional sources (of any kind). *At least two of these sources should present contrasting perspectives.*
Artistic Representation:	Do you represent your experience artfully?
Ethical Consideration:	Do you explicitly consider any ethical issues and resolve them appropriately, *referring to sources* to support your position?
Grammar:	Do you write without errors and *cite your sources properly*?
Style:	Do you write engagingly?
Justification for autoethnography:	Do you indicate why autoethnography is appropriate for this topic, referring to sources to support your position?

References

Adams, T. E., Holman Jones, S., & Ellis, C. (2015). *Autoethnography: Understanding qualitative research.* New York, NY: Oxford University Press.

Ellis, C., Adams, T. E., & Bochner, A. P. (2011). Autoethnography: An overview. *Forum: Qualitative Social Research, 12*(1).

Jago, B. J. (2011). Shacking up: An autoethnographic tale of cohabitation. *Qualitative Inquiry, 17*(2), 204–219.

Tolich, M. (2010). A critique of current practice: Ten foundational guidelines for autoethnographers. *Qualitative Health Research, 20*(12), 1599–1610.

Appendix D

Additional Student Autoethnographies

When I started writing this book, I planned to include examples from a few student autoethnographies in each of Chapters Five through Twelve. However, it became clear that I needed to narrow my focus. Eventually, I realized that any more than one student example per chapter would be distracting and confusing.

But I simply can't let all my other students' work go without at least some attention. Hence this appendix, where I share the titles, topics, and brief excerpts from each autoethnography that was not covered in the book's main body. These can only be glimpses, but hopefully they will give some sense of the strength, depth, and breadth of the work.

For convenience, I arrange the entries according to the outcome they most manifested.

Reflexivity

Hannah

Hannah's autoethnography, "Identity Tug: A Reflection of Gender, Culture, and Relationships Between Siblings," shows how the cultural factors of language, food, and music illustrated her conflicted family dynamic. Throughout the essay, Hannah reflects on how the element of choice—for example, choice of which language to use: Spanish or English—factors into identity, both individually and socially.

For Hannah, as for her family, the element of choice was crucial to connecting the self with the community. For example, she writes about having to choose how to represent herself while filling out forms that ask for her ethnicity:

> There is still a part of me that wants to hang onto the idea, especially under the current presidential administration, that I am in some way different from the rest of Americans. I do not want to be bracketed by a single ethnicity check for job applications that puts me alongside racists or misogynists.
>
> Still, I pause before checking "Hispanic/Latino." I don't want to be viewed or judged differently because of my last name, something my dad made sure we understood.

How Hannah illustrates her conflicted impulses when it comes to this choice demonstrates reflexivity on the ways identities are formed, both as individuals and in relation to others.

Much of Hannah's autoethnography explores the choices made by her sibling, Roan. In a section called "Palabras," Hannah recalls Roan's frustration at their (Roan's pronoun) difficulty adapting to the U.S. American school system. Roan reacted negatively to pressure to conform, and they also rejected the unofficial English-only rule of Hannah's home, choosing to use Spanish instead. This decision prompted Hannah to reflect:

> From my perspective, Roan is choosing to speak Spanish to make more of their heritage. The language doesn't quite flow out of their mouth, but pushes itself against the molars and tongue, making them pause every time before speaking. Roan has chosen language to be an identity factor, something different from the English they have grown up speaking.

Roan's perspective on language, and other cultural factors, created a kind of rift in Hannah's family. So did Roan's non-cis gender identity, an identity Hannah notably never describes as based on choice. The nuance of this distinction demonstrates powerful reflexivity through awareness of both self and contributing social/cultural factors.

In her interview, Hannah emphasized how practicing autoethnography had made her recognize the strong emotions she felt about the situation: "There are a lot of things that I haven't thought in depth about, about my own life." She wrote a poem and placed it near the end of her essay:

> *Still Angry*
> They stated they did not consider us family.
> They said true family is chosen, and theirs came from their queer community.

At first, we responded with quiet denial.
It must have been miswording, a misspoken idea that wasn't fully developed.
It hurt, cut deeper than I could have imagined.
Then came the anger.
It still stings today.

This poem, which brings stinging tears to my eyes even as I copy and paste it, once again demonstrates Hannah's remarkable reflexivity. Though Hannah emphasizes Roan's choice in some matters of identity—their choice of family (as, before, their choice of language)—she shows how choice contributes to some aspects of identity, but not others.

As I have mentioned, before sending this manuscript to print, I asked all the students if there was anything they would want to change. A few suggested small adjustments. Hannah asked that a note be added reminding readers that reflexivity never ends, and if she were to write her autoethnography "now" (then two years after its original composition), it would be different, just as if she had written it 20 years later. For Hannah, it was hard to review her own writing because it had come from, at that time, "a place of hurt and not understanding or separating many of the elements that go into identity, relationships, and everything in life." Since that time, her relationships with her family had, of course, evolved, but Hannah wanted the record of her experience to remain.

Sam

In her essay, "Justice at the Discretion of Imperfect Men," Sam critiques criminal procedures as applied to juvenile cases. In her interview, when I asked which aspects of practicing autoethnography were most important, Sam answered, without pause, reflexivity: "I learned that when you're in the moment, or even a whole year after it, you won't take the time to reflect on yourself and how you behaved and how other influences made your situation happen." The situation Sam refers to is her experience of being convicted in juvenile court of third-degree assault. For Sam, practicing autoethnography was a way to process that experience, and reflexivity was both a crucial tool in that process and an outcome from it.

The first words of Sam's autoethnography are blunt: "The American criminal justice system has failed me." Sam does not balk in asserting her innocence, despite her conviction, and she maintains that innocence throughout the essay. However, she also acknowledges that others involved in her case probably perceive it differently: "I would also like to recognize that their perspective of my autoethnography and the role they played in it may differ from my own." She further states that she does not mean to blame all the people involved in her individual experience, but rather to show how that experience reveals bigger problems in the social/cultural context that frames it:

> While I do draw conclusions that describe the issue with the American criminal justice system itself, it is important to state that it is in the job description of the police department, judges and department heads to fulfill their duties. As much as I may hold resentment towards them, I recognize that they did not design the system and the issues I present are more systematic than personal.

To articulate this kind of understanding requires substantial reflexivity, both into one's self, and into the social/cultural forces that have hurt one's self.

Sam tells the story of her personal experience, from the inciting incident to the end of the trial. For example, here is her depiction of the setting of the initial conflict:

> The hot summer air makes the decrepit shed feel even smaller. … As I walk around the room socializing with friends, meeting new people, my Old Navy flip flops stick to the floor and I can feel the soot from previous parties under my shoes. Broken glass, old cans, and cigarettes are collected in the corners of the room as if someone swept them to the side as an effort to make the place look more presentable. The shed is holding way more high schoolers than it should, and the crowdedness of the room is overwhelming.

Her description is impressive, both in detail, and in demonstrating critical self-awareness: This is not an innocuous environment. Furthermore, Sam phrases the fight carefully, deliberately using passive voice: "After several punches are thrown between us, my friends pull me away and her friends pull her limp body to the side." This is the voice of someone acutely aware of the power of language to represent—and influence—experience.

Following the narrative, Sam provides substantial research to contextualize the experience. She explicitly states her overall motivation:

> My frustration with the criminal justice system and resentment with those who participate in its operation is not only founded in my own experiences, but in the fact that there are many lives that have been affected in the same way as my own.… I want to make my story heard in order to inspire change, yet I recognize the institutionalization of the system as core to American culture and politics.

Referring to legal theory like Stuntz's (2013) notion of "official discretion" and Koppl and Sacks' (2013) reports on overzealous police action, Sam observes, unfortunately, hers is only one of many such stories. Her autoethnography ends as bluntly, and as reflexively, as it began:

My experience with the criminal justice system is just one of many incidents in which it has failed the citizens of America. These voices such as my own need to be heard and taken seriously within the academic world in order for significant change to be made. The criminal justice system is flawed and will continue to damage lives unless we listen to those whom it oppresses.

Writing

Jocelyne

Jocelyne's essay, "Cruzando La Frontera: Achieving A Higher Education," documents the experience of a first-generation college student. In her interview, Jocelyne admitted that she found the process of writing her autoethnography difficult. It was hard just to meet the minimum requirement for number of words—her first draft was just at the edge of that bottom margin. However, her second draft, like many others, met and surpassed that minimum.

Quantity is no guarantee of quality, of course, but Jocelyne proved capable of crafting evocative description, as in this passage:

> Splattered paint and plaster made its way across his strong arms and gentle hands. The dried-up dirt created the illusion of half-moons on his nails. Those same arms that picked me up when I was first born and that enveloped me in hugs whenever my brother would fight with me, are the same ones that he used to build a comfortable lifestyle for his children.

The alliteration, the parallelism, the imagery, the verbs: All serve to create a powerful portrait of her father.

Another distinctive aspect of Jocelyne's writing is her use of her first language. In our conversations during drafting and revision, Jocelyne and I discussed the options of translating the Spanish she included. Though I pointed out that some readers might not understand precisely what was written, I said that most would get the idea and that sometimes curiosity is worth more than certainty. I left the decision to her. As in her title, here and throughout the essay, Jocelyne leaves the Spanish untranslated—a deliberate and, I think, effective choice.

> "I'm proud of you *mama. Te quiero mucho.*" My mother never doubted that I would make it this far in my educational career. The days leading up to my departure for college were some of the most exciting and saddest days for the both of us.
>
> From the moment I was born, my mother and I have been inseparable. She has been there for me since my first day of pre-K and she continues to be here for my college journey.

In every letter and phone call from her and my family, I am reminded of my life motto that I adopted since elementary school: *Estudia, sigue estudiando y échale muchas ganas, solo así te puedes mejorar.* I am reminded that the only way to better myself is by getting an education and working hard.

To some, the idea of college is just another step in the process of landing a well-paying job and career. But for people like me, a child of immigrant parents and someone who comes from an underserved part of Los Angeles, the idea of college holds more significance. College means the security of a well-paying job, college is living proof that you can and will be better off than your parents.

It is a means for providing for your family, for giving back to your community, it is an escape and a future, it is what sets you apart.

Lynne

Lynne wrote about her experience growing up in a rural environment. In "Under the Apple Tree, Big Apple Dreamin,'" she reflected on the intersection of such aspects of identity as geographic, ethnic, and economic privilege. In her interview, Lynne said that an important aspect of practicing autoethnography involved descriptive writing: "to give a lot of details and make it artistic" because that "catches readers' attention and allows them to be engulfed in the situation themselves." Here is the beginning of Lynne's essay:

> Fields of corn and trees of green surround an old white farm house with black shutters. Close to the road is a red pig pen with a compost pile on the backside of it. Next to that is a large three story barn and next to that is a red shed for storage. Across from that shed is another shed for lawnmowers and a tractor. And next to that shed is a red chicken coop with a nearby patch of dirt where the deteriorating outhouse was recently removed.
>
> I hear the stalks of corn swaying and the beagles howling. I am just the right temperature in my khaki pants and navy polo shirt school uniform. "Ho, ho, ho it's magic, you know" lingers into the yard as I wait for my lab to return his ball.
>
> I live in the middle of nowhere. The nearest Chipotle or Panera is an hour away. The nearest mall is an hour away. The nearest arts programs are an hour away. The nearest presence of dialogue other than English and races other than white are an hour away.
>
> The only way that I can get an hour away is by car. The only way I can attain a car is by buying one. The only way I can buy one is by having money. The only way I can have money is by working. Or by growing up with guardians who have money.

The vivid detail in this description of Lynne's rural environment certainly allows me to be "engulfed" in her world. I can see what she sees, smell what she smells, and hear what she hears. Also, I admire her use of repetition throughout, creating a distinctive rhythm—that sense of "same old, same old."

Lynne made substantial changes to her essay during the revision process. For example, her original title, "A Liberal Living in a Redneck World," showed her focus on the political side of her rural upbringing. While I acknowledged the catchiness of the title, I did note in my feedback that not much of the rest of the essay actually developed the idea of political affiliation, but rather broader attitudes associated with rural life.

Lynne changed her title—for the better, I thought—and dropped most explicit references to politics. She also shifted her structure substantially. In her first draft, she presented several scenes—a football game, a high school curricular meeting, and a vacation trip to Sedona, Arizona—back to back to back, and then provided her research and analysis. Through revision, she alternates scenes with research and analysis, which I find much more effective.

Finally, in her interview, Lynne said that one aspect of writing autoethnography that was both challenging and satisfying was the genre's open-endedness: "there weren't many guidelines, it was all what you thought was best." Students are often used to (and tend to prefer) extensive and explicit instructions on how to write, so the experience of receiving less direction is both a privilege and pressure to perform under unfamiliar circumstances.

Research

Allison

Allison's autoethnography, "Mom's Little Helper: In Vitro Fertilization and Families," shows the challenges for families—and especially siblings—surrounding the IVF experience. In her interview, Allison stressed the unexpected difficulty of the research process: "My research was so hard and I remember thinking it wasn't going to be." I was also surprised by her statement, since her research—and specifically, the effective way she incorporated her research into her essay—was what struck me most on reading her essay.

One thing I've noticed undergraduates struggle with is integrating more than one source into any given paragraph. Their paragraphs become a parade of single-source summaries punctuated by block quotes. There is no synthesis, no comparison between or combination of sources to make a point. Allison proved a skilled synthesizer, making connections between multiple sources in many paragraphs.

Another of Allison's strengths in using research was her ability to paraphrase effectively. I remember finding paraphrasing difficult as an undergraduate, and I have observed many students similarly lacking the ability to put a source's information into their own words. Hence, I was impressed by how well Allison honed that skill in her essay.

The following excerpt provides an example both of Allison's ability to synthesize sources in individual paragraphs, and to paraphrase effectively:

> It is a private thing, and I understand that, but in my experience, "in vitro fertilization" has been somewhat of a dirty word; I never tell anyone the truth about my sister out of fear of my family being laughed at or called weird, a fear I've carried with me throughout my childhood. Because of this perceived stigma, either unique in my family's case or indeed a cultural phenomenon, most likely both, I have never talked to another family that is very open about their history with in vitro fertilization or other alternative methods of conception (Ginsburg & Racowsky, 2012). Smith (1998) suggests that this may be because families are generally wary to admit that they are different when trying to fit into social circles.
>
> Another reason could be that the process of in vitro fertilization is a very private, emotional and time-consuming one (Mann, 2014). While the United States is more accepting of alternative reproductive methods than other countries, such as Poland (Radkowska-Walkowicz, 2012), it has still been said in the United States that in vitro fertilization negatively affects parent-child relationships and children's psychological well-being (Golombok, MacCallum, & Goodman, 2001, p. 604). I have not found this to be true in my own experience, and the scenes that follow, along with the research pertaining to them, will demonstrate this.

Despite the difficulty, Allison expressed satisfaction with what she had learned through her research, especially regarding how common IVF is. That fact, she said: "puts my sister into this community that I didn't know about before ... and me too, as her family."

Cooper

Cooper, too, found research hard, and not much fun. About his autoethnography, "My Eye-Opening Mishap Behind the Wheel," he was blunt: "My least favorite part of this probably was having to look for the sources." However, he also acknowledged that the research helped him better understand his experience of being in an automobile accident: "I know obviously in the end, it's worth it."

In his interview, Cooper commented on how especially satisfying it was to be able to use different kinds of sources in his research: "You really get a different perspective … for instance if I look at a news article that was a different type of information I come across during my research." Cooper uses news articles, and more, in these paragraphs about how his gender and age may have influenced his accident:

> An additional fact, supported by a CBS news article, compares and contrasts the driving techniques and causes of accidents by both men and women. While women typically have distracted driving accidents involving cell phones (either calling or texting), men are typically distracted by the thrill of driving and operating large machinery (Edgerton, 2011). The mixture between being a teenager and being a male, based on my research, demonstrates the idea that my gender and age combination plays a role in determining my incident. Males, statistically, have nearly double the amount of car accidents annually in the United States than women do; however, it is very unlikely that my gender is the primary reason for my incident based on the nature of the situation (Edgerton, 2011).
>
> The final possibility for my car accident, and likely the most self-explanatory, is that teenagers, and anyone who drives, mainly have accidents based on the *reason* that they are driving (Carlos, 2009, p. 210). For example, if a person were to be driving to a funeral, they would probably be driving slowly because they are most likely in a sensitive state where need for speed is not necessarily a priority. A student trying to raise their social status would likely drive extremely recklessly in order to maximize their given attention (National Research Council, 2007).

In his interview, Cooper said that he learned from practicing autoethnography that "it's important to be able to look back at something that happened in your life and connect it to actual research and everything." He paused, then continued: "If someone asked me about the car accident, I think I have a more deep understanding and a better explanation of it after having done this project." So even if the research had been "definitely … a struggle," it had been worth it.

Ethics

Taylor

Taylor's essay, "How Socioeconomics Shapes a Life," shows how her parents' circumstances (especially their educational opportunities) had an impact on her own identity formation. In her interview, Taylor said the hardest part of practicing autoethnography was "remembering that I'm talking to an audience that could totally interpret it a different way than what I meant …. You need to be aware of who's reading your work, and you have to be considerate of all the people involved." This sensitivity is remarkable for an undergraduate.

Much of Taylor's essay focused on the socioeconomic difference between her and her father's childhoods, particularly regarding education. Taylor grew up in the privileged Main Line environment; her father's upbringing had been less privileged. About her own education, Taylor wrote:

> In most private schools on the Main Line, you are distinguished by "Delco" (Delaware County), Main Line or "city kids." More often than not, the "Delco" and "city kids" were outcastes because they were seen as not having as much money as the Main Liners. That's why image mattered. If you dressed the part, most often times you were accepted. All you needed were the newest J-Crew sweaters, the latest Sperrys, or a flashy Patagonia.

The theme of clothing as an indicator for socioeconomic status runs throughout Taylor's essay. In one scene, for example, she describes her father working at his second job, in a liquor store:

> my father was going about his work, scanning the products. A woman dressed in, as my father would explain, fancy clothing, approached him. My father never really cared about fashion. He wore what made him happy. He's simple like that, and I love that about him. Without a greeting, the woman approached him and questioned the navy Episcopal Academy Softball hoodie he was wearing. He loved that sweatshirt. He loved representing me because he was proud of me. He always reminded me of that.

The scene continues, illustrating Taylor's father's pride in the opportunities he has been able to give his children, as well as his playful teasing of the woman in "fancy clothing."

Taylor cared greatly about how audiences might perceive her work: "since I'm writing about social classes, [I] try not to offend anyone of another class by speaking down upon them." She followed the scene with this qualification: "To be clear, the Main Line may consist of people that allow their affluence to consume them, but there are also genuine, humble people that have impacted my life in the most positive ways."

Because Taylor's autoethnography focused on her father, in her essay she described her "constant checking with him" from first to final draft to "make sure he feels comfortable." She noted that his reaction to one section stood out: his surprise at being referred to as a "minority" in his predominantly non-Caucasian high school. In her interview, Taylor said he had not asked her to change anything and that he found it "interesting ... to hear it from someone else's point of view."

Lydia

In "Life with Laura," Lydia chronicles her rich and complex relationship with her twin sister.

In her interview, Lydia talked about sharing her essay with her sister, and their mother. First, however, she faithfully followed Tolich's (2010) advice to prioritize proactive over retroactive consent. Lydia told her family about her topic when she was beginning her research, and the following paragraph describes that decision, and her sister's reaction:

> I'm staying over at Laura's college before going home for spring break. Writing this autoethnography has been on my mind for some time and I need Laura's help in defining and analyzing our relationship. I explain to Laura what my project consists of and ask her if she feels the same way about our healthy twin relationship.
>
> Laura agrees with me; she explains that being a twin has been nothing but positive in the development of our selves. She too thinks we are "soul mates who naturally provide love and support" (Mathias, 1992, p. xi). I then tell her about how I need consent to create an ethical autoethnography, and that once I finish thinking of the stories I will show and tell, that I will be asking for her approval.... She responds with excitement. This project sounds "special" and makes us both feel very nostalgic.
>
> Laura approves of me writing anything; in fact she states, "What's the worst you can say about me?"

Lydia follows this rhetorical question with a humorous reply: *"Well Laura, now that you ask..."*

She then proceeds to recount a memory of her sister suffering from a night of hard drinking, and how she (Lydia) handled the situation. The portrait is comic, graphic, and a poignant illustration of Lydia's desire to protect her twin:

> I'm happy that she was in my care. No one else could take care of her like I could. I could have easily left her to her own devices and risk her getting in trouble with my parents. It does cross my mind a few times, being that I had a volleyball tournament the following morning that I had to wake up early for. But as Barbara Mathias (1992) explains, "sisters rarely totally abandon each other. Their love may be ambivalent for periods of time, but it is not in their feminine character to turn their backs and never return." (p. 7)

Also, apparently, when Lydia did show the scene to her sister and her mother—continuing to follow Tolich's (2010) guidelines for subject consultation—it was appreciated by both: "What I enjoyed most was reading it after to my sister and I showed it to my mother ... and I think that was really special. It was cool."

Though their mother said about certain events portrayed that she would "rather not know that," Laura "loved it." For Lydia, revisiting the autoethnography was "like looking through my old pictures."

Empowerment

Kim

In her essay, "Don't Be a Follower: Autoethnography on Effects of Social Media," Kim recounts her struggle with the issue of body-image and her exploration of that all-too-common phenomenon on social media. Kim cared a lot about contributing to a common good. Throughout her interview, she kept returning to her desire for her autoethnography to be helpful: "I don't want to write about something that's not going to help anyone, or benefit anyone." She explicitly expresses that goal in the abstract of her essay:

> My purpose is to hopefully show people that they are not to blame for how they feel about themselves, they have been raised and nurtured to believe that they are not good enough or never will be good enough. My intended audience is for young girls and anyone in general because it is something that is seen everywhere.... I intend on making it clear that no one has the right to tell you how to be, you are your own judge.

Kim's autoethnography alternates between anecdotes and analysis. Here, for example, she recalls an upsetting childhood experience:

> As I stepped off the scale in the doctor's office, I looked up to see my Mom and Dad shaking their heads side to side with disappointment. All I thought was, I know and I'm sorry. My mom specifically told me to not eat too much when she dropped me off at the airport, but I did it anyway. I did not listen and I should have. The doctor started talking to my parents in Mandarin, I think he had forgotten that my Mandarin has improved significantly since my trip to China, and I understood every word he said.

Kim grounds her account in her own pain, desiring to spare others the same experience. However, she also provides compelling research to frame her narrative:

> Self-objectification can lead to many negative outcomes, like body shame and anxiety, which can lead to depression, sexual dysfunction, and eating disorders (Fardouly et al., 2015, p. 447). Facebook creates a great opportunity for people to compare themselves to their friends and family members. Fardouly et al. (2015) continue, "greater usage of sexually objectifying media may be associated with higher levels of self-objectification because these media focus on women's physical appearance and place pressure on women to focus on their own appearance" (p. 448). I agree with her and I can see this

within myself. If I see a friend receiving a lot of attention from people, I am likely to be triggered to try and do or look like her.

Having shared her own experience and her research into others', Kim's conclusion includes a direct exhortation to readers:

> Everyone has had a battle with their worst critic, themselves. There will be days that will be hard to get through because people will always tell you to be a certain way, but your opinion matters the most …. You are your own person and you should do what makes *you* happy.

Between the poignant storytelling and the insightful analysis of research, Kim builds a case against the kind of social pressure she finds so damaging. In her interview, she spoke about how she shared her autoethnography with friends, and how impressed they were. Their positive response convinced her "my voice is very powerful."

Indeed, it is.

Haley

Haley hadn't yet shared her autoethnography, "Learning Differences in the Real World," but in her interview she said she planned to. She emphasized "how important it is to share personal things because putting it out there can teach someone so much." In her case, her personal experience was overcoming the obstacles posed by her learning difference, a significant challenge.

Haley begins her essay by recalling the day she found out she had been accepted into her first choice college:

> When I looked around my college counselor's room, I saw the same thing I saw in every other room of the entire building except the signs had all become colleges that I was meant to be looking at. The room was large, full to the brim with pamphlets, brochures and posters of schools all over the country showing off the professional and pristine images they had paid for to get students to want to attend. Each senior's name was written on white boards surrounding the room, 27 students, 27 adults headed off into the real world in less than 7 months. I saw my name printed in large purple letters, and underneath my name, there was only one thing written. Franklin and Marshall College, Lancaster, PA.
>
> "I got in," I said as my counselor looked up from her computer. She smiled widely and stood up to hug me. I hugged her back more than excited.
>
> "I told you that you would!" She laughed. I squeezed my eyes shut as I pulled away feeling the tears welling up in my eyes. I tried to laugh remembering all the times that she told me if I just sat down and finished my application I would totally get in.

"What's wrong?" She asked concerned, seeing a single tear fall on my cheek. I opened my eyes and looked at her through blurred eyes and said a simple phrase I knew she would understand,

"No one ever thought I could do it."

Haley portrays her struggle by referring both to her personal experience and to research on learning differences. In her interview, she commented on the impact of practicing autoethnography: "it taught me how to write both in the scholarly form and the free-form, fun way, and putting them both together." She embraced the approach wholeheartedly: "I like the blend because the blend can make both more powerful." She concludes her essay by looking ahead:

> As I look at my future as a student with a learning difference I have no problem admitting who I am and how my brain works. No, I do not have the same processing speed as everyone else but that does not mean I am incapable .... My learning differences have helped me to grow into a strong self-advocate. I know it is okay to ask for help when no one else will and I believe that has taken my potential as a student to a whole new level .... My learning differences taught me the determination that I would have never been able to have without my learning difficulties. I am thankful for who I am as a person and what my learning differences have brought out in my potential as I continue my college education and move on to the workplace.

Mariama

Mariama's autoethnography, "In Unity Lies Strength: An Autoethnographic Exploration of the Women's March," demonstrates the power of political protest through its depiction of the Women's March on Washington. Sadly, black and white print cannot completely convey Mariama's title: "Unity" is colored red, "Strength" green, "An Autoethnographic Exploration" gold, and "Women's March" pink. The coloring is clearly deliberate, intended to evoke emotional associations: the first three colors represent Mariama's West African roots—these are the colors of the Guinean flag. The purpose of the pink is plain, as is Mariama's overall purpose, stated early in her essay:

> my end goal is to build off the foundations that Civil Right activists have set forth and capitalize on this momentum. Thus, I hope for my personal experience at the Women's March to serve as pushing the envelope when it comes to addressing the intersectionality that comes along with ... the nation's state of contemporary politics.

In her interview, Mariama said the thing she liked best about practicing autoethnography was "being able to articulate my opinion." Her essay is full of her opinions, and while they are far from subtle, they are also couched in compelling narrative and careful research.

For example, Mariama emphasizes the context of the Women's March within a larger history, as well as her own personal background:

> West and Blumberg (1991) shed light on the type of protests that are recognized and that is usually white, men, and cis-gendered. But, that was not the case that Saturday day. We did the unexpected….
>
> Growing up as the oldest to West African immigrants, they instilled strength and focus in me. Though I was born in America, English was neither my first or second language. Fulani and French were my first two languages. I was made fun of throughout kindergarten and first grade for it. Thus, instilling strength, focus, and heart was the way for my resistance to be felt. Through education I could resist….
>
> And that was what this Women's March in D.C. was about. Social citizenship. Social citizenship is said to have been the "strong thread running through the full history of the March on Washington Movement" as Jones (2013) explains ….

Mariama said that in her experience, historical context of these issues has not been sufficiently addressed, and she was glad that the research and reflection in these paragraphs contextualizes her experience, connecting the present with the past.

In her interview, Mariama talked about how helpful it was to learn about the way she thinks and talks through "putting that in writing and trying to explain it to people." Mariama concluded her essay with a fascinating mixture of bitter humor, history, hope, and anger, all elements eminently appropriate to her topic and each reflecting empowerment, experienced through the autoethnographic process:

> Here we were. At the White House. Chanting: "This pussy grabs back" and "BLACK LIVES MATTER." We did it. We left Mr. Donald Trump gifts. The White House gates were flooded with the pussy, pink hat … As I turned away from the White House, I cannot help but I have a smirk on my face. It reminded me of Phillip Randolph and how he was the head organizer of the first March on Washington, where Martin Luther King Jr. gave his famous "I Have a Dream" speech (Jones, 2013). As I think about his speech and go back to listen to it, it is the epitome of denouncing respectability politics ….

CATHARSIS

Caroline

Caroline had one of the best attitudes I've ever encountered in a student—consistently cheerful and enthusiastic—so it was surprising to me that in her interview, she heavily emphasized the therapeutic effect of writing her autoethnography, "The Impacts on Charter Education Because of Redlining." From her positive demeanor, I would not have guessed at the more difficult feelings the genre exposed, and helped address. Yet Caroline wrote at the beginning of her essay: "Through my findings, I found relief as I wrote about my high school experience and the anger I have towards the high school that failed me as a student."

Caroline attended a charter school in a suburb of Boston. She paints a grim picture of her surroundings growing up: "I feared where I lived. I was raised in the streets called the 'hood.' No safety at night, and an occasional gunshot with cops infesting the city." Articulating these dire circumstances must have been difficult for Caroline, but it was necessary to convey the impact that her education would have on her.

Caroline knew that education could be a way out, a fact that was instilled in her by inspirational teachers and programs at her charter school. She describes one of her teachers, Mr. Kith:

> *He studies our faces, ensuring that he has made eye contact with each individual. He begins to speak in a mellow tone. However, his strong, brown face shows discontent.* "Look around you. There are 100 students in this grade. Only one of you will have a PhD. *He begins to point out students while raising his voice steadily.* Only 13 of you will go to and THROUGH college. The rest of you, well, maybe go into labor jobs. Maybe the other half go into drugs?… Will you graduate? Society thinks you are destined to fail. *He preaches.* Will you fail me?"

Mr. Kith's fiery rhetoric motivated Caroline to do the hard work she knew was necessary to succeed: "I dedicated my life and soul to this by attending school five days a week and ten hours a day." And she did excel. Depicting Mr. Kith's exhortation, and her own subsequent accomplishment, must have been emotionally satisfying to Caroline.

However, the education Caroline's charter school gave her, while inspiring, seemed inadequate during her transition to the more rigorous college environment. Caroline expressed her frustration simply, but eloquently: "I fail every time I write. I cannot make a simple sentence without my grammar becoming an issue. [My teachers tell me:] 'You have amazing ideas Caroline, but your grammar downplays your potential.'" I winced as I read that, since I probably wrote something close to the comment myself on her essays. Caroline had persevered, no doubt, but it was still painful:

> In this institution, I fight every day to acknowledge that I deserve to be here. I fight with myself to enunciate my words correctly. I fight to believe that I am good enough. Every day, I see the ease of how people who had more opportunities and better education can write better. I cannot tell my parents about my "small struggles."

> "You can do it. It's not that hard."
>
> Well, it is. I fight with my grammar every day. I fight for the privilege I do not have. I fight for the barriers of the future. And that is what KIPP taught me. To fight.

Apparently, writing these words reaffirmed for Caroline the value of persistence. In her interview, Caroline talked about how practicing autoethnography was not "venting" exactly, but that the genre helped her find "peace in myself, letting the past go a bit." She said she had been "mad at the fact that my school failed me," but that her research and writing had calmed that anger and had led her to the conclusion: "I do deserve to be in this institution."

Marian

Marian's essay, "A Mom's (Not So Gentle) Touch," is a portrait of a conflicted mother-daughter relationship. When I asked Marian what aspects of practicing autoethnography were difficult, she answered that it was hard because it involved getting "really emotional," but, she said, it also "helped me understand my mom's behavior to me."

Marian begins by describing a trip she took to Iceland with her mother. Marian had planned the trip as an attempt to bond. However, the reality of the trip was not as positive as she hoped:

> The aura of negative energy between us began with me telling her not to bump into me so much because she has a bad habit of subconsciously nudging people, and it is a pet peeve of mine, which she did not understand. When someone nudges me frequently, I feel disturbed and I lose focus …. Because I told her how uncomfortable I felt, she exclaimed, "Oh so you don't want me to touch you anymore, then so be it. I won't ever touch you or give you hugs again."

Marian uses the trip to Iceland to illustrate the problems in her relationship with her mother. Practicing autoethnography helped Marian better articulate some of those problems.

Marian identifies some specific aspects of her relationship with her mother that have been influenced by their shared social/cultural context. Here, for example, Marian identifies one issue, the fact that she had been sent to live away from her parents at a very young age:

> I am known as a satellite baby …. Bohr & Tse (2009) conducted a study about satellite babies and … accounted for the depression or stress parents endure when they are separated from their young (p. 270) …. my mom pushed me away because she felt that I was not her daughter anymore. I do not remember what happened during those eighteen months, but I do know that when I came back to live with my family, my

> mom did not feel close to me, so I did not receive the nurturing I needed as a child, and I felt alienated from the family. My mom told me a couple of years ago that she regretted sending me away, but she had no choice.

Another influence on Marian's strained relationship with her mother might have had to do with her cultural heritage:

> Maybe my silence from not speaking up for myself stems from filial piety, which is a virtue where the child is supposed to unconditionally respect and take care of the parents when they age because the parents are older than the child. It is an important aspect of Chinese cultural and social tradition. (Evans, 2008, p. 172)

Marian said she had known about some aspects of Chinese culture that could have contributed to her situation, but seeing those ideas in print was different. Knowing about the existence of other "anchor babies," and that "there's other people like me" was helpful for Marian. Contextualizing her experience helped Marian come to terms with that experience.

Selena

In her autoethnography, "Through Salsa: Your Legacy Lives," Selena shares the significance of salsa music to her family, particularly in the wake of her father's death. In her interview, Selena said that the most important aspect of practicing autoethnography for her was "definitely the therapeutic component …. I learned a lot about vulnerability: it's scary, but it's so important for self-healing and self-learning."

For Selena and her family, Salsa was a source of joy and unity, as she depicts in a scene from her childhood:

> The air filled with laughter as my family took turns sharing stories and reminiscing on their childhood experiences. I'd laugh and smile along with them while trying to play the stories they shared in my head like a movie.… Is this what people meant when they said: "One day you're going to look back and finally understand why you had to go through so many hardships to get to where you are today?" *Was this their happiness?*
>
> After sharing stories, my dad and my aunt found their way back to the center of the backyard. As if it was a dance floor, they danced. Side to side, back and forth, their feet moving in-sync with one another, their hips swaying to the beats of African drums and Cuban sounds, and their arms swinging freely allowing for each other to turn. A brave warrior covered in the bright colors of our flag—red, white, and blue—and a queen with glowing skin and a head full of bantu knots dripped unapologetic honor in all that she was. Watching them dance was my favorite part of family gatherings.

No doubt recalling these moments was painful, given her loss since. Yet the bittersweet memories also seem to bring Selena a sense of belonging to a community united in its love of Salsa.

Throughout the essay, Selena carefully connects her personal experience with the social/cultural context of her Puerto Rican heritage and Salsa's historical roots. Here she presents some of her research, and how it affects her:

> Salsa is a mixture of mixtures (Duany, 1984). It not only contains elements of rhythms and beats originating from the Caribbean, Southern Spain, and Western Africa. It also contains elements of history, oppression, and stories of our island and our ancestors.... Growing up listening to Salsa and watching my family dance is how *I* witnessed firsthand strength. It was in those moments where everything fit together perfectly. It was the understanding of all that we were not only as members of the Puerto Rican community, but as individuals and as a family.

According to Selena, discovering these roots and reflecting on this heritage was therapeutic, as she said in her interview: "I realized there were a lot of parts of myself that I neglected for a long time," parts like not speaking Spanish or listening to Salsa. Practicing autoethnography, she said, was a chance to "hone in on my roots" because "I want to embrace this side of me, I want it to be a part of my everyday life." For Selena, the therapeutic outcome was especially valuable because of her ethnic background: "Communities of color don't normally have the time and the space to invest in emotional labor and what we're going through, so to be in a class to be devoted to strictly that, was like, wow!"

Ultimately, the impact of Selena's work was acutely personal. Near the end of her autoethnography, she reflects on her father's legacy:

> My childhood was full of great, great songs. Songs that inspired love and laughter. Songs that spoke of the human condition and more than anything, songs that spoke to our ability to bounce back from all that life throws our way. I remember Saturday morning cartoons interrupted by the record player pumping out Salsa tunes and upsetting me but dad just laughed and danced. He'd scoop me up and dance with me in his arms until my pouting mouth turned into a smile....
>
> My father used to say "Selena you think you know the world, but you don't. You think you're grown, but you're not." And although I never wanted to admit it, he was right because the day he passed away was the day I realized how much I didn't actually know.

For Selena, recognition brought no clichéd closure, but it did help her to handle her grief, as her essay indicates:

> People often say, "time heals all wounds," but I disagree. Time does not heal all wounds and all wounds most certainly do not heal. We learn how to cope and learning how to cope is never black or white. Coping is a method of trial and error, and for me, coping took place through the sounds of Salsa.

References

Bohr, Y, & Tse, C. (2009). Satellite babies in transnational families: A study of parents' decision to separate from their infants. *Infant Mental Health Journal, 30*(3), 265–286.

Carlos, R. M., Borba, J. A., Heck, K. E., Nathaniel, K. C., & Sousa, C. M. (2009). Survey explores teen driving behavior in Central Valley, Los Angeles high schools. *California Agriculture, 63*(4), 208–214.

Duany, J. (1984). Popular music in Puerto Rico: Toward an anthropology of "Salsa." *Latin American Music Review/Revista De Música Latinoamericana, 5*(2), 186–216.

Edgerton, J. (2011, October 11). Men vs. women: Who are safer drivers? *CBS News*. Retreived from https://www.cbsnews.com/news/men-vs-women-who-are-safer-drivers/

Evans, H. (2008). *The subject of gender: Daughters and moms in urban China*. Lanham, MD: Rowman & Littlefield.

Fardouly, J., Diedrichs, P. C., Vartanian, L. R., & Halliwell, E. (2015). Social comparisons on social media: The impact of Facebook on young women's body image concerns and mood. *Psychology of Women Quarterly, 39*(4), 447–457.

Ginsburg, E. S., & Racowsky, C. (2012). In vitro fertilization: A comprehensive guide. New York, NY: Springer.

Golombok, S., MacCallum, F., & Goodman, E. (2001). The "test-tube" generation: Parent child relationships and the psychological well-being of in vitro fertilization children at adolescence. *Child Development, 72*(2), 599–608.

Jones, W. P. (2013). *The march on Washington: Jobs, freedom, and the forgotten history of civil rights*. New York, NY: W. W. Norton.

Koppl, R., & Sacks, M. (2013). The criminal justice system creates incentives for false convictions. *Criminal Justice Ethics, 32*(2), 126–162.

Mann, M. (2014). *Psychoanalytic aspects of assisted reproductive technology*. London: Karnac.

Mathias, B. (1992). *Between sisters: Secret rivals, intimate friends*. New York, NY: Delacorte Press.

National Research Council, Institute of Medicine, and Transporation Research Board. (2007). *Preventing teen motor crashes*. Washington, DC: The National Academic Press.

Radkowska-Walkowicz, M. (2012). The creation of "monsters": The discourse of opposition to in vitro fertilization in Poland. *Reproductive Health Matters, 20*(40), 30–37.

Smith, G. P. (1998). *Family values and the new society: Dilemmas of the 21st century*. Westport, CN: Praeger.

Stuntz, W. J. (2013). *The collapse of American criminal justice*. Cambridge: The Belknap Press of Harvard University Press.

Tolich, M. (2010). A critique of current practice: Ten foundational guidelines for autoethnographers. *Qualitative Health Research, 20*(12), 1599–1610.

West, G., & Blumberg, R. L. (1991). *Women and social protest*. New York, NY: Oxford University Press.

Appendix E

Author's Autoethnography

Coming "Home": An Autoethnographic Exploration of Third Culture Kid Transition
Justin B. Hopkins

Abstract

Born in the United States, I grew up in Senegal, West Africa, where my parents worked as missionary linguists. "Coming 'Home'" tells the story of my return to the United States after graduating from high school. I frame my personal memories, shared in the form of poems (following the methodology outlined by David Hanauer's *Poetry as Research*), with reflexive analysis (using the theory of David Pollock and Ruth Van Reken's *Third Culture Kids*). I examine the difficulty of leaving particular places and people from the "host culture," as well as the challenge of transition back into the "home" culture.

"Increasingly, we are becoming aware that putting closure on the overseas experience is the first step in making a comfortable transition home" (Eakin, 1998, p. 78).

Figure 1: Photo by Betsy Barbour, 2001

INVOLVEMENT: SOME TIME BEFORE LEAVING SENEGAL

Sitting in a frangipani tree,
Settled into its branches,
Feeling the knots in my side,
Against my neck,
Feeling the sun on my face and arms,
Remembering ...

Sleeping surrounded by mosquito netting and mud brick,
Hearing the scorpion scuttling across the vinyl floor,
Playing soccer in the sand at twilight,
Hiding from a man in a costume made of bark, shrieking and clashing machetes,
Laughing at baby parrots fighting for food from a yoghurt cup,
Listening to Mom or Dad reading aloud by the glow of a hissing gas lamp,
Riding a bicycle over a bridge with a crocodile living under it,
Taking a bucket bath,
Climbing the baobob tree,
Speaking Jola, the local language,
Dancing to the djembe drums,
Relishing the sound of rain on a tin roof,
Seeing soldiers walking and tanks rolling into the village,
Leaving the village,

Giving candy and bread to beggar boys,
Riding in taxis with cracked windshields and without floorboards,
Watching falling stars while camping out on rocky beach cliffs,
Swallowing bitter malaria pills,
Haggling in the marketplace for a watch or a calculator,
Making tea with my brother on a thatch mat,
Drinking Coke from a perspiring bottle,
Wearing brightly colored trousers made for tourists,
Learning French, the colonial language
Eating rice and fish and vegetables from a communal bowl,
Sweating, always sweating,
Swimming in the sea, dodging Portuguese Man-of-War jellyfish,
Smelling the eucalyptus, the smoke …

***

I identify as an Adult Third Culture Kid (ATCK).

Working in India in the 1950s, social anthropologists John and Ruth Hill Useem coined the term "Third Culture Kid," and David Pollock and Ruth Van Reken (2009) developed the idea further, defining a TCK as "a person who has spent a significant part of his or her developmental years outside the parents' culture … build[ing] relationships to all of the cultures, while not having full ownership in any" (p. 13). I met David Pollock when he visited the missionary school where I was a junior. He looked like Santa Claus in blue jeans, except that he had sad eyes. He told me and my peers that we were special, that we had an identity, a name that distinguished us. "You're TCKs," he told us. According to Pollock and Van Reken (2009), TCKs share several characteristics, including "being raised in a genuinely cross-cultural" and "highly mobile world" where they are distinctly, often "physically different from those around them" and from which they "usually expect at some point to return permanently to live in their home country" (p. 17). Furthermore, TCKs typically grow up in a "neither/nor world," a world initially defined as a negative construction: "neither fully the world of their parents' culture (or cultures) nor fully the world of the other culture (or cultures) in which they were raised" (p. 4). For TCKs, the question, "Where are you from?" is difficult to answer.

I lived in Senegal, West Africa, where my parents worked as missionary linguists, from about 6 months of age until just before my 18th birthday. Every few years we would return to the United States, my birth and passport country, for a furlough, but the majority of my formative years were spent in Senegal. For the first 10 years, we were based in a village, Sindian, in the southern part of the country, the Casamance. Then a civil war forced us to relocate to the capital city, Dakar, where we spent the next eight years.

In particular, this autoethnographic essay explores my experience of leaving Senegal, examining what happens during TCK reentry—transitioning from life abroad to life in the "home" country. Davis, Suarez, Crawford, and Rehfuss (2013) point to their own empirical findings as well as to "decades of literature purporting that the experience of repatriation can be a difficult time fraught with feelings of depression, anxiety, and stress" (p. 134). Although my own experience was not as dire as some, there were difficult aspects to it. Gilbert (2008), analyzing manifestations of grief in the TCK experience, writes about how many TCKs frequently feel homeless, and reentry can highlight that feeling: "The absence of a home in their life becomes most apparent when participants ... moved to their passport country" (p. 105). I can certainly relate.

Melles and Schwartz (2013) observe, "With the burgeoning globalization over the last century, TCKs and ATCKs are becoming more common" (p. 261). Not only more common, TCKs and ATCKs are becoming more publicly visible. U.S. President Barack Obama, for example, is an ATCK, as were and are many members of his first and current cabinets. With more visible and just more members, the TCK and ATCK groups become more important to the cultures they inhabit—interacting with them productively requires understanding them, and vice versa. In addition, academic interest in the TCK experience, begun in the latter half of the twentieth century, has continued growing, as evidenced by the number of studies published over the last decade.[1] In addition to contributing to the scholarly dialogue, my research should interest anyone who identifies as a TCK or an ATCK. It should also interest anyone who interacts with anyone in those categories, perhaps leaving few who would find this material irrelevant.

Denzin (2014) defines the subject matter of autoethnography as "the life experiences and performances of a person" (p. 1), specifically, the researcher—in this case, me. In particular, I chose to write a poetic autoethnography because, as Hanauer (2010) asserts, "Poetry writing is particularly suited for the exploration of research questions that address experiences with emotional content ..." (p. 84) and "for eliciting succinct, emotion-laden understandings of self-experience" (p. 134). Perhaps poetry goes where prose cannot, straight to the heart of the matter. I hope, as Hanauer (2010) puts it, my poetic and performative autoethnography can "capture a moment of self understanding of past experience through the performance of poetic identity at the moment of writing" (p. 88), or, as Denzin (2014) describes, "capture, probe, and render understandable problematic experience" (p. 36). In addition, Anderson (2006) asserts that autoethnographies often provide opportunities for individuals to work through their "emotionally wrenching experiences"

(Anderson, 2006, p. 377). My experience was certainly problematic, often difficult, and occasionally even emotionally wrenching, and I am grateful for the chance to confront the issues artistically and academically.

My methodological approach was simple. Although I never thought of myself as a poet, David Hanauer guided me through an established procedure to produce poetic data, summarizing "the poetry writing process [as] a form of inquiry in which meanings of personal experience are discovered" (p. 25). In a seminar titled "Life Writing," and according to the method outlined in his *Poetry as Research* (2010), Hanauer directed me to pick provocative prompts related to my topic, to use those prompts to generate as much raw material as possible, and to sculpt that information gradually into its final form for analysis.

Following Hanauer's (2010) instructions, I collected and listed memories surrounding the experience of leaving Senegal. This was the Activation stage, "in which an experiential and/or associative process triggers the writing process" (p. 19). Next, through freewriting, I fleshed out the memories with as many details as possible during the Discovery stage, "in which the writer finds new underlying meanings and gives new directions to the emerging poem" (p. 19). Then I drafted and re-drafted the actual poems in the Permutation stage, "in which the poem develops through a series of rewritings" (p. 19) for aesthetic refinement. Finally, during the Finalization stage, I "produce[d] the last version of the poem[s]" (p. 19). Analysis followed.

It's worth noting that, serendipitously, I discovered after the fact that the five poems I composed correspond precisely to Pollock and Van Reken's (2009) stages of transition from culture to culture: involvement, leaving, transition, entering, reinvolvement (p. 66). I included these stages in the poem's titles. Using the poems as data for my autoethnographic study (Hanauer, 2010, p. 81), I analyzed them, comparing the themes to current research on TCKs, and asking myself the question, "How does this poem position me?" In the answers, I referred again to Pollock and Van Reken's (2009) stages of transition. So, for example, as I look back at my first poem in this piece, "Involvement," I find it positions me as the involved TCK, feeling "settled and comfortable, knowing where [I] belong and how [I] fit in" (Pollock and Van Reken, 2009, p. 66), reflecting on the many, powerful, nearly overwhelming sensations of living in Senegal. Humor dances with danger, the beautiful with the bizarre and the grotesque, and hopefully a general sense of satisfaction prevails over the moments of inconvenience, discomfort, and trauma.

***

Leaving: Shortly Before Leaving Senegal

My friend leaves Senegal before I do.
We have pictures of us together as children,
Playing Legos,
Practicing martial arts.
Now he poses alone for a going-away photo,
Wearing his multi-color patchwork pants,
His dark blue suit jacket,
His Bob Marley beret.
He looks funny.
He wears rings too,
One his parents gave him,
Gold, with an inscription of Africa on it,
And a tiny ruby for Senegal;
One I gave him,
The copy of which I wear myself,
Much less grand,
A simple, silver band,
With a friendship knot woven into one side.
He smiles widely.
Later, probably close to midnight, at the airport,
We hug goodbye.
And then he is gone.
On the ride back to the Center, where I live,
I struggle to hold back tears.
Back at the Center, where I live,
I climb the wooden stairs to the roof,
Sit in a corner, alone,
And cry,
Feeling the cool brick against my back,
The hot breeze against my face.
He was my childhood.
He was my Africa.
And now he is gone.

***

Pollock and Van Reken (2009) write, "TCKs usually place a high value on their relationships" (p. 136). Some say it's hard for TCKs to form strong relationships in the first place. Lijadi and van Schalkwyk (2014) studied TCK commitment and reticence in interpersonal interactions, concluding that, because of frequent moves, often "the only stable relationship for TCKs was within their own family" (p. 9), and their research subjects "could not reach a deep level of friendship as they were constantly on the move" (p. 11). I don't doubt their research, but I was lucky, for a long time. Although my family moved frequently, it was usually just from the village to the city or vice versa, with occasional visits to the United States. While I did my fair share of bonding and breaking away, I did not suffer quite the same level of "repeated patterns of forming friendship and of saying goodbye" (Lijadi and van Schalkwyk, 2014, p. 2) due to the "constant state of flux" (Gilbert, 2008, p. 99).

Furthermore, throughout most of the moving, my friend Ibu (his adopted Senegalese name) was as constant as anyone besides my family. His parents were my parents' work partners, and their moves often mirrored ours. In the village, his family lived only about a forty-minute drive away. In the city, they were even closer. Here was the flip side of TCK relationship potential: "A positive relationship between friends and family in terms of social bonds was also observed" (Ittel and Sisler, 2012, p. 490). Perhaps this potential is a result of the increased social sensitivity that Lyttle et al. (2011) documented, in comparison to monocultural individuals. Hence the pain of parting that I, like many TCKs, experienced: "When returning to their home country, they may grieve over relationships and environments that belong to their host country" (Hoersting and Jenkins, 2011, p. 19). Lijadi and van Schalkwyk (2014) second the observation: "For TCKs every farewell was difficult, as it entailed grieving the loss of friends" (p. 13). The poem "Leaving" positions me as the grieving TCK, as "life begins to change" (Pollock and Van Reken, 2009, p. 67), remembering good times with a good friend, the devastating reality of separation settling in only after the fact. We would remain friends, of course, but in those moments there was only the unrelenting absence. After Ibu left, I felt as though I wasn't really present anymore in Africa. It was like an out-of-body experience—an out-of-country, off-of-continent experience: I remember walking around half-wondering where I was.

***

TRANSITION: LEAVING SENEGAL

My turn at the airport comes,
And I feel ready.
I carry my beat-up backpack,
And other luggage.
18 years weighs a lot.
There are more friends to bid farewell.
We exchange gifts,
Hugs.

> I drink a Coke.
> I ride the bus to the plane.
> I notice my last step on African soil.
> My foot moves from the ground
> Onto the steel staircase to the plane.
> I slump into the window seat.
> The lights on the continent fade.

***

Although after Ibu left I already felt absent from Africa, my actual parting was more difficult than I anticipated. As Moore and Barker (2012) observe, "Detriments of the third culture experience include … having to say goodbye to friends, the pain of leaving what is familiar" (p. 558). I had already said goodbye to friends, and I said goodbye to more, some who would be following me soon, some who would be staying on. The repeated pain of parting was expected, but I had no idea how it would feel to physically walk off of Africa, to leave and lose everything familiar in an instant. Gilbert (2008) comments on that experience: "Moving from the country they lived in as TCKs was a commonly cited loss. The smells, tastes, cultural rituals, site-specific opportunities, in addition to the physical aspect of the country—geography and climate—were noted as elements of what was then missing in their lives" (p. 100).

The poem "Transition" positions me as the TCK in transit, "begin[ning] the moment I leave one place" (Pollock and Van Reken, 2009, p. 69), the neither/nor immigrant/emigrant carrying an old life to a new place.

***

ENTERING: SHORTLY AFTER ARRIVING STATESIDE

> I was born on the 4th of July,
> A real, live nephew of my Uncle Sam.
> Tomorrow I turn 18.
> I will be an adult,
> Celebrate my own independence on Independence Day.
> Tonight we eat at a Chinese Buffet,
> And go to Blockbuster,
> Across the Parking Lot,
> The sky darkens.
> A storm rolls in.
> I am excited to rent movies:
> *From Here to Eternity*,

A Streetcar Named Desire,
The Graduate.
I don't remember cake or presents.
I remember watching movies:
Yankee Doodle Dandy.
James Cagney sings and dances
About the grand old flag,
And I remember …

***

Performing a sociological self-exploration, TCK Kate Russell (2011) reflects, "Moving back to the United States … proved to be one of the more difficult transitions for me" (p. 32). She is not alone. Limberg and Lambie (2011) concur, citing Kotesky (2008), "Anxiety and depression are prevalent diagnoses of individuals who transition into a new culture" (p. 48). Pollock and Van Reken (2009) write, "one of the factors that distinguishes the TCK experience from that of a true immigrant is the full expectation that after living for a significant period of their developmental years outside their passport culture, there will come the day when TCKs make a permanent return to that country and culture" (p. 225). I anticipated returning to the United States at the end of my high school years, and I even looked forward to it at times, especially during those many moments of challenge specific to living in a developing country—anything from lack of electricity and running water to evacuating a war-zone. However, my hopes, like those of many, were complicated by the attendant unrealistic expectations Pollock and Van Reken (2009) assert TCKs often carry back to their passport culture, along with their more material luggage. Some expect a "dream world" (p. 226), associating the passport culture with furloughs or vacations of the past, during which residence was temporary and so, often, idealistic. (I did—America was the land promising fast food and film stores galore.) Some expect to fit right in to their passport culture, and they are frequently met by similar expectations from others—after all, they are "coming home," right? They don't expect what Pollock and Van Reken (2009) call "reverse culture shock" (p. 227), being alienated by elements of the passport culture, from small differences like "slang or idioms that mean nothing to the returning TCKs" to "deeper levels of cultural dissonance" like lackadaisical attitudes towards food waste (p. 228). Moore and Barker (2012) put it bluntly: "When returning to their passport countries, TCKs often perceive themselves as culturally marginal and terminally unique" (p. 555). I did.

But film helped. About a year before I returned to the United States, I started cultivating an interest in film. I didn't think this at the time, but in retrospect I wonder if I was already trying to build a bridge of some kind with my passport culture, a way to relate to America. In any case, when I arrived in the U.S., the first thing I wanted to do was to watch movies. Having had access to relatively little film in Senegal, I was amazed by the wealth of choice. Also, turning 18 and reaching (legal) adulthood, I was finally able to watch what I wanted to watch, not what my parents allowed me to watch. I celebrated my coming-of-age with cinema, and for a long while after, my strongest connection with my passport culture was through movies. The poem "Entering" positions me as the arriving TCK, "feel[ing] a lot of ambivalence" (Pollock and Van Reken, 2009, p. 72), and gorging myself on the delicacies the new country offers, perhaps in an attempt to satisfy a craving that can actually be satisfied as opposed to one that cannot.

***

REINVOLVEMENT: SOME TIME AFTER ARRIVING STATESIDE

Just a few days before starting my new job,
Cashier at a grocery store,
Ibu was visiting.
How wonderful to walk and talk with him again.
I woke up,
Excited to spend another day with him.
I walked out of my room,
And met my mom.
She said something had happened.
Her voice was tense.
We went to the TV.
We watched the second plane hit.
We watched the towers fall.
I was shocked,
And afraid.
But as I saw the flags unfurl,
And shared the shock, fear, and awe with my neighbors,
I thought,
I live here now.

***

I have wondered what impact 9–11 would have had on me had I still been living in Senegal. Senegal is a mostly Muslim country, but, like many other Muslim countries, the general response of the populace was one of sympathy with the United States. Senegalese culture places a high priority on peace, but still the American school I attended introduced new security measures—armed guards at the gates and higher walls. I wonder how I would have felt to witness these changes in person. Probably like something good had been spoiled.

In any case, I wasn't living in Senegal. I was living in the United States, albeit for less than six months at the time. I had already attended a week-long TCK reentry seminar, led by David Pollock. We talked a lot about what it means to be a TCK returning to the passport culture. We shared our personal backgrounds and found many similarities. Davis et al. (2013) note that these seminars can lead to drastic reduction in feelings of depression, anxiety, and stress, and indeed the week helped me feel more acculturated. However, I believe it took 9–11 to truly bring me "home." Sharing the fear of a nation has a powerful acculturative effect. Now I find myself not entirely comfortable with this perception, as I have since confronted the problematic aspects of nationalism. Retrospectively, I balk at the particular brand of patriotism that flared during those days of shared fear. But it happened, and I was a part of it. The poem "Reinvolvement" positions me as a TCK in the final stage of transition, a time when "[I] once again become part of the permanent community" (Pollock & Van Reken, 2009, p. 73), settling, and experiencing a moment of identification with the culture around me.

***

Anymore

Anymore, I blend in.
Anymore, people are surprised when they learn I grew up in Africa.
"Why don't you have an accent?"
But if you listen carefully, I still do.
When someone sneezes, I say "Maas."
When I like something, I snap my tongue against my soft palate in a glottal click.
When I don't want to do something, I bend my arm at an angle and jerk my elbow back, Muttering "Imangut."
These are Jola words, Jola gestures.
And I've adapted to other cultures, adopting from other places I've lived since Senegal.
For "thanks," I may say the Great British "cheers" or the Finnish "kiitos."
American winters don't seem so harsh, anymore,
After London's brutal damp and the dry frigidity of Helsinki.
I still watch movies, but not as many, anymore.
I don't feel the need to connect with American culture that way, anymore.
Instead, I binge-watch TV shows, on Netflix, or Hulu.
Very American.

> The last time I visited Senegal, I told people trying to sell me over-priced souvenirs:
> "Je ne suis pas touriste, moi."
> "I'm not a tourist, me."
> And I'm not
> But I don't live there, either, anymore.

***

Being a TCK certainly comes with benefits. Straffon (2003) showed that students attending an international high school tested at high levels of intercultural sensitivity. Sheard (2008) compared TCKs and "gifted children" and found they share many of the same characteristics, including "knowledge beyond that of their classmates" (p. 31). Dewaele and van Oudenhoven (2009) found TCKs tested higher on measurements of "Openmindedness" and "Cultural Empathy" than did "monoculturals." Moore and Barker (2012) believe being a TCK "makes it a lot easier to adapt to new situations and environments" (p. 560). I can't claim all of these advantages, but I am grateful for whatever positives my experience entails—the compulsion to travel, if nothing else: after growing up overseas, I spent a good chunk of my young adulthood abroad also, studying performance in Europe. Yet these benefits come with a cost. Hoersting and Jenkins (2011) write, "The literature on cross-cultural childhood experiences supports the argument that such experiences can lead to feeling suspended between cultures, cultural membership uncertainty, and CH [cultural homelessness]" (p. 20). I can attest to those difficult feelings, and I am glad to have had the opportunity to confront and bring closure, or at least balance, to some of them through the course of this autoethnography. As Art Bochner (2013) puts it, "the question of happiness is the most urgent calling of autoethnography" (p. 53), and while I won't assert any absurd level of happiness from my study, I believe it has brought me substantial satisfaction. Autoethnography, according to Adams, Holman Jones, and Ellis (2014), allows practitioners to better understand "how we come to know, name, and interpret personal and cultural experience" (p. 1). I am grateful for the insight the form has provided me.

Not all TCKs fare so fortunately. Pollock and Van Reken (2009) observe, "In spite of the growing efforts to help current TCKs to better understand and use their cross-cultural experiences, many ATCKs ... have grown up with little assistance in sorting out the full effect of their third culture upbringing" (p. 249). These ATCKs struggle to make sense of their experiences, for one reason or another, or many. On the other hand, "many ATCKs have successfully found their way through the morass of conflicting cultures and lifestyles, come to terms with the inherent losses, and developed a positive sense of identity" (p. 249). I hope I have done so.

One of the ways I have incorporated my past into my present identity is by teaching a course called "In and Out of Africa." In this seminar, in which we explore writing from and about Africa, we encounter the poetry of Léopold Sédar Senghor, Senegal's first president, and one of its finest artists and academics. In "Que m'accompagnent koras et balafong" ["To the music of Koras and Balaphon"] Senghor evokes "Paradis mon enfance africaine" (p. 282) ["Paradise my African childhood" (p. 17)] and how his home "reçoit l'enfant toujours enfant, que douze ans d'errances n'ont pas vielli" (p. 291) [Receive the eternally childlike child who has not aged/ In twelve years of wandering" (p. 24)]. I never considered my African childhood Paradise, and when I returned after not quite a dozen years away, I felt comfortable, but not at home. I've moved on, or moved forward, or moved away, or something.

Note

Author's autoethnography is re-published with permission of *Qualitative Inquiry*: Hopkins, J. B. (2015). Coming "home": An autoethnographic exploration of Third Culture Kid transition. *Qualitative Inquiry*, *21*(19), 812–820.

1. Lijadi and van Schalkwyk (2014), Melles and Schwartz (2013), Davis et al. (2013), Moore and Barker (2012), Ittel and Sisler (2012), Russell (2011), Lyttle et al. (2011), Limberg and Lambie (2011), Hoersting and Jenkins (2011), Pollock and Van Reken (2009), Peterson and Plamadon (2009), Dewaele and van Oudenhoven (2009), Sheard (2008), Gilbert (2008), Fail et al. (2004), and Straffon (2003).

References

Adams, T. E., Holman Jones, S., & Ellis, C. (2014). *Autoethnography: Understanding Qualitative Research*. Oxford: Oxford University Press.

Anderson, L. (2006). Analytic autoethnography. *Journal of Contemporary Ethnography*, *35*, 373–395.

Bochner, A. (2013). Putting meanings into motion: Autoethnography's existential calling. In S. Holman Jones, T. E. Adams, & C. Ellis (Eds.), *Handbook of Autoethnography*. Walnut Creek, CA: Left Coast Press.

Davis, P. S., Suarez, E. C., Crawford, N. A., & Rehfuss, M. C. (2013). Reentry program impact on missionary kid depression, anxiety, and stress: A three-year study. *Journal of Psychology and Theology*, *41*(2), 128–140.

Denzin, N. K. (2014). *Interpretive autoethnography*. Los Angeles, CA: SAGE.

Dewaele, J., & Van Oudenhoven J. P. (2009). The effect of multilingualism/multiculturalism on personality: No gain without pain for Third Culture Kids? *International Journal of Multilingualism*, *6*(4), 443–459.

Eakin, K. B. (1998). *According to my passport, I'm coming home.* Washington, DC: U.S. Department of State, Family Liaison Office.

Fail, H., Thompson, J., & Walker, G. (2004). Belonging, identity, and Third Culture Kids. *Journal of Research in International Education, 3*(3), 319–338.

Gilbert, K. R. (2008). Loss and grief between and among cultures: The experience of Third Culture Kids. *Illness, Crisis, & Loss, 16*(2), 93–109.

Hanauer, D. I. (2010). *Poetry as research: Exploring second language poetry writing.* Philadelphia, PA: John Benjamins.

Hoersting, R. C., & Jenkins, S. R. (2011). No place to call home: Cultural homelessness, self-esteem, and cross-cultural identities. *International Journal of Intercultural Relations, 35*, 17–30.

Ittel, A., & Sisler, A. (2012). Third culture kids: Adjusting to a changing world. *Diskurs Kindheits, 4*, 487–492.

Lijadi, A. A., & van Schalkwyk, G. J. (2014). Narratives of third culture kids: Commitment and reticence in social relationships. *The Qualitative Report, 19*(49), 1–18.

Limberg, D., & Lambie, G. W. (2011). Third culture kids: Implications for professional school counseling. *ASCA, 15*(1), 45–54.

Lyttle, A. D., Barker, G. G., & Cornwell, T. L. (2011). Adept through adaptation: Third culture individuals' interpersonal sensitivity. *International Journal of Intercultural Relations, 35*, 686–694.

Melles, E. A., & Schwartz, J. (2013). Does the third culture kid experience predict levels of prejudice? *International Journal of Intercultural Relations, 37*, 260–267.

Moore, A. M., & Barker, G. G. (2012). Confused or multicultural: Third culture individuals' cultural identity. *International Journal of Intercultural Relations, 36*, 553–562.

Peterson, B. E., & Plamadon, L. T. (2009). Third culture kids and the consequences of international sojourns on authoritarianism, acculturative balance, and positive affect. *Journal of Research in Personality, 43*, 755–763.

Pollock, D. C., & Van Reken, R. E. (2009). *Third culture kids: The experience of growing up among worlds.* Boston, MA: Nicholas Brealey.

Russell, K. M. (2011). Growing up a third culture kid: A sociological self-exploration. *Human Architecture: Journal of the Sociology of Self-knowledge, 9*(1), 29–42.

Senghor, L. S. (1991). Que m'accompagnent koras et balafong. In *Léopold Sédar Senghor: The collected poetry* (Dixon, M., Ed. and Trans.). Virginia: The University Press of Virginia.

Index

A

Adams, Tony xiv, 24, 34, 36, 40, 49, 60, 81–82, 91, 99–100, 112, 133
Allison. *See* student autoethnographers
Alvarez, Steven 5, 16–17
analytic rigor of autoethnography, lack of. *See* critiques of autoethnography
artistic writing 3–4, 12, 32–33, 37–39, 61, 152, 158
assessment/evaluation of autoethnography, challenge of. *See* critiques of autoethnography
audience awareness 59–68

B

Bartholomae, David 5, 14, 132
Bean, John 1–2, 69–70
Betty. *See* student autoethnographers

Bochner, Art xiii–xiv, 3, 10, 13–14, 99, 112, 121, 126, 184
Brodkey, Linda 5, 15–16

C

Camangian, Patrick 5, 16
Canagarajah, Suresh 5, 17, 132
Caroline. *See* student autoethnographers
Chang, Heewon 5, 13, 21–28
Christa. *See* student autoethnographers
Cooper. *See* student autoethnographers
community, developing a sense of. *See* outcomes of practicing autoethnography
critical empowerment. *See* outcomes of practicing autoethnography
critiques of autoethnography
    analytic rigor of autoethnography, lack of 11–13, 121
    assessment/evaluation of autoethnography, challenge of 11, 13–14, 121–122

ethical implications of autoethnography, consideration of 11–12, 37, 81–83, 121, 152
student surveys 122–123
student anxiety. *See* vulnerability, emotional

D

Danielewicz, Jane 5, 14, 16
data analysis 24–26
data collection 22–24, 37
definition of autoethnography xiii–xiv, 3, 9–10, 33, 134–135
Delamont, Sara 11, 37, 49, 81

E

Edward. *See* student autoethnographers
Elizabeth. *See* student autoethnographers
Ellis, Carolyn xiii–xv, 3, 10, 11, 14, 24, 34, 36, 40, 49, 60, 81–82, 91, 99–100, 112, 133
Emily. *See* student autoethnographers
enjoyment. *See* outcomes of practicing autoethnography
epiphanies 24, 36
ethical consideration. *See* outcomes of practicing autoethnography

F

freewriting 23, 33, 37, 177
Franklin & Marshall College 31–33, 87–88, 96–97, 128–129

G

Goldblatt, Eli 3–4

H

Hairston, Maxine 133
Haley. *See* student autoethnographers
Hanauer, David ix–xii, xiii–xiv, 5, 21–29, 34–35, 37, 134–135, 173, 176–177
Hannah. *See* student autoethnographers
Holman Jones, Shirley 24, 34, 36, 40, 49, 60, 81–82, 91, 99–100, 112, 133
Hood, Carra 5, 17

I

informed consent 11–12, 81–84, 95, 139–140

J

Jocelyne. *See* student autoethnographers

K

Kaitlyn. *See* student autoethnographers
Kim. *See* student autoethnographers

L

literacy autobiography 17
Lydia. *See* student autoethnographers
Lynne. *See* student autoethnographers

M

Mahala, Daniel and Jody Swilky 15–16
Mariama. *See* student autoethnographers
Marian. *See* student autoethnographers
meaningful literacy xi, 134–135

N

narrative elements 3, 37–40, 61–68, 72

O

outcomes of practicing autoethnography
    community, developing a sense of xv, 6, 45, 109–120
    critical empowerment xv, 6, 16, 45, 91–98, 111–112, 164–167
    enjoyment xv, 6, 45, 109–120
    ethical consideration xv, 6, 45, 81–90, 112–113, 161–164
    reflexivity xv, 6, 15, 41, 45, 49–58, 114–115, 134 153–157
    research skills improvement xv, 6, 17 45, 69–79, 113–114, 159–161
    therapeutic catharsis xv, 6, 16, 45, 52, 99–107, 111–112, 126, 167–171
    writing skills improvement xv, 6, 17, 45, 59–68, 115–117, 157–159

P

Pagnucci, Gian 3
Park, Gloria 3
peer feedback 36–43, 60, 65, 117–118, 134
poetry xiv, 26–29, 176–177
Pollock, David and Ruth Van Reken xiv, 23–28, 173–186

Q

qualitative inquiry/research 10

R

Reflexivity. *See* outcomes of practicing autoethnography),

research skills improvement. *See* outcomes of practicing autoethnography
research topic 2, 22, 35–37, 69
research writing 1–4, 32, 37, 69–79
revision 4, 41–42, 60–61, 65, 134

S

Sam. *See* student autoethnographers
Selena. *See* student autoethnographers
Senghor, Léopold Sédar 26, 185
Sikes, Pat 9, 13
Soliday, Mary 15
Sophie. *See* student autoethnographers
Spencer. *See* student autoethnographers
student autoethnographers
    Allison 91, 159–160
    Betty xvi, 70–79, 82–83, 100, 119, 123, 131
    Caroline 123, 167–170,
    Christa xvi, 50–60, 99, 119–120, 123, 136
    Cooper xvi, 160–161
    Edward 60–68, 70, 100, 132, 136
    Elizabeth 100–107, 117–119, 132
    Emily 4, 6, 38–43, 69, 118, 135–136
    Haley 119, 123, 132, 165–166
    Hannah 136, 153–155
    Jocelyne 157–158
    Kaitlyn 83–90, 92, 100, 109, 123
    Kim 59, 123, 164–165
    Lydia 137, 163–164
    Lynne xvi, 125, 158–159
    Mariama 166–167
    Marian 169–170
    Sam 118, 155–157
    Selena 109, 131–132, 170–171
    Sophie 111–120, 123, 136–137
    Spencer 7, 81, 120, 123–127, 132
    Tania 49, 92–100, 118–120, 125–126, 131
    Taylor 118–119, 136–137, 161–162

T

Tania. *See* student autoethnographers
Taylor. *See* student autoethnographers
Third Culture Kid (TCK) xiv, 22–28, 173–186
therapeutic catharsis. *See* outcomes of practicing autoethnography
Tolich, Martin 11–12, 81–83, 112–113
Tombro, Melissa 5, 18
Tullis, Jill 12

V

vulnerability, emotional 7, 36, 43, 100, 117, 124–127, 129
vulnerability, professional 127–129

W

Writing Program Administrators Council (WPA) 133–134
writing skills improvement. *See* outcomes of practicing autoethnography